VICTORIAN JEWELRY, IDENTITY,
AND THE NOVEL

for Tony

Victorian Jewelry, Identity, and the Novel
Prisms of Culture

JEAN ARNOLD
California State University, San Bernardino, California

ASHGATE

Published by
Ashgate Publishing Limited
Wey Court East
Union Road
Farnham
Surrey, GU9 7PT
England

Ashgate Publishing Company
Suite 420
101 Cherry Street
Burlington
VT 05401-4405
USA

www.ashgate.com

British Library Cataloguing in Publication Data
Arnold, Jean.
  Victorian jewelry, identity, and the novel : prisms of
  culture.
  1. Diamonds--Social aspects. 2. Social values--History--
  19th century. 3. Collins, Wilkie, 1824-1889. Moonstone.
  4. Eliot, George, 1819-1880. Middlemarch. 5. Thackeray,
  William Makepeace, 1811-1863. Great Hoggarty diamond.
  6. Trollope, Anthony, 1815-1882. Eustace diamonds.
  7. Jewelry in literature.
  I. Title
  823.8'09353-dc22

Library of Congress Cataloging-in-Publication Data
Arnold, Jean, 1939-
  Victorian jewelry, identity, and the novel : prisms of culture / Jean Arnold.
    p. cm.
  Includes bibliographical references and index.
  ISBN 978-1-4094-2127-6 (hbk) -- ISBN 978-1-4094-2128-3
(ebk.) 1. English fiction--19th century--History and criticism. 2. Material culture in literature. 3. Gems in literature. 4. Jewelry in literature. 5. Object (Aesthetics) in literature. 6. Identity (Psychology) in literature. 7. Gems--Symbolic aspects. 8. Values in literature. 9. Values--Great Britain--History--19th century. 10. Material culture--Great Britain--History--19th century. I. Title.
  PR878.M38A75 2011
  823'.8093564--dc22

2010052523

ISBN 9781409421276 (hbk)
ISBN 9781409421283 (ebk)

Printed and bound in Great Britain by
TJ International Ltd, Padstow, Cornwall.

Contents

List of Figures

Acknowledgments

Deep thanks go to all those who have contributed to this volume. A form of Chapter 5 has appeared in *Victorian Literature and Culture*, Volume 30, Number 1, 2002, and I am grateful to Adrienne Munich and John Maynard, editors, and to Richard Stein, reader, for their interest and suggestions in bringing this chapter to print. I thank the editors for their permission to reprint the material here.

The book has evolved in response to written resources in the field of literary criticism, cultural criticism, theory, anthropology, economics, sociology, and philosophy, and so it is to some extent a product of its times. At the same time the work has developed organically as writers, readers, and friends have contributed ideas and references. The book is therefore offered as a gift to all those who have read and responded to various drafts; their encouragement, belief, and insights have been an integral part of its growth. John Briggs, Jean Gillingwators, Jennifer Manion, and J'nan Sellery have all responded thoughtfully to the working manuscript. Special thanks also go to Wendy Belcher and Margaret Waller for their friendship and suggestions over several years. Writers' Group colleagues at California State University, San Bernardino, offered their insights and suggestions to various drafts, vital contributions that mean more me to than I am able to express. Luz Elena Ramirez, our group's driving force and organizer, Jenny Andersen, Anne Bennett, and Nancy Best will see their superlative ideas and suggestions on many of these pages.

Members of Victoria Listserv have been supportive and interested, engaging in lively conversation about Victorian jewelry, available in the list's archives at http:listserv.indiana.edu/archives/victoria.html. With over 50 entries on the search topic "Victorian Jewelry," this inspiring and authoritative source was constructed from the listserv's community of experts. One list member wrote that, after his students had joined the online discussion and then completed a survey, "Victorian Jewelry" turned out to be their favorite topic. Here my thanks go to Patrick Leary, list moderator, who for many years has guided the list with a firm, diplomatic hand as he has developed it into a professional model of its kind.

I thank colleagues in NAVSA, VISAWUS, and PAMLA who have given feedback and suggestions for new sources in response to my oral presentations. California State University, San Bernardino, has supported my research, and my special thanks go to Rong Chen, former department chair, whose generous support helped this project along at a crucial juncture.

I also give thanks to longtime friends in The Shakespeare Club who have provided positive interest during the course of this project. To Anita Arnold, I give credit for her specialized consultation and expert work on some of the images appearing in the book, and to Mary Anntiques.com for sharing their fabulous collection of cameos and miniatures. To my whole family, I give my thankful appreciation for always being there, and to Tony, I give profound thanks for his singular support; his presence and encouragement made the book possible.

My deep thanks go to Ann Donahue, editor extraordinaire, and the anonymous reader at Ashgate for many formative ideas in building the final version of this work. Marc Redfield has given me inspiration and excellent advice over a number of years, so that his diffused influence fills many of these pages.

To all these people, then, I offer the gift of this book, in reciprocation for their many gifts of support in the form of friendship and critical input. The book belongs to you all, and my appreciation goes beyond words or any means of representation, as it stretches across global distances and passing years.

Chapter 1

Introduction:
Jewels and the Formation of Identity in
Victorian Literature and Culture

In Charles Dickens's *Little Dorrit*, Mrs. Merdle's jewels enable her to "represent and express Society so well" (I.33). What sustains this portrayal of Mrs. Merdle is her husband's exalted position within a materialist culture based on free-wheeling capitalism. Mr. Merdle is variously hailed "the mastermind of the age," "an illustrious man and great national ornament," "Gigantic Enterprise," "The Wealth of England," "Credit," "Capital," and "Prosperity": in short, the very personification of prodigious capital accumulation (II.24). In the London high society depicted in the novel, Mrs. Merdle's role as wife of the prestigious and wealthy Mr. Merdle is to display her valuable jewels as class markers. With revealing, typical hyperbole, Dickens informs his readers that Mrs. Merdle possesses "a capital bosom to hang jewels upon," so that "the Bosom moving in Society with the jewels displayed upon it, attracts … general admiration" (I.21).

As Dickens portrays the power of a woman's bejeweled image to signify class rank in the socioeconomic hierarchy, his commentary on jewels also marks the Merdles's narrowly rigid gender roles in their marriage as situated within a capitalist value system: "Mr. Merdle wanted something to hang jewels upon, and he bought it for that purpose" (I.21). As gender roles developed in response to industrial capitalism of the Victorian age, men had renounced the wearing of conspicuous jewels; by contrast, women continued and developed the practice. Writers on fashion and clothing of the period alternatively note that the early British nineteenth century featured a "great masculine renunciation" or "fashion's new gender disjunction," in which men wore business suits, while women wore colorful jewels and changing fashions.[1] Because cultural practices of Dickens's

---

[1]   Frances Rogers and Alice Beard, *5,000 Years of Gems and Jewelry* (New York: J. B. Lippincott Company, 1947) 142. They write, "Whereas in the past [men] had rivaled women in the splendor of their adornments, they now contented themselves with bunches of seals at their fobs, a ring or two and little else." See also Kim M. Phillips, "Masculinities and the Medieval English Sumptuary Laws," *Gender & History* 19.1 (April 2007). She notes that "the realm of high fashion and sartorial adornment was not primarily focused on women until the 'great masculine renunciation' of the early nineteenth century" (23); the phrase is Flugel's term: J. C. Flugel, *The Psychology of Clothes* (New York: International University Press, 1930). Gilles Lipovetsky, *The Empire of Fashion: Dressing Modern Democracy*,

reading audience did not allow Mr. Merdle to display his wealth by wearing jewels, the narrator had needed to supply Mr. Merdle with a wife who would fill this class-marking function for him; her expensive jewels could reveal, in Veblen's words, "pecuniary strength."[2]

The circulation of jewels in Victorian culture assured some very specific visual messages so that Dickens and other writers of his time could depend upon their readers to recognize meanings about class and gender in anecdotes such as this one referencing Mrs. Merdle. His sketch is one of many examples in which jewels contribute to identity formation of characters in Victorian novels. This role for jewels in fiction points toward a whole range of private and social behaviors that could be classified as Victorian object relations.

In the Victorian era, women's practices of wearing jewelry became so widespread that jewels served as a focal point in novelistic narratives; recall, for instance, titles such as *The Moonstone* and *The Eustace Diamonds*, among others.[3] We can trace the very *raison d'être* of these works to the pervasive signifying power of jewels in the culture, and to the resulting insights that authors were prompted to communicate about the jewels' established meanings. This focus in Victorian novels also reflects—and in fact is an instance of—an increasing cultural

---

trans. Catherine Porter, foreword Richard Sennett (Princeton: Princeton University Press, 1994) 74. Lipovetsky's term for this nineteenth-century change in dress codes is "fashion's new gender disjunction." Shirley Bury, *Jewellery, 1789–1910: The International Era* (Woodbridge, Suffolk: Antique Collectors' Club, Ltd., 1991). On the other hand, some noblemen on the continent did wear jewels early in the nineteenth century. For example, in 1816, "Lady Shelley observed Count Palffy wearing a turquoise and diamond necklace." She describes it as "'extremely ridiculous in a man,' but she had never seen turquoises so large. The Count told her that he had spent a lifetime amassing the stones" (Bury quoting Shelley 180). For more on Count Palffy, see also fn 48, this chapter.

[2] Expensive jewels functioned as status symbols in Victorian times. See Erving Goffman, "Symbols of Class Status," *The British Journal of Sociology* 2.4 (December 1951) 294. Goffman argues that "Specialized means of displaying one's position frequently develop. Such sign-vehicles have been called *status symbols*." Also see Thorsten Veblen on conspicuous consumption in *The Theory of the Leisure Class* (Toronto: Dover Publications, 1994) 52; originally published (New York: Macmillan, 1899). Veblen argues that "the basis on which good repute in any highly organized industrial community ultimately rests in pecuniary strength; and the means of showing pecuniary strength, and so of gaining or retaining a good name, are leisure and a conspicuous consumption of goods."

[3] For other nineteenth-century examples of this literary focus on gems, see William Collier, "The Queen's Jewel; or The Interrupted Ball," a petite comedy in one act adapted to the English stage, produced at Queen's Theatre (April 6, 1835). Thomas Carlyle, "The Diamond Necklace," Guy de Maupassant, "The Diamond Necklace," and A. Lang, "Historical Mysteries." In addition, see S. M. Burnham, *Precious Stones in Nature, Art, and Literature* (Boston: Bradlee Whidden, 1886) 182–3, for discussion of a French pre-revolutionary plot involving the theft of a diamond necklace carried out by Jeanne de St. Remy de Valois at court. Rogers and Beard note that "the story of the famous necklace has provided endless material for history and fiction" (141).

fascination with objects of all kinds in the British nineteenth century, and in recent times, critics have taken note. Catherine Waters points out that "Dickens's peculiar treatment of subject-object relations in his fiction has fed into a growing interest in Victorian material culture over the last decade or so."[4] Furthermore, in *Ideas in Things: Fugitive Meaning in Victorian Novels*, Elaine Freedgood investigates the extratextual history of material goods found in Victorian fiction:

> While recognizing that the Victorian historical context of jewels plays a necessary role in their appearance in the literature, I will also investigate the meanings of jewels inside the text, where both personal and public object relations become manifest, and I will argue that novelistic characters interact with their jewels with creative emotion in the process of building their identities.[5]

I. Jewels Interpreting Culture

Many cultures throughout history have assigned unusually high value to jewels, and it could be argued that the Victorians are no different in this regard. However, this premise, which posits a kind of stability of value through time, bypasses the idea that the accepted meaning of jewelry and gems changes from one culture to the next. A single type of gem may surface in a succession of cultures through history, and consistently remain highly valued, while content or meaning of the gem's high value varies emotionally, materially, economically, and politically from one culture to another.

Gems thus carry designated meanings assimilated from their particular cultural contexts: "Each society classifies objects in its own way," Roland Barthes writes, "and this way constitutes the very intelligibility it grants itself."[6] Therefore an understanding of the meanings that a gem absorbs and projects must arise from an understanding of its specific historical and cultural context. As a Victorian object, a valuable gem was charged with meaning in a strikingly unique way, a way that can only be fully understood by grasping key features of the Victorian cultural scene and psyche.

Not surprisingly, then, exploring why certain Victorians commonly wore jewels yields insights into values, attitudes, and beliefs circulating in the culture. Socio-archaeologist Grahame Clark offers his approach to examining jewels as a form of cultural critique:

---

[4] Catherine Waters, *Commodity Culture in Dickens's* Household Words: *The Social Life of Goods* (Burlington: Ashgate Publishing Company, 2008) 4.

[5] *Ideas in Things: Fugitive Meaning in Victorian Novels* (Chicago: University of Chicago Press, 2006) 1.

[6] Roland Barthes, *Mythologies*, trans. Annette Lavers (New York: Hill and Wang, 1972) 113.

the prime purpose of wearing [jewelry is] ... to symbolize status. It follows that the nature of jewellery is bound to reflect in some measure the structure and activities of the society in which it [is] ... current. In other words the history of jewellery and of the precious substances incorporated in it needs to be studied in the context of social history *and vice versa.*[7]

Because the practice of wearing jewelry indicates underlying values that grant status, Clark argues not only for the study of jewelry in the context of its culture, but for a critique of culture that arises from an interpretation of its jewelry.

My inquiry adopts this method of cultural analysis with a careful caveat concerning class: although precious, expensive jewels were worn only by Victorian upper class women, these gems represented the values of class differentiation deployed throughout the entire culture. As late Victorian writer Georg Simmel puts it, fashion, including jewelry, "unites ... those of a social class and segregates them from others"; furthermore, contemporary writer Guy Debord notes that the appearance of objects as possessions "conceals their true character as relationships ... between classes."[8] The lack of significant jewelry among economically disadvantaged people in this era would thus reveal immense cross-class disjunctions. At the same time, the lack of significant jewelry worn among men argues an immense disjunction in gender roles; however, while working class women's lack of jewelry may have evinced their disadvantage, men's lack of jewelry evinced their privilege. Some ownership changes of jewelry in novels thus follow this pattern: we find servants stealing jewelry in order to elevate their class standing, whereas men give jewelry as gifts to women in a show of privilege

---

[7]   Grahame Clark, *Symbols of Excellence: Precious Materials as Expressions of Status* (Cambridge: Cambridge University Press, 1986) 166. (My emphasis.)

[8]   George Simmel, "Fashion," *The American Journal of Sociology* 62.6 (May 1957) 541; originally published in *International Quarterly* X (October 1904) 130–55; also in *On Individuality and Social Forms: Selected Writings*, ed. Donald N. Levine (Chicago: University of Chicago Press, 1970) 294–323, 541. Guy Debord, *The Society of the Spectacle*, trans. Donald Nicholson-Smith (New York: Zone Books, 1995) 19. Debord writes, "Fashion is a form of imitation and so of social equalization, but paradoxically, in changing incessantly, it differentiates one time from another and one social stratum from another ... The elite initiates a fashion, and, when the mass imitates it in an effort to obliterate the external distinctions of class, abandons it for a newer mode—the process quickens with the increase of wealth." Thorsten Veblen writes about the quest for a higher socioeconomic status as characterized by a tendency to copy those positioned above: "With the exception of the instinct of self-preservation, the propensity for emulation is probably the strongest and most alert and persistent of the economic motives proper. In an industrial community this propensity for emulation expresses ... itself in form of conspicuous waste. The need of conspicuous waste, therefore, stands ready to absorb any increase in the community's industrial efficiency or output of goods, after the most elementary physical wants have been provided for" (68). Certainly, the wearing of jewels would be considered a form of conspicuous consumption or "waste."

and prerogative. For working class women and for men, even a lack of jewelry projected meaning, for jewelry had become ubiquitous as an object of desire.

Given the possibility according to their socioeconomic circumstances, Victorians wished to own jewelry or to wear it. With the rise in manufacturing in the nineteenth century, more affordable forms of secondary jewelry proliferated so that a transfer of markers of wealth trickled down to the middle classes.[9] Through emulation, fashion became an increasingly democratic phenomenon, and manufactured or secondary jewels were now within reach of a rising middle class, who purchased them with enthusiasm. Gilles Lipovetsky notes that, even though fashion was

> an instrument of social discrimination and a manifest mark of social superiority, fashion was … also a special agent of the democratic revolution. On the one hand, it blurred the established distinctions and made it possible to confront and confuse social strata. On the other hand, it reintroduced—although in a new way—the timeless logic of signs of power, brilliant symbols of domination and social difference. Here is the paradox of fashion: its flashy displays of the emblems of hierarchy played a role in the movement toward the equalization of appearances.[10]

In a convergence of circumstances, Victorian jewelry thus circulated as a sign of wealth at the same time capitalism's newly rich urban business people wished to visually verify their status through the wearing of jewels.[11] While the older aristocracy owned inherited land and titles that signified its ascendant position, newly rich upper classes without these historically significant markers to announce

---

9   Charles Babbage, "On the Identity of the Work When it is of the Same Kind, and its Accuracy When of Different Kinds," from *On the Economy of Machinery and Manufactures* (Philadelphia: Carey and Lea, 1832), in *Factory Production in Nineteenth-Century Britain*, ed. Elaine Freedgood (New York: Oxford University Press, 2003) 152. Babbage describes the manufacturing process of jewelry in a paragraph entitled "Gold and Silver Moulding": "Many of the mouldings used by jewelers consist of thin slips of metal, which have received their form by passing between steel rollers, on which the pattern is embossed or engraved; thus taking a succession of copies of the device intended." See Walter Benjamin, "The Work of Art in the Age of Mechanical Reproduction," *Illuminations*, intro. Hannah Arendt (New York: Harcourt Brace Jovanich, Inc., 1968). He writes, "By making many reproductions, [mechanical reproduction] substitutes a plurality of copies for a unique existence. And in permitting the reproduction to meet the beholder … in his own particular situation, it reactivates the object reproduced. These two processes lead to a tremendous shattering of tradition" (II).

10   Lipovetsky, 31.

11   See Colin Renfrew, "Varna and the Emergence of Wealth in Prehistoric Europe," *The Social Life of Things: Commodities in Cultural Perspective*, ed. Arjun Appadurai (New York: Cambridge University Press, 1986) 141–68, 163 for a discussion of the "multiplier effect"[s] of social conditions that can predict the circulation of objects of status.

their social position moved around the city with the visual marker of jewels to signify rank.[12] In this way, jewelry's significance was shaped by a consumer culture, which, while showing its democratic values through the constant redistribution of money that could buy expensive gems, also refashioned class stratification through the display of jewels that only money could buy.

Lipovetsky's integrated vision of democracy and hierarchy thus centers on the access of the nouveau riche to symbols of royal power. His account actually has roots that extend to sumptuary laws that became so prevalent in fourteenth-century Europe, when medieval values and practices were giving way to more active economic exchanges in the early modern period.[13] In medieval times, sumptuous attire had been generally rejected because it was viewed as an embodiment of the deadly sin of pride, according to the powerful Catholic Church. As a result,

> from the end of the Carolingian empire until mid-twelfth century, no secular European governments passed sumptuary laws … Yet as the economy began to develop, and the consumption of luxuries and public displays of social standing became increasingly common, there was a growing perception that these were social problems that needed to be addressed through new laws.[14]

Although a person's choice of clothing had previously been self-regulated according to religious and moral pressures, now, as commoners acquired the capital needed for discretionary expenditures on fine cloth and jewels, the kings of England, France, Germany, and Italy passed laws that forbade the middle classes to display these visible symbols of power, reserving for royalty and its entourage the right to dress in sumptuous clothes, such as ermine and jeweled crowns.[15] Sumptuary law and its negotiations affirmed the symbolic importance of cloth and jewels to represent social and political power in European culture, and, as early modern cities grew more populous, visual representations of power in the form of dress and jewels became more widespread among the city's upper classes and the newly rich who resided there. Yet Alan Hunt makes an important observation: while sumptuary

---

[12]   Marta Braun, "The Victorian Eye: A Political History of Light and Vision in Britain, 1810–1910 by Chris Otter," *Victorian Studies* 52.2 (Winter 2010) 324–7.

[13]   See Catherine Richardson, ed., *Clothing Culture, 1350–1650* (Burlington: Ashgate Publishing Company, 2004).

[14]   Judith C. Brown, "*Sumptuary Law in Italy: 1200–1500* by Catherine M. Kovesi Killerby," *Renaissance Quarterly* 57.1 (Spring 2004) 177–8. Also see Gerhard Jaritz, "*Ira Dei*, Material Culture, and Behavior in the Late Middle Ages: Evidence from German-speaking Regions," *Essays in Medieval Studies* 18 (2001) 53–§66.

[15]   Pascal Bastien, "'Aux tresors dissipez l'on cognoist le malfaict': Hierarchie sociale et transgression des ordannance somptuaires en France, 1543–1606," *Renaissance and Reformation/Renaissance et Reforme* XXIII.4 (1999). Sumptuary laws thus activated questions of "obedience vs. transgression at the heart of these exchanges between power and the [symbolic] representation of power" (24).

laws had been a direct and important result of changing economic conditions, the very existence of these laws can be perceived as evidence of anxiety over social change and the signifying power of these conspicuous symbols.[16]

II. "Sermons in Stones"

By the nineteenth century sumptuary laws had disappeared and the display of jewels practiced by Victorians lavishly exceeded previous centuries, when such displays had been reserved for kings and queens to symbolize political power.[17] Converging historical conditions—importation of new materials, the manufacture of secondary jewelry, increased income from expanding economic activity and trade, and expanding city populations—yielded a remarkable array of jewels in all price ranges, and because manufacturers produced less expensive jewelry for the first time ever, "the quantity ... of jewelry produced in the nineteenth century probably exceeded the output of all previous ages together."[18]

Now jewels became widely owned as commodities, mined and traded around the globe, and valued as signs of wealth, class, empire, gender roles and relations, and aesthetic refinement.[19] A newly creative selection of materials was used to fashion the less expensive jewelry: metals included gold, steel, iron, aluminum, wire, and gunmetal; other materials included tortoise shell, bird feathers, papier mâché, and gutta percha.[20] Ladies in the home even learned the art of weaving hair into bracelets and brooches.[21]

---

[16]   Alan Hunt, "The Governance of Consumption: Sumptuary Laws and Shifting Forms of Regulation," *The Consumption Reader*, ed. David B. Clarke, Marcus A. Doel, and M. L. Housiaux (London: Routledge, 2003) 62.

[17]   See, for instance, the discussion of the jewels of Henry VIII in "Jewels for Royalty," Rogers and Beard, 94–100; on clothing, Maria Hayward, "Fashion, Finance, Foreign Politics and the Wardrobe of Henry VIII," *Clothing Culture, 1350–1650*, ed. Richardson, 165–78. See also Christopher Hibbert, "The Tower of London: A History of England from the Norman Conquest" (*Newsweek*, 1981) 112–15. No collection "has ever aroused more interest than the crown jewels and royal regalia. These have been housed in the Tower [of London] ever since the beginning of the fourteenth century" (112).

[18]   Ginny Redington Dawes and Corrine Davidov, *Victorian Jewelry: Unexplored Treasures*, Photographs Tom Dawes (New York: Abbeville Press Publishers, 1991) 9. They write, "Victorian secondary jewelry [is] bold, playful, and romantic." Marie-Louise d'Otrange Mastai, *Jewelry*, ed. Brenda Gilchrist (Cooper-Hewitt Museum: The Smithsonian Institution's National Museum of Design, 1981) 99.

[19]   For example, diamonds were shipped to Europe and Britain from India, Brazil, and Southern Africa, while cameos came from Italy and France.

[20]   Gutta percha is a flexible latex material made from a Southeast Asian tree, used also in this period to wrap transatlantic telegraph cables, and, more recently, in dental work.

[21]   Dawes and Davidov, 2, 141. See Galia Ofek, *Representations of Hair in Victorian Literature and Culture* (Burlington: Ashgate Publishing Company, 2009).

Not only was jewelry made from an abundance of materials, but it was made to replicate many forms. For example, the entire collection of jewels at the 1867 Exhibition in Paris presented "imitations of nature" that included a variety of animal species. One account reports:

> a diamond spotted salamander, a pearl butterfly, ear-rings or brooches, which are golden webs with emerald or opal spiders at their centers and sapphire flies entering them; a little peacock with spread tail made into a pin; a lyrebird breast pin; a jeweled serpent for a bracelet, with a tiny watch devised in its head.[22]

A British journal (1876) describes earrings in such whimsical shapes as "monkeys, acorns, saucepans, birdcages, candelabra, cockroaches, tortoises, tongs, and [even] shovels."[23] The level of experimentation in materials and forms—what Lipovetsky terms "the headlong quest for novelty as such"—was beyond any previous creative attempts to fashion jewels into exquisite, unusual ornaments (41).

Exploring the cultural context still further, one finds that, not only did Victorian jewelry circulate extensively in urban social circles, it became the focus of books and periodicals that extolled the glories of gemstones as well. For example, in his 1886 comprehensive descriptive work, *Precious Stones*, S. M. Burnham describes gemstones as "the crowning glory of nature's handiwork, the rarest of all her material production, and those invested with the greatest fascination, either as objects of careful study or a treasure to be won at great sacrifice" (6). A poem from a monthly periodical asked, "What are Jewels but flowers that never decay/With a glow and a glory unfading as fair/And ... should they now speak their minds, if they may/These are 'Sermons in Stones' as all sages declare."[24] This flow of rhetoric in praise of jewels may seem excessive to twenty-first century ears, but it accurately reproduces the singular allure that gems possessed for Victorians. Jewels had become linked to experiences of aesthetic desire in the culture at large.[25]

---

[22]   *Harper's New Atlantic Monthly Magazine*, "More of the Great Show at Paris," 35.210 (November 1867) 787. See also "Paris 1867 Exhibition," *English Reports*, Class 36, Maskelyne, 616. Digitized by Google Books.

[23]   Margaret Flower, *Victorian Jewellery*, foreword Margaret J. Biggs, Chapter on collecting by Doris Langley Moore (New York: A. S. Barnes and Company, 1973) 129.

[24]   Mrs. Osgood, "The Language of Gems," *The Magnolia, or, Southern Apalachian [sic]: A Literary Magazine and Monthly Review*, Charleston, new series 1–2, 1.3 (July 1842–June 1843) 150–1.

[25]   See Suvir Kaul's discussion on the aesthetics of gems in his chapter, "Contesting Values: Gray's 'Elegy in a Country Churchyard'," in *Thomas Gray and Literary Authority: A Study in Ideology and Poetics* (Stanford: Stanford University Press, 1992) 122–3. In analyzing the lines "Full many a gem of purest ray serene/The dark unfathomed caves of ocean bear," Kaul notes that the "'Elegy' claims the gem has value without being a commodity, without coming into contact with the social labour that creates value." The "natural sublimity" of the gem in the poem derives from its hidden location and a catachrestic

Throughout the era, writers thus drew upon a tradition of extravagant statements about the significance of gems. Evaluating this Victorian fascination for jewels with a more critical eye in his contemporary work *Diamonds and Precious Stones* (1867), Harry Emanuel reasons that

> when the immense amount of capital, which lies dormant in the Imperial and Royal Treasuries, and in private hands, is considered, and when the fact is remembered that there is scarcely a home where jewels of one sort or another— all representing a money value—are not to be found, the subject assumes an importance, which it lacks at first sight.[26]

While Emanuel regarded jewels as a reserve for monetary value, John Ruskin interpreted jewelry as an artifact saturated with the huge burden of Victorian moral and aesthetic consciousness. In his autobiographical *Praeterita* (1885–9), Ruskin recounts a visit to Mr. Bautte's jeweler's shop in Geneva, Switzerland, where you "went … with awe, and of necessity, as one did to one's bankers … [and] you came away with a sense of duty fulfilled, of treasure possessed, and of a new foundation to the respectability of your family."[27]

In the scene, Ruskin perceives the jewelers' attendants as representatives of a "Ruling power," these culturally formed values Ruskin perceives as duty, monetary wellbeing, and respectability. He places an order, though he sees no displays, and he comes away with nothing material, for the package will be sent. Instead of dwelling on the visual aesthetics or the materiality of his purchases, Ruskin jumps straight to the moral meanings the jewelry reflects in his estimation: the mere idea of possessing new jewelry renews his faith in the public virtues of duty, wealth, and respectability. For much of the nineteenth century, aesthetics was often defined as having a moral, social component, so that jewels could be seen as symbolizing these cultural values. In a diffusion of Kantian ideas, the beautiful and the moral combined to define qualities that were universally pleasing.[28] Ultimately, the contrast between Emanuel's interpretation of jewels as monetary value and Ruskin's interpretation of jewels as moral consciousness shows how,

---

transference from economic value to aesthetic mystification. I thank Marc Redfield for suggesting this resource.

[26]   Harry Emanuel, F.R.G.S., *Diamonds and Precious Stones: Their History, Value, and Distinguishing Characteristics*, 2nd edn (London: John Camden Hotten, 1867) xi.

[27]   John Ruskin, *Praeterita: The Autobiography of John Ruskin*, intro. Kenneth Clark (Oxford: Oxford University Press, 1949) 295–6. I thank Timothy Peltason for suggesting this passage to me.

[28]   Immanuel Kant, *The Critique of Judgement* (1790), trans. James Creed Meredith (Oxford: Clarendon Press, 1952) I.9. For much of the nineteenth century, the aesthetic was defined as having a moral, social component. Kant writes "the beautiful is that which, apart from a concept, pleases universally."

in the Victorian era, jewels were talked about and analyzed through a variety of lenses.

In sum, a number of enabling historical factors activated the circulation of jewels in Victorian culture and its literature. Manufacturing capabilities boosted consumerism; trade from around the world had supplied the Victorians with precious stones and new materials from which to make jewelry; and urban culture had become an arena of spectacle. The nouveau riche donned splendid jewels and clothing in order to define their new class status through fashion, so recently developed at midcentury. Charles-Frederic Worth had begun the first haute couture fashion house in Paris in 1857–8.[29] In essence, this increasingly commercial society wore jewels as a visible way to alternatively differentiate and equalize classes in the social hierarchy, while the practice of dressing with jewels also further refined separate gender roles for women.

In the introductory close reading that follows, I begin to draw out themes of affect, identity, and object relations that I develop more fully in the subsequent chapters. In the first reading, Amelia Sedley and Becky Sharp in *Vanity Fair* reveal their developing personal identities in relation to the society in which they live, through their creative interpretations and interactive use of their respective jewels.

III. "Getting up the Genteel": A Reading of *Vanity Fair*

In the course of this inquiry, we face a paradox in the ways cultures view a material object such as a gem: the stone's physicality produces no intrinsic meaning, yet its cultural and personal meanings are everywhere apparent, encircling the gems like their precious-metal settings. We can view these antimonies—no inherent meaning on the one hand and profound significance on the other—straightforwardly as a gap between the object's materiality and its culturally assigned symbolic meaning. In this study, jewels serve as an example of a material object that contains symbolic meaning on multiple levels, and prompts personal identity in the culture. For

---

[29]   Lipovetsky, 57. Carol T. Christ and John O. Jordan, eds, *Victorian Literature and the Victorian Visual Imagination* (Berkeley: University of California Press, 1995) xxvi–xxvii. Christ and Jordan claim that "spectatorship … was directly linked to the development of a consumer culture, but, even more important, gave access to cultural life in general." See also Jonathan Crary, *Techniques of the Observer: On Vision and Modernity in the Nineteenth Century* (Cambridge, MA: MIT Press, 2001) 6. Crary claims that "what determines vision at any given historical moment is not some deep structure, economic base, or world view, but rather the functioning of a collective assemblage of disparate parts on a single social surface." While his claim is well taken, I would argue that those "disparate parts" available for spectatorship exist as present cultural effects of unseen causes, the effects of "cultural life in general," as Christ and Jordan see it. See, for example, Lipovetsky on fashion, 76: he argues that the study of "haute couture has to be resituated within a much broader historical movement, precisely that of the rationalization of power in modern societies."

instance, when considering Thackeray's *Vanity Fair*, we see the potency of the diamond and its particular ability to convey the value of wealth and high social status. In this novel, the diamond, the hardest of all objects, achieves a stunning porosity, as it absorbs and retains cultural values, and, in turn, participates in producing emotion and identity by injecting these values into individual experience. *Vanity Fair* thus presents a fictional version of the way that, as Renfrew notes, "high status can actually be achieved by the manipulation of material goods and by displays of wealth."[30] In Thackeray's novels, fashionable clothes, jewels, carriages, and the location and size of housing symbolize various levels of social status to the new urban business classes. Material evidence signifying wealth appeals to the eye when people congregate in cities and must visually assess one another according to class; in this urban interactive dynamic, "free, mobile and potentially self-aware individuals monitor one another" in public spaces.[31]

Responding to these visible cultural conventions, Thackeray inscribes in his text the experiences of this middle class on the rise. The main characters of *Vanity Fair* occupy various positions in this new middle class: the Osbornes, who are permanently established as wealthy and financially secure; the Sedleys, whose rich economic fortunes fall precipitously; and Becky and Dobbin, who begin the narrative with no established family background or money, but fill the narrative with their desires to be accepted as members of this new class. In the text, Becky Sharp believes that donning the visible accoutrements of money makes for success in climbing the social ladder. When Lord Steyne informs Becky, "You've got no money, and you want to compete with those who have," he is a "have" speaking to a "have-not" (562–3). Yet Becky could believe "herself to be a fine lady, and forgot that there was no money in the chest at home ... no ground to walk upon, in a word" (556). In her quest, Becky has to be hardhearted, self-centered, and immoral to work toward comfortable respectability and financial security. As a result, she reveals to herself in a moment of contemplation, "I think I could be a good woman if I had five thousand a year" (495). The novel thus highlights the fact that Becky will be naughty until she can bankroll a new morality, and be a "good woman." Of course, the irony here is that morality cannot suddenly be assumed, or put on, like a piece of fashionable jewelry; Becky does not understand that a positive moral identity promotes consistent and sensitive behavior toward others, practiced over time. In her active social arena, Becky depends entirely on appearances made from a visual language of signs in which fashion and jewelry function to project membership in the upper classes. As Erving Goffman notes, these "class symbols serve not so much to represent or misrepresent one's position, but rather to influence in a desired direction other persons' judgment of it."[32] Above

---

[30]   Renfrew, 144.

[31]   Braun, 325 quoting Otter 255. In discussing Otter's book, Braun also makes note of "a pattern of collective perception that [Otter] terms an *oligoptic* visual economy," and which takes place "in spaces such as libraries and museums or gardens and streets."

[32]   Goffman, 297.

all, Thackeray disparages the spectacle of Victorian urban consumer culture: only in an anonymous and immoral urban society could Becky's appearances count for so much, leading her—even if temporarily—into its exalted echelons.

In the society called "Vanity Fair," members of new middle classes had developed and adopted a consumer-oriented semiotic language to designate their rising ranks within the society, and Thackeray records these signs with profusion. As narrator, he endorses the importance of the fashion statement that diamonds make to his Victorian reading audience, as he pens a thinly veiled comment about his own narrative project in *Vanity Fair*: "the pursuit of fashion under difficulties would be a fine theme for any very great person who had the wit, the leisure, and the knowledge of the English language necessary for the compiling of such a history."[33] We can regard Thackeray's reference to "knowledge of the English language" in this brief passage as pointing not only to his own project of writing this novel, but to a Victorian language of signs, composed of diamonds and other desired material objects. It is a language whose nuances and connotations his heroine, Becky Sharp, well understands.

Other displays of this language of signs occur in the society called Vanity Fair; for example, the Sedleys and the Osbornes who live in large houses on the same city block see and understand it well. The families appear to be equally wealthy members of the business class. Yet the narrator warns,

> Be humble, my brother, in your prosperity! Be gentle with those who are less lucky, if not more deserving. Think, what right have you to be scornful ... whose success may be a chance, whose rank may be an ancestor's accident, whose prosperity is very likely a satire. (663)

For as long as the two families live in this material environment, their strivings will always be in vain, their rewards always tenuous. If, in Thackeray's cynical view, this representative quest for wealth carries with it a probable deviation from traditional moral behavior—from humility to vanity—the novel's search for an authentic moral foundation within the culture can only end with ironic questions and inconclusive observations. As Andrew Miller notes, "objects of desire are inaccessible in Thackeray's world, or, if acquired, unsatisfactory" (49). Accordingly, the Sedley family loses its fortune and must auction their household furnishings.

Yet, after the fall from their economic height, the family unity is not fleeting, but permanent. The Sedleys move to a humble abode, where Amelia faithfully tends to her mother and father in their old age. By implication, the narrator castigates a society based on impermanence and change: "that lottery of life which gives to this man the purple and fine linen, and sends to the other rags for garments and dogs for comforters" (662). For Thackeray, the permanence of their family

---

[33]   Thackeray, *Vanity Fair*, ed. J. I. M. Stewart (New York: Penguin Books, 1968), first published in 1848. In the chapter entitled "How to Live Well on Nothing a Year," 441–2.

loyalty despite their newfound poverty is the quality that redeems the Sedleys. Yet the contemporary material culture still betrays Amelia Sedley who embodies the old upstanding values, and maintains traditional family unity at all costs. As she wrongly convinces herself that her husband George Osborne had been a loyal and honorable person, Amelia's mistaken perception of her deceased husband nearly ruins her life as she naively grieves for someone who never existed. All the while, the loving but self-deprecating Dobbin suffers from a distance and in silence, having secretly given Amelia her piano, and supported her financially.

Perhaps we might think the Sedleys should be rewarded for their traditional family loyalty, yet they are nevertheless victims of the vast, uncontrollable changes the economy and its material culture undergo. In the fluctuating fortunes of the novel, the wealthy in-laws, the Osbornes, take the fatherless little Georgy, their grandson, from his destitute mother, Amelia. They raise and educate Georgy, showering him with sumptuous upper middle class possessions in spite of the fact that his other grandfather, Grandfather Sedley, had once been the better man "by ten thousand pounds," according to Grandfather Osborne (704).

Readers witness the quickly developing pathos of little Georgy's visits to the humiliated and humbled Sedleys as they read of little Georgy's clothes and his glittering accessories: he had "a fine gold chain and watch," and "gilt spurs, and a gold-headed whip, and a fine pin in his handkerchief; and the neatest little kid gloves which Lamb's Conduit Street could furnish. He had little jeweled buttons in [his] … shirt-fronts" (505, 651). These extravagant accessories convey a message of the new class division between the Osbornes and the Sedleys. Further underscoring both the class rift between the families and the separation of child and mother, Georgy gives his poverty-stricken mother a miniature of himself, a small bejeweled painted image she keeps under her pillow and over which she expends excessive amounts of maternal emotion, that "bootless love of women for children in Vanity Fair" (582).[34]

---

[34]   See John Plotz, *Portable Property: Victorian Culture on the Move* (Princeton: Princeton University Press, 2008) 27. He writes, "To analyze Victorian novels via any kind of thing theory, then, apparently requires focusing on the way that an object's singularity calls forth unsuspected reservoirs of emotion." Miniatures are jewels with painted images of particular people, used before the onset of photography.

Figure 1.1 Hand painted miniature copy of an 1825 14" x 30"
           commissioned portrait of Charles William Lambton (1818–31)
           by Sir Thomas Lawrence. The boy pictured in the portrait died
           at age 13 of consumption, but his popular image at age seven
           dressed in a red velvet suit has appeared on a British stamp,
           and on biscuit tin lids

Source: © Anita Arnold (2010), courtesy of MaryAnn-tiques

In contrast to the traditional and loyal Amelia, Becky does not take a liking to the role of motherhood, knowing that motherly duties might work against her project of social self-promotion, and never having had a mother of her own on which to model her behavior. As with Amelia Sedley and her miniature, Thackeray uses interactive images of jewelry to crystallize Becky's motherly role and to depict its tensions. Although Becky's son, little Rawdy, thinks of his mother as an "unearthly being ... to be worshiped and admired at a distance," she remains cool and unmoved toward him; in fact, "his very sight annoy[s] her" (522). And he feels this. "You never kiss me at home, Mamma," he complains. When he wanders into her bedroom, he looks at "the jewel-case, silver-clasped and the wondrous bronze hand on the dressing table, glistening all over with a hundred rings" (448). Like the jewelry on her dressing table, Becky has become a stone, and here was little Rawdy "who was worshipping a stone!" (449).

In Amelia's and Becky's divergent subjectivities, jewels become the axis of representation for diametrically opposed affective relations between mother and child.[35] Character interactions with jewelry thus form a nexus around which the narrative reveals character relations and emotions. The miniature that Amelia sleeps with under her pillow encapsulates her personal response to the sentimental value of jewelry, as it brings out an emotion that the narrator valorizes as crucial to her maternal identity.[36] The miniature is a graphic representation of her beloved son; the son, in turn, is a miniature representation of his father on whom Amelia has so selflessly lavished her devotion and for whom she continues to feel loyalty to a fault. While Amelia lacks jewelry as ornaments for herself, the miniature of little Georgy liberates her powerful maternal bond; by contrast, Becky, though positively glistening in jewels, values them only as signs of her advancing social status, but not for any personal ties to her son or husband.

Meanwhile, Becky pursues "fashion under difficulties," as she endures a carriage ride with her husband and a former admirer, who are related as son and stepfather. These three traverse London together in a carriage to attend an evening at the royal court, and during the ride, Becky's husband, Rawdon Crawley, asks her, "'Where the doose did you get the diamonds, Becky?' ... admiring some jewels he had never seen before, and which sparkled in her ears and on her neck with brilliance and profusion" (558). Some of the diamonds had been given to her secretly by her former admirer, her husband's stepfather, Sir Pitt Crawley, also riding along in the carriage. In answer to her husband, Becky replies that she

---

[35]   Diane Elise, "Beauty and the Aesthetic Impact of the Bejeweled Mother: Discussion of Papers by Debra Roth and Elaine Freedgood," *Studies in Gender and Sexuality* 7.2 (2006) 207–15. Elise argues that "jewelry is a concrete representation of the mother's most interesting bodily surfaces" in the experience of their children (207), and that "the mother's superiority, sexual and otherwise, is exemplified in her bejeweled body" (212).

[36]   Renfrew, 158–9. Renfrew notes that "often the term 'sentimental value' is used to refer to the estimation that a specific person accords an object when the high estimation is not widely shared."

"hired them" (558).[37] Yet, Lord Steyne, a third and currently active admirer of Becky and dignitary at court, knows "whence the jewels came, and who paid for them" (559). In this situation, Becky is in her element, "getting up the genteel with amazing assiduity, readiness, and success" (556). She sees nothing inappropriate in lying to her husband and saying that she had rented the jewels; she would wear diamonds to court regardless of their source, for their communicative value as a sign of upper class affluence is an indispensable aid to her social-climbing ambitions. Becky recognizes that her husband will believe her lie about renting the diamonds, because the diamonds' slippage of meaning along a signifying chain leaves much to interpretation: while the jewelry is of great value to Rawdon and Becky who were hoping to "live well on nothing a year," Becky finds it convenient to ignore an alternative interpretation of wearing these gems: that Lord Steyne expects favors in return for his gifts of these gems. Hiding under the safety of numerous interpretations of wearing diamonds, Becky has no qualms about lying to her husband, and the moral questionability and sign of disloyalty in wearing jewelry given to her by another admirer.

The narrative power of diamonds to enhance and explain Becky's quest for social position is only as forceful as the general cultural beliefs of the reading audience that creates these fashions. Here, while she is in attendance at the king's court, she makes a visual statement that dazzles and delights those who appreciate her fashionable accessories. Thackeray writes, "The particulars of Becky's costume were in the newspapers—feathers, lappets, superb diamonds, and all the rest" (560). The news, however, is not received with unanimous admiration; in the world of the novel, divisions persist between ascending materialists who use jewelry to project class, and securely titled people, such as the Bute Crawley family, in residence in the countryside. Mrs. Bute tells her daughter that diamonds are only for the socially ambitious nouveau riche: "you might have had superb diamonds forsooth ... but you're only a gentlewoman, my poor dear child. You have only some of the best blood in England in your veins, and good principles and piety for your portion" (561). In this novel, jewelry and fashion are solely for the likes of Becky Sharp and similar urban social climbers, while the landed gentry would wish to differentiate themselves from the parvenu.

While Thackeray often creates images of jewels in *Vanity Fair* as admired objects that are held, worn, or kept on a dressing table, he also narrates the

---

[37]   While Becky lies that she rents her jewels from Mr. Polonius, in Chapter Three of this book, Samuel Titmarsh also uses Mr. Polonius to reset his "Hoggarty diamond." For an extended description of Thomas Hamlet's (alias Mr. Polonius) jewelry store, which actually existed at the time, see Richard D. Altick, *The Presence of the Present: Topics of the Day in Victorian Novels* (Columbus: Ohio State University Press, 1991) 217–18. Jane Roberts, ed., *Royal Treasures: A Golden Jubilee Celebration* (London: The Royal Collection, St. James's Palace, 2002) 232. Renting jewels was actually a common practice among royalty at the time: "stones were regularly hired for use at coronations up to 1837 – computed on the value of the stones."

movement and displacement of jewels, disturbing them from their conventional positions and hence from their accepted norms and usage. This displacement symbolizes an equal displacement in character relations the jewels represent. The disordered, alternative depiction in subject/object relations is richly represented in the scene when Rawdon Crawley surprises his wife Becky in the act of singing in her drawing room for Lord Steyne, whose role in the text is to be the enabler for Becky's class-climbing ambitions, and the giver of diamonds, and all that such gifts imply.

At the moment of Rawdon Crawley's entrance on the scene, Thackeray carefully crafts an image of Becky "in full toilette, her arms and all her fingers sparkling with bracelets and rings; and the brilliants on her breast which Steyne had given her" (620). When caught in the act of having a tête-à-tête with Lord Steyne, Becky tries to proclaim her innocence to her husband, a ploy which in turn causes Lord Steyne to become infuriated. He delivers a tirade: "You innocent! Why every trinket you have on your body is paid for by me. I have given you thousands of pounds." Finally realizing the true tenor of Lord Steyne and Becky's relationship, Rawdon dispenses serious blows to Lord Steyne. Then, turning angrily on Becky, he dictates, "Take off those things" … "Throw them down." He wrenches the "diamond ornament" from her bodice and throws it at Lord Steyne. Thackeray succinctly relates, "It cut him on his bald forehead. Steyne wore the scar to his dying day" (621).

The violence centering on Becky's diamond jewelry signifies the rupture of relations between these three characters. In the text, the image of jewels thrown to the floor, and the diamond pin being hurled across the room to cause injury to Lord Steyne, break the dramatic irony built into the scene, revealing new and disturbing knowledge the characters now have about each other. Rawdon has discovered his wife's deception, that all along she had been accepting gifts of jewelry from another man; as she attempts to hide behind her weak pleas of innocence, Lord Steyne has spoken the truth about Becky's behavior. Lord Steyne himself has discovered that his attentions to Becky must come to an end, and all the money he has spent on diamonds for her will come to naught. Becky's dishonest maneuvers could last only so long as the other two characters could be kept unaware. In this scene, the characters' relations to the jewels have taken on new and drastically changed symbolic meanings, causing the diamonds to be spatially rearranged in the text. Rawdon demands the jewels be removed from Becky's body; Lord Steyne loses his privileged possession of both Becky and her indebtedness to him because of his gifts; and Becky can no longer pretend that the jewels have come to her in a legitimate manner, such as renting them. In *Vanity Fair*, the diamonds' new arrangement on the drawing room floor reveals that they are tainted with the dishonor of Becky's apparent sale of herself for social advancement.

At the close of the scene, Rawdon leaves Becky, Lord Steyne leaves Becky, and Becky is alone upstairs in her bedroom. However, the diamonds have not finished their interactive relation with the novel's characters; they become the vehicle by which the housemaid, Mademoiselle Fifine, transforms her own life.

The maid gathers the diamonds from the drawing room floor and leaves the house with them along with a few other objects of value; the narrative suggests that she begins a milliner's shop in Paris. Andrew Miller notes that in Thackeray's texts one finds a "desire of servants for their master's 'movables,' [or chattel]."[38] In this instance, the master/servant relation central to the novel's society is turned upside down by the movement of diamonds. If, as Bruce Robbins notes, "servants are signs of money, itself a sign," Mlle. Fifine rejects that identity as she leaves the house. Here she takes on a new middle class identity in her own right. In this fictional portrayal of the trickle-down effect of class status symbols, the narrator disparages Victorian urban upper classes who base their status on the appearance of signs such as servants or jewels, for both may be easily obtained or lost, like the class status they signify.

IV. Prisms of Culture

Of the many new types of jewelry that circulated through Victorian culture, diamonds were often among the most highly valued. Even by the end of the eighteenth century, a French countess, in a letter to the King of Sweden, had noted that "no one will buy anything but diamonds anymore." Translucent jewelry was becoming fashionable for evening life, a social phenomenon resulting from the rise of "more efficient candles."[39] After the turn of the century, the geometric facets of diamonds reflected the light radiating from the newly installed gas lamps on city streets and in theaters, further enhancing the translucence of the jewels worn to evening events.[40] Enacting the "Society of the Spectacle," this example of diamonds reflecting the new gas lights allows us to understand how an impressive visual experience made its stand as a power to determine the real; spectacle as the real, in Guy Debord's view, is solely a one-way communication, "inaccessible to review or correction."[41] Gleaming diamonds thus enter the lives of characters in Victorian fiction as signs and symbols of established cultural values; in *Vanity*

---

[38]   Andrew Miller, *Novels Behind Glass: Commodity Culture and Victorian Narrative* (Cambridge: Cambridge University Press, 1995) 16.

[39]   Mastai, 99, 94.

[40]   Andreas Bluhm and Louise Lippincott, *Light! The Industrial Age 1750–1900*, Art & Science, Technology & Society (Amsterdam: The Van Gogh Museum; Pittsburgh: Carnegie Museum of Art, 2000), 239–40. In 1802 in London and Paris, there were exhibitions of gas lighting, and the first gas street lamps were installed in Pall Mall, Westminster, in 1809. In 1850, in England, Burghley House is among the earliest private homes to light paintings with gas picture lights.

[41]   Debord, 17, 19. Victorian fascination with vision and the developing technology of lighting have been well documented. See for example Crary, as cited above; Christ and Jordan, as cited above; Kate Flint, *The Victorians and the Visual Imagination* (Cambridge: Cambridge University Press, 2000); Chris Otter, *The Victorian Eye: A Political History of*

Fair, Becky Sharp's jewels are an integral part of her performance in determining her public identity in society and, sadly, within the nucleus of her small, temporary family. As we will discover, the gems catalyze individual emotion, action, and ultimately identity formation in many Victorian novels.

Translucent gems can thus be perceived as prisms of culture. In fact, their prismatic effect insists on analogy: prisms and translucent gems receive monochromatic light, refracting or bending it, changing it into a rainbow of colors. Rogers and Beard elucidate:

> A ray of light striking a diamond is split into a band of colors ranging from red to violet, because a cut diamond, like a glass prism, has the power to separate the light into rainbow hues. The spectrum produced by the prism, however, is a comparatively narrow strip, while the diamond is able to separate colors, one from another, to such an extent that under favorable conditions the eye may catch the burning intensity of one color at a time. (172)

A historical precedent for the analogy resides in the image of the Kohinoor Diamond and a glass replica of it displayed at the Great Exhibition of 1851. Dena Tarshis compares the prismatic qualities of these objects: "Due to its excellent cutting, [the glass replica] ... acted as a prism, in a manner that rivaled the gem itself."[42] Isobel Armstrong evaluates glass at the Exhibition as the "spectral double of diamonds," and rightfully argues that "Glass destroys the ... 'thought' around the diamonds. [... Glass is] free of attachment to privilege and power, free of a history of labour, free of violent extrinsic meanings" (231).[43]

However, the diamond does signify the crystallization of Victorian "thought" or cultural beliefs, and we can conceive that the gem undergoes a symbolic process parallel to the prism: while individual members of a culture may receive what appears to the critic's eye as uniform cultural belief systems, each individual integrates these values into his or her particular life. The seemingly uniform

---

Light and Vision in Britain, 1800–1910 (Chicago and London: University of Chicago Press, 2008).

[42] Dena K. Tarshis, "The Koh-I-noor Diamond and its Glass Replica at the Crystal Palace Exhibition," *Journal of Glass Studies* 42 (2000) 143; Patrick Voillot, *Diamonds and Precious Stones*, Discoveries (New York: Harry N. Abrams, Inc., Publishers, 1998) 33; Isobel Armstrong, *Glassworlds: Glass Culture and the Imagination 1830–1880* (Oxford: Oxford University Press, 2008) 229–32. Today the prismatic glass copy of the diamond is on loan and displayed at the Corning Museum of Glass, Corning, New York, and the Kohinoor Diamond is mounted in the crown of Queen Elizabeth the Queen Mother, and displayed with the Crown Jewels.

[43] For a full and interesting discussion of the Exhibition, see *Victorian Prism: Refractions of the Crystal Palace*, ed. James Buzard, Joseph W. Childers, and Eileen Gilooly (Charlottesville: University of Virginia Press, 2007). The introduction in this anthology of essays discusses previous publications about the Exhibition, including works by Richards, Miller, Auerbach and Davis, and Hobhouse.

beliefs transform into a variety of colorful, subjective experiences. The narration of a particular subjective experience of jewels shapes Victorian fiction's plots and scenes, creating this type of symbolic action, and it can be read across a range of works. In these works, translucent gems create a spectrum of affect, a gamut of emotions that both produce and reveal individual identity.

On the other hand, the jewels equally produce cultural cohesion as they embody agreed upon cultural meanings. For example, in the late Victorian period, Georg Simmel wrote that "genuine jewels ... have their roots in the value ideas of the whole social circle and are ramified through all of it."[44] His reasoning held that

> material products of culture ... in which natural material is developed into forms which could never have been realized by their own energies, are products of our own desires and emotions, the result of ideas that utilize the available possibilities of objects.

Circulating as objects that carry public meanings, jewels reveal a culture's moving history of "desires and emotions"—individual feelings and experiences that accumulate and become embedded in historical practices in the mining, production, marketing, and wearing of jewelry. "By cultivating objects ... we cultivate ourselves," Simmel observes. Jewelry's contextual "value ideas" thus become objectified in the gem's materiality.[45] Along Simmel's line of reasoning, affect experienced repeatedly by different individuals as a response to the meaning of their jewels can give rise to cultural practices that become fixed over time. Under these conditions, objects like jewels would constitute a site of tension insofar as their public and private meanings diverge: while Victorian jewels symbolized established public values of money, class, gender roles, and empire, they also symbolized private personal emotions through gifts, inheritances, and as aesthetic objects. An object like a piece of jewelry opens itself to a double reading—it is an object with personal meaning for the individual, and with an established meaning for the culture at large; therefore, its reading is located in the space between private and public domains. Read doubly in this way, Victorian jewelry may function as a symbolic representation of the individual's relation to the society.

---

[44]   Georg Simmel, *The Sociology of Georg Simmel*, trans., ed., and intro. Kurt H. Wolff (New York: The Free Press, 1950) 343. Simmel began publishing his works on sociology in Leipzig, 1890, followed by multiple editions of his works, until 1923.

[45]   Georg Simmel, *The Philosophy of Money*, ed. David Frisby, trans. Tom Bottomore and David Frisby (New York: Routledge, 1978) 446–7. The first complete translation of the revised edition (1907) of *Philosphie des Geldes*, first published in 1900. Wolff, "Introduction," *The Sociology of Georg Simmel*, xx. Wolff argues that, "Simmel's relation to things—'things,' 'objects,' 'the objective,' 'objectivity' occupied him in many of his writings" toward the end of the nineteenth century. Because Simmel viewed culture as a whole, he linked abstract ideas of a culture to the artifacts or objects a culture produced.

With this double reading of jewels, we can understand Victorian culture's organizing principles and their tensions from outside and inside at once: from outside, seeing the diamond's historical development produces a visual object with the power to project cultural norms, and from inside, witnessing the way Victorian literature portrays characters' subjective experiences and reactions to those cultural norms through symbolic interactions with their jewels. This study thus creates a historicist interpretation of novels, evaluating the cultural history integral to the wearing of jewelry; at the same time, however, analysis of the fiction elicits an aesthetic interpretation, for the affect that arises from the fictional characters' subjective aesthetic experiences of their jewels occupies a "utopian space" of dazzling "free play" politically situated inside a discrete realm of unmediated experience.[46] In fact, the historicist and aesthetic critiques together form a holistic evaluation of jewels across Victorian culture and literature; this evaluative unity is embodied in the visual unity of a jewel, which contains diverse cultural and personal meanings that often confront one another.

V. Turquoise and Diamonds: A Reading of *Daniel Deronda*

Focusing on a few scenes from George Eliot's *Daniel Deronda* illustrates this confrontation between the individual and society, as Gwendolen Harleth interacts with the symbolic dimensions of her gems. In the novel, a turquoise necklace plays a key role in building Gwendolen's identity as it symbolizes her desired goal of developing internal moral awareness and a personal direction in opposition to the prevailing pressures of her social environment.[47] Turquoise and diamonds are jewels that actually represent opposed cultural values within the text, ultimately confronting one another on Gwendolen's body.

At the narrative outset, Gwendolen pawns her turquoise necklace, for she has run out of money at the roulette table and must win enough to pay for her journey home. As Deronda approaches the table, Gwendolen senses that he judges her

---

[46]   George Levine, "Introduction: Reclaiming the Aesthetic," *Aesthetics and Ideology*, ed. George Levine (New Brunswick: Rutgers University Press, 1994) 17. In addition, see "the politics of affect" in Ann Cvetkovich, *Mixed Feelings: Feminism, Mass Culture and Victorian Sensationalism* (New Brunswick: Rutgers University Press, 1992). This "free play" is considered a discrete realm that is politically constructed. Again I refer to Benjamin's concept of "aura," defined as awe or reverence in viewing art, as "outmoded" concepts such as "creativity and genius, eternal value and mystery" come into play. See also John Briggs, *Francis Bacon and the Rhetoric of Nature* (Cambridge, MA: Harvard University Press, 1989).

[47]   Rogers and Beard, 255. "Turquoise was considered particularly appropriate as a jewel for the very young ... worn ... proudly by slightly older little girls. It was the fashion." Turquoise came from Persia (as well as the US Southwest), was a "Jewel known and loved by the ancients," and has been thought to protect its wearer while promoting feelings of kindness, wisdom, and understanding. The name turquoise comes from "Turkish stone."

gambling as wrong; then she begins to lose. Although Daniel has "cast an evil eye on [her] play ... at the roulette table," he later redeems the necklace and anonymously returns it to Gwendolen (462).[48] As he and Gwendolen later come to a mutual understanding that "it was he who sent [back] the necklace," Deronda associates his return of the necklace with the moral rejection of gambling. However, in the subsequent narrative, Gwendolen does gamble, losing once again; her marriage to Grandcourt gives her and her mother much-needed financial security, but she must pay a price: submission to her husband's dominance. Even more detrimental, in the process of marrying Grandcourt, she denies any chances for legitimacy to the children Grandcourt has fathered with Lydia Glasher, a move that drastically lowers Lydia and her children's economic and social prospects. The moral point Daniel upholds is that we must not seek out actions that will hurt others, for "there are enough inevitable turns of fortune which force us to see that our gain is another's loss:—that is one of the ugly aspects of life" (383).[49] Therefore, as the developing narrative highlights Gwendolen's growing fondness for the turquoise necklace, it correspondingly highlights her growing moral awareness with which this jewelry is associated. The narrator relates this "purifying restraining influence" and moral awareness with Gwendolen's father, from whose family Gwendolen had originally inherited the turquoise necklace. Gilbert and Gubar express a parallel between Gwendolen's initial lack of moral moorings and George Eliot's note in a letter, in

---

[48]   Jane Irwin, ed., *George Eliot's Daniel Deronda Notebooks* (New York: Cambridge University Press, 1996) xxvii, 280. Eliot's gambling notes for *Daniel Deronda* find their source in Richard Anthony Proctor, *Cornhill Magazine* 25 (June 1872) 704–17. See also Gordon Haight, *George Eliot: A Biography* (New York: Penguin Books, 1968), who notes that "the germ of *Daniel Deronda*, planted in September 1872 when George Eliot was watching Miss Leigh at the roulette table in Homburg began to grow at once." She made notes on "Gambling Superstitions" from the article in *Cornhill* (Bury, 180). As explained above, Count Palffy's turquoise necklace had been noticed and written about in the England of the early nineteenth century. An interesting parallel to the plot of *Daniel Deronda* is that Count Palffy lost his necklace by using it as collateral while gambling or speculating in the theater. "Metternich and other friends paid his debts and kept the necklace as security, permitting the Count to borrow it on special occasions."

[49]   Deronda's statement here foreshadows the narrative end in which he chooses to marry Mirah, while rejecting Gwendolen who is depending on him to continue to encourage her independence, ultimately an unworkable relation: "She was a victim of his happiness" (877). Also see Martha C. Nussbaum, "Flawed Crystals: James's *The Golden Bowl* and Literature as Moral Philosophy," *Love's Knowledge: Essays on Philosophy and Literature* (New York: Oxford University Press, 1990). Nussbaum claims that instead of being consistent, loyal, and dutiful in her morals, a character like Gwendolen must be willing to "burst out of the tight circle of harmony" of given structures to achieve "love's knowledge" (129). I thank Jennifer Andersen for referring me to this source.

which the author writes, "What shall I be without my Father ... It will seem as if a part of my moral nature were gone."[50]

Pitted against the idea of moral redemption inherent in Gwendolen's attachment to the turquoise necklace is the idea of moral degeneracy associated with the Grandcourt family diamonds. When Gwendolen marries Grandcourt, Lydia's children become legally disinherited.[51] Lydia sends the Grandcourt diamonds to Gwendolen, but when Gwendolen opens the container, she experiences "a spasm of terror," as the diamonds "roll out of the 'casket' onto the floor." The scattered diamonds rob Gwendolen of her expected joy, for the "poisoned gems" symbolize for Gwendolen the psychic consequences of her immoral marriage and the resulting disastrous material consequences for Glasher and her children (407).

Like the diamond jewelry flung across Becky's drawing room in *Vanity Fair*, the image of falling, displaced jewels hitting the floor in *Daniel Deronda* has similarly forged a new recognition of changed relations between the novel's characters Gwendolen, Grandcourt, and Glasher. Indeed, the jewels appear to have an entirely unexpected meaning, even an agency, in representing the new marriage. The diamonds, as a family heirloom, should rightly pass from one Lady Grandcourt to the next. Their temporary ownership by Lydia Glasher—presumably with the expectation that she would be the next Lady Grandcourt—taints the honor they should confer of membership in a titled aristocratic family. The transfer of the jewels from Lydia to Gwendolen, on the contrary, equates the new bride with a kept mistress and consequently signals the loss of her moral inheritance.

The image of the displaced and dispersed jewels occurs in the text at the moment the narrative begins its argument against repressive male practices within marriage. The transfer of diamonds constitutes communication between the two women who suffer at the hands of Grandcourt: Lydia Glasher, who is in "the melancholy position of [someone] who depended on [Grandcourt's] will [and] made a standing banquet for his delight in dominating," (389), and Gwendolen, who "had neither devices at her command to determine his will, nor any rational means of escaping it" (480). Then, when Gwendolen dresses for an evening event, she rejects the spousal tradition of wearing the family diamonds, saying they "don't

---

[50]   Sandra M. Gilbert and Susan Gubar, *The Madwoman in the Attic: The Woman Writer and the Nineteenth-Century Literary Imagination* (New Haven: Yale University Press, 1979) 467, qtg. *Letters*, I:283–4.

[51]   Barbara Leigh Smith Bodichon, "A Brief Summary, in plain language, of the most important laws concerning women: together with a few observations thereon" (1854), Appendix One in Tim Dolin, *Mistress of the House: Women of Property in the Victorian Novel* (Brookfield: Ashgate Publishing Company, 1997) 129. Bodichon writes, "The rights of an illegitimate child are only such as he can acquire; he can inherit nothing, being in law looked upon as nobody's son, but he may acquire property by devise or bequest. He may acquire a surname by reputation, but does not inherit one." At the narrative end, it becomes known that Grandcourt left the larger share of his property to Lydia Glasher's son, and also gave the illegitimate son his last name (782–3).

suit" her; her comment implies a moral stance in opposition to the diamonds' cursed meaning. However, Grandcourt replies, "What you think has nothing to do with it ... I wish you to wear the diamonds" (481), asserting his dominance. The narrator pursues the problem as she explores the methods by which Grandcourt wields such power. Throughout the novel, Gwendolen's affect takes the form of a subordinate Other who identifies with her oppressor: "she might as well have tried to defy the texture of her nerves and the palpitation of her heart. Her husband had a 'ghostly army' at his back, that could close round her wherever she might turn" (503). The ghostly army can be perceived as the abusive power behind class and wealth that Grandcourt personifies and to which Gwendolen has chosen to give her allegiance through marriage.

Opening the casket of jewels exhumes Grandcourt's "ghostly army" at the same time that Gwendolen reads the letter from Lydia Glasher, declaring that Lydia is the "grave in which [Gwendolen's] chance of happiness is buried"; in fact, "the willing wrong" Gwendolen committed would be her "curse" (406). The images of death suggest the rigid appearance which Gwendolen must now assume as she wears the diamonds, an appearance which precludes any moral agency or useful function within the culture at large. She must live out a life of visual display of apparent respectability, personifying class position "like a statue" rather than embodying any self-made moral virtue (745). In assuming the comforts of gentility and money, she has also assumed a static position in which, according to Daniel Cottom, "society lived on its traditional basis is entirely a visual effect."[52] This public position embodying tradition is outside any moral value that Deronda has tried to inculcate in Gwendolen through his gaze, his counsel, and his redemption and return of the turquoise necklace.

The narrative conflict surfaces as a confrontation between Gwendolen's father's family turquoise necklace and the Grandcourt family diamonds, both forms of jewelry handed down through generations: the turquoise acts as Gwendolyn's affirmative reminder that she must form an identity answerable to her own inward moral compass, while the Grandcourt diamonds act as Gwendolen's negative reminder of her harmful moral decisions and the male dominance within her marriage. This conflict further embodies what Eagleton views as a Victorian typology: bourgeois "England ... in precarious transition from the institutions of ... political coercion to the apparatuses of moral-psychological consent."[53] More particularly, Cottom explains, "the downfall of the old notion of gentility would make sense only if one could look inward within individuals."[54] While the eighteenth century had valued universal discourses representing a timeless human nature—a

---

[52]   Daniel Cottom, *Social Figures: George Eliot, Social History, and Literary Representation*, foreword Terry Eagleton, Theory and History of Literature, 44 (Minneapolis: University of Minnesota Press, 1987) 91.

[53]   Terry Eagleton, "Foreword," *Social Figures: George Eliot, Social History, and Literary Representation*, xii.

[54]   Cottom, 90.

mode of knowing that supported static class positions—the nineteenth century developed and valued discourses of individual experience, a mode of knowing that tended to bypass categories of class in favor of *Bildung* of the individual self.[55] In her object relations with her diamonds and turquoise, Gwendolen experiences an emotional transition from one epistemological mode to the other as she moves from a titled position representing nobility to a singular life of analytical and moral perception. Grandcourt personifies the political privilege of class distinction, while Deronda, seeming to be a marginal member of the upper class, is an advocate of the value of moral-psychological consent. So conceived, these two types of jewelry—the turquoise necklace and the Grandcourt diamonds—play a symbolic role not only in the rivalry between Deronda and Grandcourt, but they speak for the conflict between changing discourses of a whole era.

The discursive duel between the turquoise necklace and the diamonds culminates in a scene in which Gwendolen wears both sets of jewelry at once. The rival discourses of gender coercion versus psychological-moral consent— personified in Gwendolen's two lovers, and further embodied in the respective sets of jewelry they have given her—clash together in the very locus of her body. Readers can observe how the conflicting ideas represented by the two types of jewelry splinter Gwendolen's fragile sense of identity. After Grandcourt insists that Gwendolen wear his family diamonds to the upcoming gathering, Gwendolen obeys his commands, but, in addition, she wraps the cumbersome turquoise necklace around her wrist, hiding it under a "burnous," or cape. The diamond/ turquoise scene shows Gwendolen's strategies for communicating through the symbolic jewels within "the enemy's field of vision."[56] In this scene, Gwendolen has altered the conventional placement of the turquoise necklace by wearing it as a bracelet and using it to signal unauthorized, unspoken intentions. Her surreptitious method allows her to show the bracelet only to Deronda, an under-cover communication, as it were. She achieves her aim of showing him the necklace by asking him to fetch a drink of water; when she removes her hand from beneath the burnous to accept the glass, Grandcourt spies the turquoise necklace on her wrist. He immediately recognizes her attempt to subvert his authority, since he had only authorized her to wear the diamonds. Grandcourt asks her, in front of Deronda, "What is that hideous thing you have on your wrist?" She answers vaguely, so that Grandcourt is mystified at the same time that Deronda understands: "It is an old necklace that I like to wear. I lost it once, and someone found it for me" (499). Deronda thinks, because she wears the turquoise, that she would "submit ... her mind to rebuke," and that she wishes to talk with him. Grandcourt permits them to have a private conversation because his egotism cannot admit to jealousy. Alone with Deronda, Gwendolen confides in him "in contrast to her habitual resolute

---

[55]   Michel Foucault, *The Order of Things: An Archaeology of Human Sciences*, a translation of *Les Mots et les choses* (New York: Vintage Books, 1973) 209, 218–20.

[56]   Michel De Certeau, *The Practice of Everyday Life*, trans. Steven Rendall (Berkeley: University of California Press, 1984) 37 (De Certeau quoting van Bulow).

concealment," whilst Deronda "utters ... thought which he had used for himself in moments of painful meditation" (501). Their silences emerge into full speech by the victory of the talismanic turquoise over the Grandcourt family diamonds.[57]

At the narrative end, Gwendolen anticipates a post-narrative future in which she will build a moral identity and will her own action: "I shall live. I mean to live," she reveals in a sort of delirium. She will live freely in consonance with her own desires, practice moral judgment, and not allow herself to be confined in a marriage that requires that she have no will or judgment of her own. This sequence of scenarios featuring the turquoise necklace in confrontation with the Grandcourt diamonds symbolizes the culture's tension between the process of development of a private female self and the received public values that solely permit the static entrenchment of women within a male dominated system of class power.

A third piece of jewelry in the novel appears as Daniel makes several visits to a pawnshop to trade in a diamond ring he has inherited. Daniel states that his errand is "to borrow," offering his "fine diamond ring to offer as security," for he is "not in the habit of wearing it." The idea of exchange of "equivocal objects" is developed into a strong undercurrent in the narrative as a symbolic process for making life changes that alter one's standing in the culture. Daniel is about to exchange his protected position within the ranks of gentility for his Jewish heritage. Developing the idea of exchange, the narrator has the pawnbroker, Mr. Cohen, note that he "wouldn't exchange [his] business with any in the world ... I wouldn't be without a pawn shop, sir ... It puts you in connection with the world at large" (432, 442). For Mr. Cohen, one can and should exchange anything at all, except the idea of exchange itself, epitomized in the shop: without exchange in the larger sense of the idea, there would be only fate. In Gwendolen's and Daniel's case, being able to grow and change forms a leitmotif in their paired narratives.

Exchanging the diamond ring conveys that Daniel is open to the idea of changing his allegiance from his vexed and subordinate position within the power structure of gentility toward an alternative position that answers to his inmost psyche within the Jewish community.[58] As Daniel counsels Gwendolen to become morally aware of the consequences of her actions, he pawns his diamond ring,

---

[57]   Jacques Lacan, "Function and Field of Speech and Language," *Ecrits* (New York: W. W. Norton, 1977) 46–8. The term "full speech" aids Lacan in his analysis of the role of speech in psychoanalysis. Full speech "is not a question of reality, but of [personal] truth." Full speech identifies and reorders perceptions of the past in order to change the future.

[58]   Jonathan Freedman, *The Temple of Culture* (New York: Oxford University Press, 2000) 48. In his discussion of Matthew Arnold's ideas concerning the alienated intellectual as cultural critic in *The Function of Criticism at the Present Time*, Jonathan Freedman argues that the Jew constitutes an "alien within, indistinguishably subversive of the cultural dominant"; indeed, he is "the alien who stands in opposition to all forms of cultural inhibition and social power, the alien who affirms his alienness as the very ground of his being." This stance is not dissimilar to the author's own position as she exits England to write and live on the continent with Lewes, who was already married.

leaves the upper class milieu in order to marry Mirah and to actively acknowledge his Jewish heritage, Daniel has become an "alien within" or an "alienated intellectual" and cultural critic outside the boundaries of any class position.[59]

Throughout the narrative Daniel disparages Gwendolen's lack of moral fiber, while at the same time he displays a sympathy for Gwendolen as a disadvantaged Other. Perhaps the springs of this sympathy are rooted in his own hidden Otherness, as a person of ambiguous parentage and as a member of a Jewish minority. The narrator, for example, chooses to note that "Deronda said he had always felt a little with Caliban, who naturally had his own point of view" (376). Indeed, he would have had to "work [himself] up to an equal standing with [his] legally-born brothers" because of his mysterious parentage (205). For both Daniel and Gwendolen, Otherness is a supreme fact, making itself known through the objection to their diamonds. While Gwendolen's diamonds "roll" onto the floor, Daniel's diamond ring finds its way to the pawnshop. They both reject the gift of diamonds because they reject narrow cultural roles and conventions the acceptance of these jewels symbolizes.

On the whole, in her treatment of the female main characters, Eliot portrays the dilemmas and tactics of the Other, by narrating her characters' refusal to wear conventional jewelry in a conventional manner, adopting instead jewels' alternative symbolic uses. In the very movement and displacement of jewelry, Eliot claims special powers to frame the argument of the Other against the deployment of coercive Victorian social conventions. Through her narratives filled with jewels, she speaks out against rigid gender and class roles that do not allow for individual difference, preference, or self-determining agency. The gem as material object plays a significant role: it becomes radically subversive in its images of unconventional placement, supplying the visual means outside of the written text to express a social identity that is opposed to conventional beliefs and practices normally attached to the jewelry. Gwendolen's affective attachment to the turquoise necklace helps her to express a preferred morality and kinship; at the same time she resists wearing the Grandcourt diamonds that represent a subject-object relation that would subsume her under her spouse's amoral value system.

---

[59] Daniel's diamond ring undergoes another exchange, too, when Mirah's father steals it (861). Here the theft would enable the father to come upon "an advantageous opening for him abroad," a motive not unlike Mlle. Fifine's theft of Becky's diamonds in *Vanity Fair* (860). When the storyline features movement and a change in the ownership of jewels, it destabilizes the status quo, such as these thefts that destabilize class boundaries, or the delivery of diamonds from Lydia to Gwendolen.

VI. Victorian Jewelry, Identity, and the Novel

This study of Victorian jewelry, identity, and the novel owes a tremendous debt to those critics who have looked at Victorian objects as economic commodities.[60] More recent criticism invites a still broader examination of the lenses through which Victorians perceived their material world, and a broader examination of the discursive implications of objects in Victorian literature and culture.[61] My study situates itself within a critical framework of deep Victorian materialism, as it aims to discover underlying causes of the human emotional investments in material objects. As I explain in the next chapter, this work on jewelry demonstrates a wide range of possibilities for literary criticism in regard to objects of all kinds that animate Victorian narratives.

Considering Victorian jewelry's role in its culture and literature allows us to conceive of jewelry as part of a visual language made of objects.[62] Bill Brown

---

[60]   See, for example, Arjun Appadurai, ed., *The Social Life of Things: Commodities in Cultural Perspective* (Cambridge: Cambridge University Press, 1986); Thomas Richards, *The Commodity Culture of Victorian England: Advertising and Spectacle, 1851–1914* (Stanford: Stanford University Press, 1990); Nicholas Thomas, *Entangled Objects: Exchange, Material Culture, and Colonialism in the Pacific* (Cambridge, MA: Harvard University Press, 1991); Jeff Nunokawa, *The Afterlife of Property: Domestic Security and the Victorian Novel* (Princeton: Princeton University Press, 1994); Andrew Miller, *Novels Behind Glass: Commodity, Culture, and Victorian Narrative* (New York: Cambridge University Press, 1995); Jean Baudrillard, *The System of Objects*, trans. James Benedict (New York: Verso, 1996), originally published as *Le systeme des objets: La consummation des signes*, Bibliotheque Mediations, 93 (Paris: Denoel-Gonthier, 1968); Martha Woodmansee and Mark Osteen, eds, *The New Economic Criticism: Studies at the Intersection of Literature and Economics* (New York: Routledge, 1999); Waters, as cited above; and a transitional work between commodity criticism and thing criticism, Elaine Freedgood, "Commodity Criticism and Victorian Thing Culture," in Eileen Gillooly and Deirdre David, eds, *Contemporary Dickens* (Columbus: Ohio State University Press, 2008).

[61]   Fredric Jameson, *The Political Unconscious: Narrative as a Socially Symbolic Act* (Ithaca: Cornell University Press, 1981) 20. Jameson argues for a criticism that "undertake[s] … the unmasking of cultural artifacts as socially symbolic acts." See also Hayden White, *The Content of the Form: Narrative Discourse and Historical Representation* (Baltimore: The Johns Hopkins Press, 1987) 147. White argues that "the ultimate referent of [moving] history … can be approached only by 'passing through its prior textualizations' to arrive at the 'absent causes of present social effects'" (White quoting Althusser). We thus engage in a study of jewelry as a material artifact as it exists in narratives, a particularly rich source in Victorian novels.

[62]   Jonathan Culler, *Ferdinand de Saussure* (Ithaca: Cornell University Press, 1986) 108. Culler notes that "semiotic analysis … required a model that insists on the conventional cultural basis of signs so as to resist the ideological forces that naturalize them. If one starts with the presumption that signs [such as words in a linguistic system or jewelry in a system of object/images) are arbitrary, one will be disposed to seek out the underlying systems of convention." Saussurian linguistics has served as a working model in social sciences and

has recently argued for "a new materialism that grants objects their potency and show[s] how they organize our private and public affection" (7).[63] In what follows, we will ask why Victorian culture expended so much energy—beyond basic needs—manufacturing, displaying, selling, buying, possessing, and discarding material objects.[64] We will consider history's events and fiction's plots as the contexts of this study about the symbolic significance of jewelry as a material object; we will see how real people and fictional characters invent culturally informed and individually elaborated practices in relation to jewels. By examining the coextensive realm of objects and their human subjects, we also embark on an evaluation of the dynamics of human relations to material objects, raising broad questions about the values, practices, and ends of Western culture. In further explanation of this conceptual approach, we can reference Baudrillard who states that "consumption is an active form of relationship (not only to objects, but also to society and to the world), a systematic activity and global response which founds our entire cultural system."[65]

Furthermore, this study recognizes that, through the characters, this literature presents a proliferation of different ideas about jewels. Some characters, for example, perceive jewels as having more or less stable cultural meanings; this perception would indicate that established conventions of the culture govern these characters' lives. Other characters relate to jewels in individually creative ways, forming subjective identities in conflict with conventions of the culture. For the most part, this study considers the second group of characters, locating its analysis in the nineteenth-century discursive space that often separates private and public realms in Victorian culture, where a character creates private meanings for a jewel that conflict with the jewel's public meanings.[66]

---

cultural criticism. See also Jean Baudrillard, "For a Critique of the Political Economy of the Sign," *Selected Writings*, ed. and intro Mark Poster (Cambridge: Polity Press, 1988; Stanford: Stanford University Press, 1988, revised and expanded 2001) 70; Baudrillard discusses the absent causes of present social effects.

63   Bill Brown, "Thing Theory," *Things*, ed. Bill Brown, 1–16. In considering Victorian jewelry's role in its culture and literature, jewelry is, in a larger conception, a representative material object. See also Elaine Freedgood, *The Ideas in Things* (Chicago: University of Chicago Press, 2006).

64   Tim Kasser, *The High Price of Materialism* (Cambridge, MA: MIT Press, 2002) 92. Kasser pinpoints the notion that "overconsumption is one of the fundamental problems threatening the well-being and integrity of Earth's ecosystem. Humans, particularly in the Western hemisphere, are consuming resources at a pace that far outweighs Earth's ability to renew these resources and absorb resultant wastes."

65   Jean Baudrillard, *The System of Objects*, trans. James Benedict (New York: Verso, 1996) 199. Originally published as *Le systeme des objets* (Paris: Editions Gallimard, 1968).

66   Hunt, 66. He attributes "the widening separation between the private and the public" as a cause for the disappearance of sumptuary law so prevalent in the seventeenth century. My discussion recognizes this separation and notes the gap as a site for formation

When individual and cultural values embodied in the jewels exist as an internal conflict for a character, his or her handling of the object constitutes a site of rich emotional production.[67] Pinpointing the causes of emotion or affect can sometimes prove difficult, since what constitutes emotions generally, and what constitutes specific emotions in particular, are widely debated. I agree with Catherine Lutz and Geoffrey M. White's claim that "the individual remains the ultimate seat of emotion"; I also maintain that emotions and affect may be considered "potential sources of correct knowledge about the social world." In contrast to the idea that emotion is "irrational," Lutz and White note that much of the research on emotion rests upon the concept of a "culturally constituted self, positioned at the nexus of personal and social worlds."[68] In this study, the emotions and affects that characters experience often arise from tensions within their personal lives and circumstances, as well as from expectations for them that are embedded in the culture; these emotions form knowledge about life that assists in characters' identity formation. As we shall see, these tensions with their manifestations and meanings are often expressed in the character's handling of specific jewels.

The ultimate goal of this cross-disciplinary study is to enlarge an understanding of how individuals construct meaning in relation to objects embedded in their cultural environment, and to recognize the affective role that material objects play in the shaping of personal identity in Victorian novels and in the formation of cultural cohesion in the West.

The book follows this organization: we first define material objects using a number of disciplinary perspectives, while also allowing "their force as a sensuous presence or as a metaphysical presence" to work their "magic."[69] The subsequent four chapters explore the colorful spectrum of affect associated with Victorian jewelry in the period fiction. The novels I discuss portray individual experiences representative enough to have resonated authentically with the novel's culture-wide reading audience. The varied approaches to these novels follow a certain progression: a reading of a novella by Thackeray that deals with economics and the

---

of individual identity in relation to public culture in the nineteenth century. See also Georg Simmel, *The Sociology of Georg Simmel*, trans., ed., and intro. Kurt H. Wolff (New York: The Free Press, 1950) 334. In writing about the separation of public and private spheres in Victorian culture, Simmel notes that "the secret is a first-rate element of individualization. It is this in a typical dual role: social conditions of strong personal differentiation permit and require secrecy in a high degree."

[67]   Catherine Lutz and Geoffrey M. White, "The Anthropology of Emotions," *Annual Review of Anthropology* 15 (1986) 405–36. They write, "When emotion is defined as a statement about a person's relationship with the world, and particularly problems in that relationship, the most commonly occurring emotions in a society can be seen as markers of the point of tension (or fulfillment) generated by its structure" (421). I thank Anne Bennett for referring me to this source.

[68]   Lutz and White, 408, 409, 417.

[69]   Bill Brown, "Thing Theory," *Critical Inquiry* 28.1 (Autumn 2001) 5.

stock market comes first, then a reading of a Collins novel about imperialism and colonialism's practices circulating in the domestic culture, and then two readings on gender, one on gender and aesthetics as narrated by Eliot, the other on gender and the law, as argued and interpreted by Trollope.

In what follows, the novels discussed reveal and valorize these critical approaches. W. M. Thackeray's *The Great Hoggarty Diamond* presents a family diamond as a commodity fetish that symbolizes capital; the work brims with commentary on the promises and pitfalls of early industrial capitalism, focusing on the swings of emotion instigated by this period's typically sporadic business fortunes. Throughout the narrative, the fate of the diamond's owner is objectified in the fate of the diamond itself. While Samuel Titmarsh, hero of *The Great Hoggarty Diamond*, looks upon his diamond as a fetish, no character in Wilkie Collins's *The Moonstone* owns the Indian diamond long enough for it to become fetishized; instead, numerous characters vie to establish a diamond's symbolic meaning. The novel narrates the fate of a single large diamond—the Moonstone— as a symbol of the fascinations and disadvantages of the British Indian Empire. The Moonstone exemplifies the object as an inherited gift, and its movement plays a crucial role in the emotions—and therefore the identity—of those who interact with the diamond in some way: characters refuse to accept it, consent to receive it, steal it, and even die for it. The final two chapters deal with gender problems. George Eliot's *Middlemarch* presents artful gems as aesthetic objects; cameos and miniatures figure in the plot while the text further extends its aesthetic judgments to sculpture and to women. Here we discover objects of male and female aesthetic judgment and the emotions they arouse in the novel's characters. Finally, Anthony Trollope's *The Eustace Diamonds* reveals the culturally-symbolic dynamics of diamonds when the heroine uses a diamond necklace to confront social and legal barriers against women and to explore possibilities for her own identity in a society in which male prerogatives and the law determine a woman's possibilities.

The chapters that follow examine the dynamics of human-object relations in shaping Western culture, for these relations form a broad emotional web that weaves the culture together.[70] This web of people cum objects continues to produce cultural configurations at a time when other forms of community such as religion and family structure have become less cohesive. Material objects form a nexus around which the culture organizes its time and energy: producing and using objects allows people to ground their sense of a culture-specific empirical reality, to work, to spend what they earn, to enact class identity through the possession and display of objects, and thus to form individual life narratives. However, as a cautionary note about object relations, Kasser argues that

---

[70] For further discussion, see Theodor Adorno, "Subject and Object," *The Adorno Reader*, ed. Brian O'Connor (Oxford: Blackwell Publishers, 2000) 137–51. Published as "Subject and Object" (1969) in *The Essential Frankfurt School Reader*, ed. and trans. Andrew Arato and Eike Gebhardt (Oxford: Basic Blackwell, 1978) 497–511.

the extent to which individuals focus on materialistic pursuits affects the way they interact with other people. When people place a strong emphasis on consuming and buying, earning and spending ... They may also become more likely to treat people like things.[71]

Just as Mr. Merdle acquires Mrs. Merdle to function as a thing upon which to hang expensive jewels, the ways in which Victorian characters relate to jewels may serve as transparent records of not only the ways Victorian reading audiences think, feel, or act in relation to jewels, but the ways they may relate to the living beings they objectify, too. A subject's affect resulting from the quest for material objects may thus symbolize scenarios for interpersonal relationships. Ideally and perhaps ultimately, developing nuanced perceptions about object-relations in novels creates an analytical distance, or a discursive space, that allows us to consider ethical attitudes and behaviors, not only about our production and consumption in the material culture, but about the emotions, beliefs, and actions that cause us to objectify others, either consciously or unconsciously, and "to treat people like things."

---

[71]   Kasser, 67. Kasser refers to Martin Buber's "I-It" relationship, in which other people become reduced to objects.

Chapter 2
Perceiving Objects

Subjectivity is ... the result of the process of engagement with objects.
—Brian O'Connor, ed., The Adorno Reader[1]

Emotions, no less than impressions of sense, can be objectified; they can be experienced as objects.
—Bill Brown, "The Tyranny of Things"[2]

To evaluate the role of jewels in Victorian literature and culture is to engage in the crucial tasks of thinking through characters' subjective perceptions of jewels in novels and appreciating the historical, culture-wide production of jewels as material objects. While during the nineteenth century, material objects were often thought to be the basis for determining what is real, other quite distinct Western points of view about material objects and the material world have circulated both before and after the Victorian era. Over the past four centuries, for example, Western culture has variously viewed jewels as objects of desire, products of empire, repositories of monetary value, representations of accepted respectability and morality, symbols of class prestige, signs of gender definition, evidence of changing fashion, ideal representations of people carved into cameos, or, in the case of miniatures, sentimental remembrances of particular individuals. This variety demonstrates that perceptions about material objects are contingent and changeable, even though the very existence of these objects is historically and culturally determined. Reviewing some ways that Western culture has perceived objects during the modern period contextualizes and deepens any study analyzing how characters in Victorian novels respond to their jewels, how we can think about those dynamic relations with these material objects, and what we can ultimately learn from such a study. Over the course of this chapter, I tap into what George Eliot terms "the provinces of masculine knowledge," the domain of knowledge inaccessible to Dorothea Brooke, heroine of *Middlemarch* (I.7.47). Consequently, in surveying a broad history of Western perceptions of the physical world that have been published and handed down, I necessarily call upon male writings, for to my present knowledge, epistemological considerations concerning the physical world appear to fall into the exclusive domain of this male tradition. I therefore refer to the two related projects that Mary Jacobus delineates concerning women's writing: first, how women, "necessarily working within 'male' discourse ... work

---

[1]   Brian O'Connor, Introduction, "Subject and Object" *The Adorno Reader*, by Theodor Adorno, 138.

[2]   Bill Brown, "The Tyranny of Things," *Critical Inquiry* 28.2 (Winter 2002) 448.

... to deconstruct it," and second, how women might "explore the extent to which patriarchal representation, by contrast, 'silences' women."[3] In response to the second project, one would have to ask, how did women who were contemporaries of Descartes in the early modern period think about the physical world and material objects? Or did they? The answers to this question would open up new and exciting areas of investigation in gender studies.

In this project, I engage in Jacobus's first named project of deconstructing "male discourse" as my ideas build away from the Cartesian *cogito*.[4] The goal here is to arrive instead at an equitable, responsible, and ecological epistemology concerning the material world.

I. Subject and Object: Bridging the Gap

In the centuries since Descartes, Rationalism in the male traditions of Western culture has located knowledge and meaning within the mind of the subject and applied to an object.[5] Even within the last 50 years, Jacques Lacan has argued that "only a subject can understand a meaning; conversely, every phenomenon of meaning implies a subject"; the symbolic "formal fixation" of the object allows the subject to "extend indefinitely his world and his power." Regrettably, Lacan's statements leave out the role of the object in the creation of meaning, allowing, even freeing, the subject to think in terms of control.[6]

Yet, in thinking historically about the location of knowledge, one can trace a movement away from this Cartesian "cogito," in which a subject is the sole determinant of knowledge and meaning. In recent times, theorists have suggested a shift in the source of meaning, and hence in the locus of meaning production: objects outside the subject's mind may actively construct meaning that can then yield knowledge for the subject. As a result, traditional subject positions have become decentered, and under these circumstances, the object or objectified Other assumes a significant role in the construction of meaning. In this view, the object contributes to the ontology and identity of the subject. Jean Baudrillard characterizes the change this way:

> Knowledge, defined conventionally, always proceeds in the same direction, from the subject to the object. But today processes of reversion are emerging

---

[3]   Mary Jacobus, "The Difference of View," *Women Writing and Writing about Women* (1979) 13.

[4]   "*Cogito*" is often used as a shortened form of Descartes' famous Latin phrase "*Cogito ergo sum*," or "I think therefore I am."

[5]   John W. Yolton, *Perception & Reality: A History from Descartes to Kant* (Ithaca: Cornell University Press, 1996).

[6]   Jacques Lacan, "Aggressivity in Psychoanalysis," *Ecrits: A Selection* (New York: W. W. Norton, 1977) 9, 17.

everywhere—in areas from anthropology to viral pathology. It is as if we had torn the object from its opaque and inoffensive stillness ... Today the object wakes up and reacts ... This duel engaged in by the subject and the object means the loss of the subject's hegemonic position ... The object becomes opposed to the classic theory of knowledge.[7]

In another example, Douglas Mao grants the object "extrasubjective integrity," as an Other whose importance we may wish to understand and support; he describes this perspective as "foundationally ecological."[8] To recognize the object's integrity is to enlarge knowledge toward a more holistic, less subject-centered point of view, and to gain insight into the relative contingency of the historical role of the individual subject in the production of meaning in the West.

In further expanding thought about subject/object relations, it may be noted that the English language normally structures its sentences so that a subject acts upon an object. Here I would refer to the "Whorf-Sapir" hypothesis that "verbal and grammatical structures are directly connected to behavior." Cognition and language are synchronized, so that agency resides within the linguistic subject. As Benveniste puts it, "it is literally true that the basis of subjectivity is in the exercise of language," and that "the establishment of subjectivity in language creates the category of person—both in language and also, we believe, outside of it as well."[9] So in a sense my argument works against the English sentence with an active verb, focusing instead on a process that is more diffuse in order to be more perceptive to environments. In this study, the very definition of "object" is at stake: although the object will always be outside the subject and in some sense

---

[7] Jean Baudrillard, *The Vital Illusion*, ed. Julia Witwer (New York: Columbia University Press, 2000) 76–7. See also Fredric Jameson, "Postmodernism and the Consumer Society," *The Cultural Turn: Selected Writings on the Postmodern, 1983–1998* (New York: Verso, 1998) 5. Jameson notes that, in postmodernism, a "new component is what is generally called 'the death of the subject' or, to say it in more conventional language, the end of individualism as such."

[8] Douglas Mao, *Solid Objects: Modernism and the Test of Production* (Princeton: Princeton University Press, 1998) 10. See also Dorothy Hall, "Aesthetics and the New Ethics: Theorizing the Novel in the Twenty-first Century," *PMLA* 124.3 (May 2009) 896–905. Here "ecology" can be interpreted in its usual meaning as an awareness of the process of nature outside human control; the word can also take on a larger scope of meaning that includes both individually specific and culture-wide environments.

[9] Hazard Adams and Leroy Searle, eds, "Benjamin Lee Whorf," *Critical Theory Since 1965* (Tallahassee: Florida State University Press, 1986) 709. See also Benjamin Lee Whorf, "Subjectivity in Language," *Critical Theory Since 1965*, 710–23. Jacques Lacan, "The Agency of the Letter in the Unconscious," *Ecrits*, trans. Alan Sheridan (New York: W. W. Norton & Co, 1977) 148. See also Lorraine Daston, ed., *Biographies of Scientific Objects* (Chicago: University of Chicago Press, 2000) 2–3. Emile Benveniste, "Subjectivity in Language," *Critical Theory Since 1965*, ed. Hazard Adams and Leroy Searle (Tallahassee: Florida State University Press, 1986) 730, 731.

different from it, relationships between subject and object can change from one moment to the next and this dynamic must be reassessed continually. As Adorno notes, "the difference between subject and object cuts through both the subject and the object. It can no more be absolutized than it can be put out of the mind."[10] The ultimate goal in this study, then, is to look for the locus of meaning neither in the rational mind of the subject nor in the opaque materiality of the object, but in the extra-rational, inclusive space across which subject and object interact. This space, created from combined subject/object production of meaning is the site of unconscious emotional responses, as people in history and characters in fiction interrelate with material objects such as jewels.[11] In support of this approach, William Sewell notes

> humans proceed, and can *only* proceed, by gathering and manipulating information
> ... stored ... in the intersubjective space of human signifying practice and in
> the objects—books, maps, clothing, tools, sacred goods, illustrations, the built
> environment—that give it material form.

The subject, the object, and the intersubjective space between them engage in a dialectic that produces Victorian culture's spectrum of affect, defined in this study as a wide variety of emotional responses to cultural beliefs and practices, as they are symbolized in objects.

While this colorful spectrum of affect is a notion that encompasses the received cultural belief system an individual brings to everyday experience, any particular affect or emotion itself arises from the individual's unique subjectivity. Simon O'Sullivan describes affects as "moments in *intensity*, a reaction in/on the body at the level of matter. We might even say that affects are *immanent* to matter. They are certainly immanent to experience." Most importantly, he argues that "affect ... connects us to the world. It is the matter in us responding and resonating with the matter around us. The affect is, in this sense, *trans*human."[12] We can consider the spectrum of affect, then, as a culture's accrued totality of emotion, formed by common experience and given back to the individual to re-form. This web of emotion creates social cohesion, and symbolic objects can play a major role in its constitution.

Functioning much like Lacan's mirror, material objects can absorb and project meaning, thereby promoting the subject's identity construction. Lacan writes about

---

[10]   Adorno, "Subject and Object," 148.

[11]   William H. Sewell, Jr., "Geertz, Cultural Systems, and History: From Synchrony to Transformation," *The Fate of "Culture": Geertz and Beyond*, ed. Sherry B. Ortner (Berkeley: University of California Press, 1999) 44.

[12]   Simon O'Sullivan, "The Aesthetics of Affect," *Angelaki: Journal of the Theoretical Humanities* 6.3 (December 2001) 126, 128.

the child's encounter with his image in the mirror ... from the sixth month. The *mirror stage* ... manifests the affective dynamism by which the subject originally identifies himself with the visual *Gestalt* of his own body.[13]

In *Victorian Jewelry, Identity, and the Novel: Prisms of Culture*, a material object takes the place of the mirror with its body image; the visible object partakes in an affective dynamism that allows the subject to form identity through its reflection of values and ideas.

In fiction and history, characters and people interact with material objects that, in turn, allow human subjects to extend their power out into the world in the form of producing, displaying, selling, admiring, showing, hiding, giving, receiving, taking, possessing, storing, using, and caring for objects. These actions reveal at once the object's culturally symbolic role and the subject's identity, formed through an interactive, affective relation to the object.[14] There are numerable ways to define an object as it fulfills this reflective cultural role, and some sections of this chapter will consider what these specific roles might be.

II. The Commodity as Object of Vision

Of course, Western cultural beliefs about material objects have fluctuated through history, and over the last two centuries, scholars within discrete academic disciplines have often focused on material objects as a source for meaning construction in their own fields. Karl Marx's mid-nineteenth century *Capital* presents an example of how material objects absorb and produce human affect. Wanting to "decipher the hieroglyphic" and "get behind the secret of our own social products," Marx represents the economic commodity in capitalism as an embodiment of the labor that went into it: "the social character of labour appears to us to be an objective character of the products themselves," he notes.[15] If the commodity embodies labor, it represents the time and effort of the worker—a living moment or day in the worker's life—that has been sold for wages. In this framework, the commodity embodies the laborer facing his or her own mortality. As Foucault notes, the "working day ... at once patterns and uses up man's life"; when the laborer produces goods, his labor circulates in the form of things, its "time and toil transformed, concealed, forgotten."[16]

---

[13]   Lacan, "Aggressivity in Psychoanalysis," *Ecrits*, 18.

[14]   For further elucidation on this argument, see Jean Baudrillard, *The System of Objects*, trans. James Benedict (New York: Verso, 1996).

[15]   Karl Marx, *Capital*, ed. Frederick Engels, revised Ernest Untermann, trans. Samuel Moore and Edward Aveling (New York: The Modern Library, 1906) I.I.4, 81–3.

[16]   Michel Foucault, *The Order of Things* (New York: Vintage Books, 1973) 225. Additionally, the laborer, as "*Homo Oeconomicus* is not the human being who represents

The emotions the worker experiences during the manufacturing process are objectified in the material form of the commodity. The sale of a commodity depends upon this objectification, which enables marketing strategies to represent any single product as an identical member of a category, such as "shoe" "hoe," or "bell." Yet a single object's history contains a sequence of these human affects, and given a voice, any object could tell a great story about the investment of human emotion in it as it follows its circuit through the lives of laborers, merchants, and owners, to other masters of its fate in a museum, pawnshop, or landfill.[17]

While Marx identifies commodities produced by Victorian capitalism as an embodiment of labor, Arjun Appadurai has recently described the Victorian commodity as an *"incarnated sign."*[18] Separated by a century, these two interpretations of the commodity reveal the authors' differing contexts as they view an object's role in Victorian culture. While Marx emphasized the commodity's process of production, subsequent adaptation of the commodity form to all facets of Victorian cultural practice allows Appadurai to emphasize Victorian consumption rather than production and to view the common array of commodities as a language whose signs generate a variety of discursive messages that appeal to consumers. Add to this view of commodities the criticism of Thomas Richards, Andrew Miller, and Jeff Nunokawa, and one finds that the Victorian material object produced by the capitalist system becomes "the focal point of all representation, the dead center of the modern world," in Richards's words (1).[19]

Taken together, Marx's and Appadurai's critical interpretations attest to the importance of the commodity, to its ability to communicate an invisible realm of meaning, yoking a visible object like jewelry to aesthetic, political, gendered, or class meanings. Writers on Victorian commodities recognize the initial signifying power generated by these objects at the Great Exhibition of 1851, held at the

---

his own needs to himself, and the objects capable of satisfying them; he is the human being who spends, wears out, and wastes his life in evading the imminence of death" (257).

[17]   Igor Kopytoff, "The Cultural Biography of Things: Commoditization as Process," *The Social Life of Things: Commodities in Cultural Perspective*, ed. Arjun Appadurai (New York: Cambridge University Press, 1986) 90. He writes, "The biography of things in complex societies reveals a similar pattern. In the homogenized world of commodities, an eventful biography of a thing becomes the story of the various singularizations of it, of classifications and reclassification in an uncertain world of categories whose importance shifts with every minor change in context."

[18]   Marx, I.I.4; Appadurai, 38.

[19]   Thomas Richards, *The Commodity Culture of Victorian England: Advertising and Spectacle, 1851–1914* (Stanford: Stanford University Press, 1990) 17–22; Andrew Miller, *Novels Behind Glass: Commodity, Culture, and Victorian Narrative* (Cambridge: Cambridge University Press, 1995) 50–90; Jeff Nunokawa, *The Afterlife of Property: Domestic Security and the Victorian Novel* (Princeton: Princeton University Press, 1994). Also see Martha Woodmansee and Mark Osteen, eds, *The New Economic Criticism: Studies at the Intersection of Literature and Economics* (New York: Routledge, 1999) and Jean Baudrillard, *The System of Objects*, trans. James Benedict (New York: Verso, 1996).

Crystal Palace in London. Calling this event "a monument to consumption," Richards explains that "capitalism was now consolidating its hold over England not only economically but semiotically. The era of the spectacle had begun."[20] Semiotic interpretations of commodities perceive these objects as more than the embodiment of productive labor Marx cited; instead, commodities circulate as symbolic representations that "stand for" ideas, as if by "social agreement" of the consumer culture.[21]

The visual effects of commodities form an essential part of Appadurai's description of them as an "incarnated sign."[22] Discussing the Great Exhibition of 1851, Richards notes the commodity's dependence on a visual realm of projected meaning for its value, as he refers to an iconoclastic Biblical verse—"Where much is, there are many to consume it; and what hath the owner but the sight of it with his eyes?"[23] Richards explains,

> until the Exhibition the commodity had not for a moment occupied center stage in English public life; during and after the Exhibition the commodity became and remained the still center of the turning earth, the focal point of all gazing … The Great Exhibition of 1851 was the first outburst of the phantasmagoria of commodity culture. It inaugurated a way of seeing things that marked indelibly the cultural and commercial life of Victorian England and fashioned a mythology of consumerism that has endured to this day.[24]

In fact, by 1899, Thorsten Veblen had documented the visibility of consumer products, tying their proliferation to sight. Using products to display class became a system of conspicuous consumption; "property [had become] the most easily recognized evidence of a reputable degree of success."[25] In recent times, a lucid description of the dependence of commodities on the visual imagination arises from the work of Guy Debord, who notes that "all effective 'having' must now derive

---

[20]   Richards, 3.

[21]   W. J. T. Mitchell, "Representation," *Critical Terms for Literary Study*, ed. Frank Lentricchia and Thomas McLaughlin (Chicago: University of Chicago Press, 1990) 13.

[22]   For discussion of the importance of Victorian visual experience and criticism on objects in visual culture in literature, photography, and art, respectively, see for example Carol T. Christ and John O. Jordan, eds., *Victorian Literature and the Victorian Visual Imagination* (Berkeley: University of California Press, 1995); Nancy Armstrong, *Fiction in the Age of Photography: The Legacy of British Realism* (Cambridge: Cambridge University Press, 1999); Kate Flint, *The Victorians and the Visual Imagination* (Cambridge: Cambridge University Press, 2000).

[23]   *The Holy Bible, Ecclesiastes* 5:11.

[24]   Richards, 18.

[25]   Thorsten Veblen, *The Theory of the Leisure Class* (Toronto: Dover Publications, 1994), 19.

both its immediate prestige and its ultimate *raison d'etre* from appearances."[26]
Going even one step further, Fredric Jameson notes, in a chiasmic turn of phrase,
that in postmodernism, "the image *is* the commodity today."[27]

The commodity thus owes its power and popularity in both Victorian culture
and current Western culture to the interpretation of objects through vision. Rather
than building an identity over time through consistency of moral action within a
community, an individual can build an amoral, instant identity in an anonymous
urban setting by projecting to others an image of material objects in his or her
possession.[28] Under industrial capitalism, the cultural emphasis on individual
identity and a concomitant erosion of communal identity has allowed commodities
to take the place of people in Western culture. For example, Marx writes, "there
is a social relation between men that assumes, in their eyes, the fantastic form of
a relation between things. So it is in the world of commodities with the products
of men's hands."[29] In this interchange between humans and things, Marx's system
of relations between material objects took the place of communal ties between
and among people. My study adds to this field of subject-object relations as it
examines the relations between people wherein objects serve as public and private
symbols simultaneously.

---

[26]   Guy Debord, *The Society of the Spectacle*, trans. Donald Nicholson-Smith (New
York: Zone Books, 1995) 16.

[27]   Frederic Jameson, *The Cultural Turn: Selected Writings, 1983–1998* (New York:
Verso, 1998) 135 (my emphasis). See also Jean Baudrillard, "Simulacra and Simulations,"
Selected Writings, ed. and intro. Mark Poster (Stanford: Stanford University Press, 1988)
170. Baudrillard takes this thought one step further: if there is no basic reality behind an
image (such as the smoke and mirrors of the Wizard of Oz), then the image refers only to
itself.

[28]   The semiotic discussion of the 1980s and 1990s plays an equally important role in
perceiving how objects project or produce meanings for their subjects. Based originally upon
the linguistic theories of Ferdinand de Saussure, semiotics defines a system of objects within
a given culture as a language of signs that point to invisible meanings. Material objects can
"stand in" for meanings. All manner of human sciences have adapted Saussure's semiotics
to their own fields, and, as a result, have produced important analyses of meaning production
in Western culture. Indeed, leading writers in the fields of psychoanalysis, anthropology,
literary and cultural theory, gender theory, and commodity theory have realized the benefits
of this method as they have sought to analyze these "underlying systems of convention" to
discover sources of meaning production. Lacan, Levi-Strauss, Barthes, de Beauvoir, and
Baudrillard, among others, have all attested to the critical resonance of looking at a cultural
sign as an artifact with a history, whether that sign is a hysterical symptom, a figure in a
dream, an ideology or cultural practice, a word, a written text, a gender construction, or a
commodity. Semiotics has opened up a multitude of new discourses in all disciplines over
the course of the twentieth century, and is also used today in cultural studies.

[29]   Karl Marx, *Capital*, I.I.4, 81–3.

III. The Object as Artifact

Moving to the nineteenth-century field of anthropology, we find that the focus on objects or cultural artifacts from cultures distant to Britain led to a "discourse of alterity."[30] In this period, differences between European and contemporary alien cultures were presumed by anthropologists to arise from their different stages of technological development. According to Susan Hegeman, "categories [of artifacts] were thought to reflect the stages of the development of human civilization, as demonstrated by the complexity of the technical 'invention' required to create each object." Serving "as signs of earlier stages of human development," cultural artifacts were thus displayed in museums with an eye to differences in levels of technological development between cultures.[31]

For centuries, Westerners had viewed material objects or artifacts from alien cultures as inferior. For example, in the seventeenth century, the French trader Tavernier wrote about his travels to a diamond mine in India:

> They have not the art of giving that fine polish to the stones, as we do in Europe. If as with us they had iron wheels … they might then give a finer polish to their stones than they are at present able to do … If the stone is clear, they only turn it on the wheel, taking no pains to shape it for fear of diminishing its weight.[32]

In fact, India valued the size and weight of the stone as a natural find, granting value to the diamond as a product of nature that could symbolize and suggest a natural order to religious and political power; in exact contrast, Europe valued the stone's geometrically cut shape and resulting translucence, granting value

---

[30]   Nicholas Thomas, *Entangled Objects: Exchange, Material Culture, and Colonialism in the Pacific* (Cambridge, MA: Harvard University Press, 1991) 3. This field of study assumed that humans across the globe possessed a universal human nature that was undergoing social evolutionary processes; differences in cultures were explained by their different stages of development on the evolutionary "ladder." This basis inferred that "savage" tribes were lower in their stage of development and that Western technological societies were at the highest stages.

[31]   Susan Hegeman, "Franz Boas and Professional Anthropology: On Mapping Borders of the Modern," *Victorian Studies* 41.3 (Spring 1998) 461. For criticism on a range of Victorian ethnography, see the special issue of *Victorian Studies*, ed. James Buzard and Joseph Childers, 41.3 (Spring 1998).

[32]   Tavernier, "Of Diamonds and the Mines and Rivers where they are found; and in the first place of the Author's Journey to the Mine of Raolconda," *A General Collection of the Best and Most Interesting Voyages and Travels in All Parts of the World* 8, ed. John Pinkerton (Philadelphia: Kimber and Conrad, 1810–12) 235–6. The Victorian view, put forth by Harry Emanuel, similarly argues that diamonds "must undergo the processes of cutting and polishing … on the regularity of the facets and the perfect polish depends the value of the stone, nearly as much as the original material" (63–4).

to the diamond as a manufactured, marketable commodity.[33] In foregrounding technological progress as the criterion for evaluating global cultural artifacts, Western ethnologists bypassed any evaluation of foreign cultures and their artifacts as self-contained.

Furthermore, these ethnologists looked at contemporary alien cultures as living examples of the past and past development, even though the cultures were contemporary. For example, in the early nineteenth century, Charles Darwin expressed these ideas in his *Voyage of the Beagle*. On a continuum of development toward "civilization" he judges the Fuegians of Tierra del Fuego, South America, as among the most "primitive" of peoples. He confesses in a footnote, "I believe, in this extreme part of South America, man exists in a lower state of improvement than in any other part of the world." He further reports, "Viewing such men, one can hardly make oneself believe they are fellow creatures, and inhabitants of the same world."[34] As a result, Darwin judges their cultural artifacts and practices negatively: the Fuegians have no home, no "domestic affection," and their "wretched canoes" are "their most ingenious work," having remained unimproved for 250 years. The berries they eat are "tasteless" and "few," and when they fish, they "jerk [them] out" of the water.

However, at the turn of the century, anthropologist Franz Boas radically changed this view of alien objects. Rather than comparing artifacts with similar functions from different world cultures, he promoted the view that artifacts should be evaluated from a historicist perspective, embedded in a relation with other objects produced in the particular culture. Strongly influenced by Boas, contemporary anthropologists focus upon objects and artifacts as cultural products that represent the values of the people who produced them. Indeed, cultural artifacts mirror and ground social behaviors. In the experience of everyday life, a cultural artifact saturated with collective meanings forms a site where public life meets private experience, where cultural value systems meet individual experience, and where history meets present action. At this intersection of what has been, what is, and what might be, individuals live their daily lives, depending on established meanings of symbolic objects as given structures by which they make sense of the world.

---

[33] Frances Rogers and Alice Beard, *5,000 Years of Gems and Jewelry* (New York: J. B. Lippincott Company, 1947) 129. "In Europe, diamonds had been cut in the form know as *rose* as early as 1520, the idea being to bring out the brilliance of the gem even at considerable sacrifice of its size; but in the Orient, size was an all-important factor. A native gem-cutter would cut small facets (placed hit or miss) to conceal whatever flaws a diamond might have, but he wasted as little as possible of the precious material in the process. Brilliance and symmetry were secondary considerations."

[34] Charles Darwin, *Voyage of the Beagle: Charles Darwin's Journal of Researches*, ed. and intro. Janet Browne and Michael Neve (New York: Penguin, 1989) 177–8. Text first published by Henry Colburn (1839).

Material objects thus play both intimately personal and broadly collective roles in Western culture, and their roles are active. In fact, human attempts to realize possibility can often be represented through the use of these objects that function as cultural symbols, while individually creative and socially unaccepted uses of symbolic objects reveal political and social conflict at the heart of a culture. Discussing this concept in relation to Clifford Geertz's work, William H. Sewell notes:

> What Geertz fails to explore is that the doubleness of symbols also raises the
> possibility of a *disjunction* between their "model of" and "model for" aspects, a
> disjunction that opens up for actors a space for critical reflection about the world
> ... This process of representation employs the symbols made available by the
> culture, of course, but these symbols may be used in a creative or open-ended
> fashion. (47)[35]

Sewell looks for the creation of new meaning through alternative uses of objects. The new uses may entirely change the role of a cultural object in order that it may represent an idea hitherto unrecognized. Here, then, is the project before us: we shall read history and fiction to discover ways that characters creatively use culturally symbolic jewelry; we shall probe character-object relations that reveal alternative uses of these symbols in the process of constructing individual identities. As we shall see, the uses of gems—the way characters hoard, hold, exchange, envy, wear, or refuse to accept them—reveal character loyalties and character discontents immersed in affective experience.

IV. The Object as Real

Objects also serve as a focus for realistic description in Victorian novels; for this culture, objects produce a "reality effect" that conveys authenticity of scene.[36] The "definite, substantial reality" objects lend to settings and characters allow the reader to perceive fiction as a ground for truth. George Eliot, for example, cites with admiration Ruskin's teachings, in which

> the truth of infinite value [is presented] ... as *realism*—the doctrine that all truth
> and beauty are to be attained by a humble and faithful study of nature, and not by

---

[35] Sewell, 47.

[36] Roland Barthes, "The Reality Effect," *French Literary Theory Today* (Cambridge: Cambridge University Press, 1982) 16. In "The reality effect," Barthes notes that "realism is only fragmentary, erratic, restricted to 'details' [or objects], and ... the most realistic narrative imaginable unfolds in an unrealistic manner ... At the very moment when these details are supposed to denote reality directly, all that they do, tacitly, is signify it."

substituting vague forms, bred by imagination on the mists of feeling, in place of definite, substantial reality.[37]

Eliot famously begins *Adam Bede* (1859) with the statement: "With this drop of ink at the end of my pen I will show you the roomy workshop of Mr. Jonathan Burge, carpenter and builder in the village of Hayslope, as it appears on the eighteenth of June, in the year of our Lord 1799."[38] Not only does Eliot's drop of ink mirror the objects of the visible scene—window-frames, doors, planks, wood shavings, a dog, five workmen—the ink also describes the light, sound, and air temperature of that particular place on that particular day. In this case, Eliot's fiction enumerates fictional facts and objects to achieve her goal of representing "definite, substantial reality."

Indeed, objects of nature in the form of data—bug collections, geological formations, or fossils—become the focus of facts in scientific knowledge at just this time.[39] For example, Charles Darwin uses the word "fact" in the first two sentences of *The Origin of Species* (1859), published the same year as *Adam Bede*. He writes:

> When on board H.M.S. Beagle, as naturalist, I was much struck with certain facts in the distribution of the inhabitants of South America, and in the geological relations of the present to the past inhabitants of that continent. These facts seemed to me to throw some light on the origin of species. (65)[40]

Thomas Huxley described Darwin's procedures as follows: "Mr. Darwin ... has endeavoured to determine great facts inductively, by observation and experiment; he has then reasoned from the data thus furnished; and lastly, he has tested the validity of his ratiocination by comparing his deductions with the observed facts of nature."[41] Eliot and Darwin base their realism and their facts on visible, touchable

---

[37]   George Eliot, "John Ruskin's *Modern Painters*, Vol. III," *George Eliot: Selected Critical Writings*, ed. Rosemary Ashton (New York: Oxford University Press, 1992) 248.

[38]   George Eliot, *Adam Bede*, ed. and intro. Stephen Gill (New York: Penguin Books, 1980), first published in 1859, 49.

[39]   Mary Poovey, *A History of the Modern Fact: Problems of Knowledge in the Science of Wealth and Society* (Chicago: University of Chicago Press, 1998) xv. She writes, "we need tools to investigate the conditions that make knowledge possible. Naming the modern fact gives us such a tool." See also Daston.

[40]   Charles Darwin, *The Origin of Species By Means of Natural Selection, or, The Preservation of Favoured Races in the Struggle for Life*, ed. and intro. J. W. Burrow (New York: Penguin Books, 1985).

[41]   Alvar Ellegard, *Darwin and the General Reader: The Reception of Darwin's Theory of Evolution in the British Periodical Press, 1859–1872*, with a new foreword by David L. Hull (Chicago: University of Chicago Press, 1990) 194–5. Ellegard quoting from *Westminster Review* 17 (1860) 566–7.

objects as they exhibit the Victorian fascination with the power and authority of the object to determine and validate "reality."

V. The *Objet d'Art*

While objects were viewed as a foundation for facts, thus constituting an authentication for knowledge in the Victorian era, beautiful objects served as a prompt for Victorian inspiration in the form of aesthetic experience.[42] In his 1790 *Critique of Judgment*, Immanuel Kant established philosophical guidelines for subjective perceptions of beautiful and sublime objects, and his influence on British aesthetics was immeasurable.[43] The following passage highlights Kant's attempt to bridge the gap between subject and object: "The ... universality of the *subjective conditions of estimating objects* forms the sole foundation ... of the delight which we connect with the representation of the object we call beautiful." Kant interprets aesthetic judgment as subjective and affective, although also universal.[44] In the tradition of Cartesian epistemology, Kant argues that "everything turns on the meaning which I can give to this representation, and not on any factor which makes me dependent on the real existence of the object." In other words, there is "no other consciousness of it ... beyond that through sensation of its effect upon the mind."[45] Kant experiences the beautiful object within the Cartesian tradition of locating meaning within the subject—though Kant's aesthetics stresses the affective experience of "delight" rather than Cartesian rational thought.

Kant's treatment of the aesthetic symbol was also applied to people, turning them into living objects.[46] Upholding the cultural interest in classical sculpture

---

[42]   For modern aesthetics, see Edmund Burke, *A Philosphical Enquiry into the Origin of our Ideas of the Sublime and Beautiful* (New York: Oxford University Press, 1990), originally published in 1757. See also Immanuel Kant, *The Critique of Judgment*, trans. James Creed Meredith (Oxford: Clarendon Press, 1952), first edition published in 1790. Ranging from about 1840 to 1890, John Ruskin's work develops a Victorian aesthetic sensibility; see, for example, John D. Rosenberg, ed., *The Genius of John Ruskin: Selections from His Writings* (Charlottesville: University of Virginia Press, 1998) with new bibliography and foreword by Herbert F. Tucker, 24. In "Definition of Greatness in Art," *Modern Painters*, Ruskin defines art as "representing any natural object faithfully" (22).

[43]   See Rosemary Ashton, *The German Idea: Four English Writers and the Reception of German Thought, 1800–1860* (Cambridge: Cambridge University Press, 1980).

[44]   Kant, I.I.9, 59. Kant's key statement in bridging the gap between subject and aesthetic object is this: "In a judgement of taste the pleasure felt by us is exacted from everyone else as necessary, just as if, when we call something beautiful, beauty was to be regarded as a quality of the object forming part of its inherent determination according to concepts."

[45]   Kant, I.I.9, 59; I.I.2, 43; I.I.9, 60.

[46]   Jacques Lacan, "Function and Field of Speech and Language," *Ecrits*, 104. Lacan argues that "the symbol manifests itself first of all as the murder of the thing, and this death

at this time, Kant argues that "the *ideal* of the beautiful [can be] sought in the *human figure*. Here the ideal consists in the expression of the *moral*." Because his concept of aesthetic judgment depends on universal agreement, he is able to make the equation that "the beautiful is the symbol of the morally good."[47] However, established morality of his patriarchal society was largely dictated from the male subject position, which imposed its political values and moral practices upon its judgment of beauty in females. Women who complied with preconceived ideals of moral behavior for females could be considered "beautiful." From a twenty-first century perspective, the practice of aesthetics in the nineteenth century, while seeking to connect material objects to a supersensible realm of moral tenets, equally became a site for male social and political domination of women as aesthetic objects.

In Eliot's *Middlemarch*, Dorothea Brooke experiences pressure to agree on what art objects are beautiful as she visits Rome with her new husband, yet instinctively she becomes uncomfortable among all the classical statues. When her husband and her uncle elicit her agreement for their "disinterested" (because empowered) aesthetic taste, art becomes a gatekeeper for ideological perspectives and moral tenets that maintain their dominant status quo. In another example, in *Middlemarch*, Dorothea questions her uncle's painting of field hands, which "makes other people's hardships picturesque"; here, paintings of romanticized, heroic field laborers could uphold class distinctions by filtering out lower class problems (288).[48]

If Kant perceived aesthetic meaning as produced by imagination and understanding, the subject thus functioned as the sole judge of aesthetic taste and the only site of aesthetic affect. However, Douglas Mao tells us that, by the early twentieth century, "modernism was ... centrally animated by ... an admiration for an object world beyond the manipulations of consciousness." This focus on the object apart from consciousness becomes apparent with the rise of Imagist poetry, for example, and with art characterized by "hardness, coldness, [and] impersonality." Here a poem could be understood as an "object in its own right ... [as] modernist polemics so often insisted it must be."[49] For example, Ezra Pound reveals his interest in objects without imposition of a subject's created meaning: "I have been a tree amid the wood/And many a new thing understood/That was rank folly to my head before." Through an empathic transference, the poet actually becomes the object, which has meaning independent of Pound's experience of it.

---

constitutes in the subject the eternalization of his desire." This description of the dialectic of aesthetic object and subject explains the affect that arises from objects as cultural symbols.

    [47]   Kant, I.I.17, 79; I.II.59, 223.

    [48]   Also see Pierre Bourdieu, *Distinction: A Social Critique of the Judgement of Taste*, trans. Richard Nice (Cambridge, MA: Harvard University Press, 1984). See, for example, nineteenth-century French paintings by Millet or Corot.

    [49]   Mao, 11, 10.

Another modernist, William Carlos Williams, lends similar independent significance to objects when he attests that "so much depends/upon/a red wheel/barrow/glazed with rain/water/beside the white/chickens." One of the most extreme statements of this view may come from Archibald MacLeisch, who argues that a poem, like an object, should be "palpable and mute/as a globed fruit, Dumb/As old medallions to the thumb,/A poem should be wordless/As the flight of birds;" like an opaque thing, "A poem should not mean/But be."[50] Some decades later, the New Criticism proved equally interested in poems as aesthetic objects removed from the socio-political realms of the culture. Critics like Cleanth Brooks, in *The Well Wrought Urn*, engaged in the aesthetic critique of poems as objects of "positive unity" and "achieved harmony," as they looked for timeless qualities that "make them *poems*." For Brooks, the "well wrought urn" of his book title is an analogy for the poem itself; he chooses the urn as a material object to represent his poetics.[51] In the Modern era, objects become so important that, in these examples, works of art and poems become more significant for their roles as aesthetic objects than for any referential meanings they conveyed or cultural problems they might express or solve.

Contemporary reconsiderations of aesthetic judgment of objects have yielded ongoing debates. According to George Levine, cultural criticism has assessed aesthetic experience as "denigrated or reduced to mystified ideology"; instead, he advocates a "rethinking the idea of the 'aesthetic' and the possibility of 'value.'"[52] Having found that aesthetics determined by the subject alone has tended toward social and political impasses, and having found that modernist sensitivity toward the object outside the subject's consciousness has reproduced an opaque environment, I suggest that the locus of new meaning production must encompass the ground that connects subject and object. As it eschews the Cartesian split, this inclusive space awaits exploration; it forms an ecological ground where understanding of the subject and the impact of the object combine to form new knowledge about the way the world works.

The discussion of jewelry as objects in novels thus situates itself across the several disciplines discussed here. Affective ties to jewels are featured in every text, as characters express their goals for identity formation. In each case, the mysterious aesthetic appeal of gems rouses emotions. As a result, the characters open themselves to the meanings the jewels carry, and impute meanings to the jewels. In each case, the jewelry is a gift, and inhabits personal interrelations and dynamic tensions within the culture. As this inquiry makes use of diverse disciplinary discourses that surround the symbolic object of jewelry itself, it

---

[50]   Ezra Pound, "The Tree," 1908; William Carlos Williams, "The Red Wheelbarrow," 1923, Archibald MacLeisch, "Ars Poetica," 1926.

[51]   Cleanth Brooks, *The Well Wrought Urn* (New York: Harcourt, Brace & World, Inc., 1947) 195, 216. The "well wrought urn" is a phrase taken from Donne's "Canonization."

[52]   George Levine, "Introduction: Reclaiming the Aesthetic," *Aesthetics and Ideology*, ed. George Levine (New Brunswick: Rutgers University Press, 1994).

explores the relations between people and their objects—or between objects and their people. Finally, the inquiry asks the all-important question: what part do Victorians assign objects to play in the processes of cultural cohesion and individual identity formation?

In the next chapter, W. M. Thackeray's character, Samuel Titmarsh, displays emotional dependency upon his fetish diamond tiepin, a dynamic that helps Titmarsh to become a member of the London business community of the 1840s.

Chapter 3

The Commodity Fetish in Thackeray's
The Great Hoggarty Diamond

The closer we come ... to the object, the more it steals away from us and finally becomes undecidable.

—Jean Baudrillard[1]

W. M. Thackeray's short novel, *The History of Samuel Titmarsh and The Great Hoggarty Diamond* (1841), focuses on a diamond tiepin that exudes the power of a commodity fetish. Its enabling historical context reflects a time when British industrial development produced newly accumulated private capital for middle class individuals, and the diamond tiepin functioned as an iconic symbol of this new excess capital.[2] Yet the Hoggarty diamond in Samuel's tiepin had not always appeared as such a fashionably potent jewel. When Samuel first inherits the family heirloom jewel as a gift from his aunt, the diamond is mounted inside a large brooch "about the size of a shaving box," and Samuel is inwardly "disgusted" and "disappointed" at having to accept politely such a gift from his aunt (5). The original configuration of the family heirloom brooch is best left to Thackeray's satirical description that merges a number of contemporary styles of jewelry into a cluster of poor taste: the oversized brooch contains the red hair from 13 family

---

[1] Jean Baudrillard, *The Vital Illusion*, ed. Julia Witwer, Wellek Library Lectures (New York: Columbia University Press, 2000).

[2] William Makepeace Thackeray, *The History of Samuel Titmarsh and the Great Hoggarty Diamond*, in *The Christmas Books of Mr. M.A. Titmarsh* (Boston: Estes and Lauriat, 1884). Originally published in *Fraser's Magazine*, September, October, November, and December, 1841 (vol. xxiv), "Edited and Illustrated by Sam's Cousin, Michael Angelo." Michael Angelo Titmarsh, a nom de plume, was "by the middle 1840's ... practically Thackeray's alter ego," according to Gordon Ray. Gordon Ray, *Thackeray: The Uses of Adversity* (New York: McGraw Hill Book Company, Inc., 1955). The full name of the work is cited in the text here, but subsequently the name cited in this text will be shortened to *The Great Hoggarty Diamond*. In this chapter, further quotations from this source will be parenthetically cited in the text. See also *The Works of William Makepeace Thackeray: Volume VIII*, Elibron Classics, Adamant Media Corporation, 2007, an unabridged facsimile of the edition published in 1872 by Smith, Elder & Co., London. The text of *The History of Samuel Titmarsh and the Great Hoggarty Diamond* is also readily available on the Internet. Not only would this novel be suitable for shorter readings in the Victorian classroom (112 pages long); the storyline is exceptionally applicable to current affairs, as it follows the ups and downs of investing, a cycle experienced by many people more than once in the first decade of the twenty-first century.

members, a painted miniature of Samuel's fat grandfather, and the diamond. Here
is how Thackeray details its history and appearance:

> [It was] a large, old-fashioned locket of Dublin manufacture in the year 1795
> … Mr. Hoggarty used to sport [it] at the Lord Lieutenant's balls and elsewhere.
> He wore it at the battle of Vinegar Hill[3] … In the middle of the brooch was
> Hoggarty in the scarlet uniform of the corps of Fencibles to which he belonged;
> around it were thirteen locks of hair, belonging to a baker's dozen of sisters that
> the old gentleman had; and, as all these little ringlets partook of the family hue
> of brilliant auburn, Hoggarty's portrait seemed to the fanciful view like a great
> fat red round of beef surrounded by thirteen carrots.[4] These were dished up on
> a plate of blue enamel, and it was from the GREAT HOGGARTY DIAMOND
> (as we called it in the family), that the collection of hairs in question seemed as
> it were to spring. (3)[5]

This bizarre piece of jewelry, depicted imaginatively to look as ridiculous as
possible, represents to Thackeray's reading audience the Irish heritage of defeat and
second-rate status at the hands of the English: the Irish rebels had been defeated in
1798 at Vinegar Hill. Through contrast, the diamond's future transformation further

------

[3]   According to *Webster's New Geographical Dictionary* (Springfield, MA: G. &
C. Merriam Company, Publishers, 1972), Vinegar Hill is in "Wexford SE Eire, East of
Enniscorthy on the Slaney river; 398 ft.; scene of defeat of Irish rebels by General Lake
June 21, 1798." According to *Brewer's Dictionary of Phrase and Fable* (Philadelphia: J.
B. Lippincott Company, 1930), "Fencibles" is "a kind of militia raised for home service
in 1759, and again in 1794, when a force of 15,000 was raised. It was disbanded in 1802.
The word is short for *defensible.*" My thanks go to Sheldon Goldfarb for helping me trace
these sources.

[4]   Ray, 178, 182. Gordon Ray informs us that Isabel Shawe, Thackeray's wife, was
of Irish descent, had many siblings, and red hair: "she was petite, red-haired, and, if not
pretty, yet decidedly attractive." Richard Altick, *The Presence of the Present: Topics of the
Day in the Victorian Novel* (Columbus: Ohio State University Press, 1991) 316–17. On
the other hand, Altick refers to an "anti-red hair bias" in these times: "no female could be
red-haired at the same time be considered attractive." Altick notes that "It is in Thackeray's
pages that we learn most about the plight of red-haired women in the marriage market, and
therefore, given the centrality of that market in the society of the time, their disadvantage
in life itself." Altick quotes Thackeray from *The Great Hoggarty Diamond* about the 13
red-haired sisters, "Biddy, Minny, Thedy, Widdy, Freddy, Issy, Tizzy, Mysie, Grizzy, Polly,
Dolly, Nell, and Bell—all married, all ugly, and all carr'ty hair (2:17)." Altick notes "That
they were all ugly, according to the current prejudice, went without saying", and that if they
indeed were married "thirteen Irishmen had to take their wives as they found them" (317).

[5]   Thackeray's emphasis. Margaret Flower, *Victorian Jewellery* (New York: A. S.
Barnes and Company, 1973) 21. Margaret Flower writes, "The finest hair brooches … ever
made belong to the forties and fifties, and so do the most exquisite pictures in hair … The
jewelry of sentiment flourished during the Romantic Period."

reveals its initial placement in the brooch as outdated and uncomplimentary: as the narrative progresses, it is refashioned into a tiepin that Samuel Titmarsh proudly wears about London as he circulates in the business world.

In this chapter the criticism of Thackeray's text centers on the diamond, as the gem's status as an object yields criticism from many points of view, a condition that holds true for jewels in fiction generally: in this instance, the diamond contains the story of battles and rebellion within Irish history; the cross-cultural transformation of the diamond's appearance; cultural studies informed by the commodity fetish; fashion in the London "society of the spectacle"; economic history of developing British Victorian capitalism and credit systems, including speculation; the ideal of the gentleman in a changing system of class definition; Christian influences in Victorian secular practices; and gender studies. Criticism centering on the diamond tiepin as a material object also brings to light broad topics such as its function in the period culture and its subject-object relations within the storyline, as all these facets of its existence in the cultural imagination open up a wide range of interdisciplinary critical materials to explore.

I. Cross-Cultural Transformation of the Diamond: From India to Europe in the Late Fifteenth and Sixteenth Centuries

As previously noted, a jewel's appearance is subject to change over time and across cultures. Not only might its setting be reworked, but a gem might be cut, polished, or faceted to create new effects within a changing cultural milieu. The diamond is refashioned in a new setting to endow it with updated fashionable currency. Yet, Samuel's diamond contains transcultural changes in its appearance even before its placement in the brooch.

To observe how Europeans accomplished the diamond's cultural transformation over time, I begin the story of diamonds in Europe at the end of the fifteenth century highlighting two major events: the discovery of a sea route to India, and the formation of the diamond-cutters' guild. While a small stock of Indian diamonds had reached the West through Venice during the fourteenth and fifteenth centuries, the dangerous land routes had remained a deterrent to any sustained volume of trade. However, in 1498, only six years after Columbus had sailed west across the Atlantic to find a shipping route from Europe to India, Portuguese explorer Vasco da Gama successfully navigated a new route to India, going south and eastward around Africa's Cape of Good Hope. Scores of Portuguese traders and colonists immediately followed in his wake. By 1510, the Portuguese had founded a gem-trading colony on the island of Goa, a base through which they traded for diamonds for export to Europe.[6] The traders' memoirs confirmed Marco Polo's earlier stories, reporting unbelievable riches in gems at the Indian courts.

---

[6]   Kathleen Prior and John Adamson, *Maharajas' Jewels* (New York: The Vendome Press, 2000) 30. Some Portuguese traders in India and their recorded dates are: Vasco da

Reports of court women so laden with jewels that they were unable to walk without assistance were augmented by descriptions of servants wearing jewels on their shoes and horses bearing harnesses heavy with gems.

The second significant late fifteenth century event took place in Burgundy, the center of courtly love, where Charles the Bold initiated events that gave rise to the jeweler's craft of diamond cutting. Charles had grown up in the Burgundian court surrounded by Italian princes and secretaries, and he had developed "a passion for everything Italian": diplomacy, warfare, art, and trade—including diamonds from India.[7] In 1475, he entrusted to Louis van Berghem of Bruges three large diamonds acquired through Italian trade. When Berghem cut facets upon the diamonds, their ability to reflect light was enhanced many times over, and his work was rewarded by King Louis XI of Paris with a charter allowing the formation of a diamond-cutters' guild. Guilds were established in Bruges, Antwerp, and Amsterdam, where their members continued to be recognized as the leading diamond-cutters of the West throughout the Victorian Age.[8]

As a result of the guild's foundation, diamonds became more than exotic stones quarried from India and traded across great distances; they were now a legally recognized, manufactured commodity in the rising mercantile economy of the West. The appearance of diamond-cutting as a profession could be viewed as a proleptic event, anticipating the growth of capitalism in the West: as a prototypical model, the guild required specialized labor and the application of innovative technology. In his economic critique of capitalism almost four centuries later, Marx would appear to have explained the formation of the diamond-cutting guild:

> That cooperation which is based on *division of labor* ... is the prevalent characteristic form of the capitalist process of production throughout the

---

Gama (1498); Pedro Alvares Cabral (1500); Duarte Barbosa (1500–16); Domingo Paes (1510); Afonso de Albuquerque (1510) captured the island of Goa.

[7] Richard Vaughan, "Chasing a Sphinx," *History Today* 37 (May 1987) 28.

[8] *Harper's New Monthly Magazine*, "Holland and the Hollanders," Second Paper, 44.261 (February 1872) 349–64. The anonymous article features an 1870s contemporary description of the diamond-cutting industry in Amsterdam, in which the author notes that: "The process of cutting and polishing ... is very slow and tedious, nearly every part of it, from the delicacy and exactness required, needing to be done by hand. The preparation of a single stone demands two months of continuous labor; and the famous Pitt or Regent diamond underwent two years of constant manipulation before it was complete" (351). Edward Jay Epstein, *The Diamond Invention* (http://edwardjayepstein.com/diamond,chap8.htm). Epstein writes, "When the Jewish diamond merchants and workers were forced by the Inquisition to flee from Lisbon and Antwerp, they resettled in Amsterdam. Since cutting factories required no equipment except for hand tools, which were portable, the Jews instantly transformed Amsterdam into the diamond center of Europe. By the middle of the seventeenth century, Jewish diamond merchants helped finance the Dutch East India Company, which organized its own trade route to India. So Amsterdam then replaced Lisbon as the port of entry in Europe for India's diamonds."

manufacturing period so called. That period, roughly speaking, extends from the middle of the 16th century to the last third of the 18th century.[9]

Of course, the guild began in the late fifteenth century—a few years earlier than Marx estimated for this form of production—but with the guild's founding, the new values of technological innovation and specialized labor transformed the ancient Indian diamond into a smaller, faceted stone that was symmetrically shaped and brilliantly translucent, qualities that appealed to the eye in the increasingly urban, visually oriented European culture.

The formation of the diamond-cutting guild had helped to guarantee the diamond's monetary value on the Western market, for the new specialty anticipated the West's priority for manufactured commodities under the growth of capitalism.[10] In his analysis of capitalism, Marx would argue that "the social character of men's labour appears to them [in a commodity] as an objective character stamped upon the product of that labour"; here, the labor of the cutters' guild was literally "stamped" upon, or cut into, the material diamond.[11] The value of the guild-cutters' art, appearing physically on the diamond itself, spoke of the exclusivity of the guild and of its legal charter granted by the monarch. Furthermore, the cutters' labor altered the appearance of the stone, adding value to an already rare and valuable trade item.[12] One might even ask if a mutuality of value was created— if the diamond, at the dawn of capitalism, revealed its agency as an object by giving value to this specialized labor, even as that labor further defined value in

---

[9]   Karl Marx, *Capital: A Critique of the Political Economy* (New York: Modern Library, 1906) IV.XIV.8b.504.

[10]   Igor Kopytoff, "The Cultural Biography of Things: Commoditization as Process," *The Social Life of Things: Commodities in Cultural Perspective*, ed. Arjun Appadurai (New York: Cambridge University Press, 1986) 72.

[11]   Marx I.I.4, 83.

[12]   Marx IV.XIV.8b.504. Diamond-cutting as a profession could be viewed as a proleptic event, anticipating the growth of capitalism in the West: as a prototypical model, the guild required specialized labor and the application of innovative technology. In his economic critique of capitalism almost four centuiries later, Marx would appear to have explained the formation of the diamond-cutting guild: "That cooperation which is based on *division of labor* ... is the prevalent characteristic form of the capitalist process of production throughout the manufacturing period so called. That period, roughly speaking, extends from the middle of the 16th century to the last third of the 18th century." Furthermore, the invention of a new cutting process, as part of capitalism's application of technology and science to the realm of manufacturing is characterized by Marx: "The principle ... of analyzing the process of production into its constituent phases, and of solving the problems thus proposed by the application of the whole range of the natural science, becomes the determining principle everywhere."

the diamond. In effect, the diamond's translucent facets radiated its new role as a highly valued Western commodity.[13]

Since no system for processing the diamond had developed in India, we can infer that it was not a priority in this country's non-capitalist culture. In fact, Marx made the case that "In the ancient Asiatic and other ancient modes of production … conversion of products into commodities … holds a subordinate place."[14] However, assuming the universality of their own culturally bound values of aesthetic translucence and technology, Europeans throughout the modern period continually commented with disdainful hauteur on Indian treatment of the stone, as noted in the previous chapter. In the nineteenth century, Harry Emanuel similarly argues that diamonds "must undergo the processes of cutting and polishing … on the regularity of the facets and perfect polish depends the value of the stone, nearly as much as the original material."[15] More recently and specifically, Rogers and Beard note that

> In Europe, diamonds had been cut in the form known as *rose* as early as 1520, the idea being to bring out the brilliance of the gem even at considerable sacrifice of its size; but in the Orient, size was an all-important factor. A native gem-cutter would cut small facets (placed hit or miss) to conceal whatever flaws a diamond might have, but he wasted as little as possible of the precious material in the process. Brilliance and symmetry were secondary considerations.[16]

Europe valued the stone's geometrically cut shape and resulting translucence, granting added value to the natural diamond as a manufactured, marketable commodity. However, throughout India, the stone had been valued for its size and weight as a natural find, granting value to the diamond as a product of nature that in turn symbolized religious and political power.

Just what were the values in Indian society that moved maharajas to amass huge collections of gems, while honoring their gems' natural size and shape? The diamond's role in India symbolized the culture's most significant values: talismanic power, political power, and divine power. Ancient Hindu astrological ideas about the gems assumed that as amulets, talismans, or charms, diamonds could ward off evil or disease, and promote good fortune. In another example, the nine-gem amulet was also thought to harness the energy of the planets in the heavens, representing the totality of the universe: diamond, pearl, ruby, sapphire,

---

[13]   Colin Renfrew, "Varna and the Emergence of Wealth in Prehistoric Europe," *The Social Life of Things*, ed. Arjun Appadurai (New York: Cambridge University Press, 1986) 144.

[14]   Marx I.II.91.

[15]   Harry Emanuel, F.R.G.S., *Diamonds and Precious Stones: Their History, Value, and Distinguishing Characteristics*, 2nd edn (London: John Camden Hotten, 1867) 63–4.

[16]   Frances Rogers and Alice Beard, *5,000 Years of Gems and Jewelry* (New York: J. B. Lippincott Company, 1947) 129.

emerald, topaz, cat's eye, coral, and hyacinth (or red zircon), combined in a single piece of jewelry, could rule the destiny of its owner.[17]

These stones were seen to influence future events and exert agency in human affairs. Interestingly, the amulet's ability to aid in attempts to manage the future is not unlike the function of the fetish of eighteenth-century Europe, when Europeans used fetishes as guarantees for future exchange contracts in colonial trade. The performative amulet and fetish executed guarantees for future events, and in so doing, could "draw on the arbitrary force of the divine."[18]

Long before Samuel Hoggarty's family had acquired the diamond to mount in a brooch that illustrated the family's Irish history, the diamond had—for centuries—undergone an acculturation to Western ideas and values. However, if the diamond had drastically changed its appearance during its acculturation to Western Europe from its Indian origins, it also assumed a cultural function that exuded emotional power as a commodity fetish.

II. The Diamond as Commodity Fetish

A history of the fetish in Western culture reveals the reasons for its cross-disciplinary flexibility.[19] The fetish originated as a religious object, entering European discourse at the end of the eighteenth century, when colonialist negotiations with "primitive" peoples demanded a form of legal security for commercial transactions. The dynamic of Victorian fetishism thus linked a religious object to the legal rhetoric of a trade agreement, as the fetish became widely diffused throughout European culture, "knotting questions of language, religion, commerce, and desire."[20] Marx had discerned the ability of the fetish to represent a doubling of the physical and metaphysical, describing the economic commodity as a fetish with "sensible

---

[17]   Prior and Adamson, 12.

[18]   Marc Redfield, *Phantom Formations: Aesthetic Ideology and the Bildungsroman* (Ithaca: Cornell University Press, 1996) 181. Redfield uses these words to describe the fetish.

[19]   For criticism on fetishism see, for example, Peter Melville Logan, *Victorian Fetishism: Intellectuals and Primitives* (Albany: SUNY Press, 2009), L. McCallum, *Object Lessons: How to Do Things with Fetishism* (Albany: SUNY Press, 1999); Henry Krips, *Fetish: An Erotics of Culture* (Ithaca: Cornell University Press, 1999); Patricia Spyer, ed., *Border Fetishisms: Material Objects in Unstable Spaces* (New York, 1998); Emily Apter and William Pietz, eds, *Fetishism as Cultural Discourse* (Ithaca: Cornell University Press, 1993); and Emily Apter, *Feminizing the Fetish: Psychoanalysis and Narrative Obsession in Turn-of-the-Century France* (Ithaca: Cornell University Press, 1991).

[20]   Redfield, 181. See also Emily Apter, "Introduction," *Fetishism as Cultural Discourse* (Ithaca: Cornell University Press, 1993); Ann Cvetkovich, *Mixed Feelings: Feminism, Mass Culture, and Victorian Sensationalism* (New Brunswick: Rutgers University Press, 1992) 191–7 ("The Mystery of the Commodity").

supersensible" social qualities inhering within its materiality.[21] Later on, Freud adapted the fetish to the field of psychoanalysis, in which he viewed the object as a metaphoric substitution for a lack; as Henry Krips describes it, the fetish "stands in the place of that which cannot be remembered directly. It substitutes for that which is and must remain repressed."[22] Even more importantly, Krips recognizes the ways in which "particular users of a cultural object may adapt it to suit their own peculiar strategic and psychic ends." While the fetish is rooted in a subjectively experienced empirical "thingness," it reveals the power of objects to prompt human emotions: as people become involved in the desire for commercial products, class status, friendship, intimacy, and personal security, they become enthralled with the object or commodity as a fetish.

Although the fetish takes part in the spectrum of affect—what Henry Krips might term an "erotics of culture"—Krips rightly calls attention to the problem of generalizing individual fetish experience into the "communual effects of cultural artifacts." The question arises whether personal affect can ever be generalized to a cultural level, and Krips asserts that "only for very basic psychic structures will the relation between the psychic and the cultural assume an effectively universal dimension" (7). William Pietz, however, clarifies the relation between individual and society regarding affect produced by the fetish: in his view, the fetish is the site of an opposition between the individual and society:

> This … historical object is … "personalized" in the sense that beyond its status as a collective social object it evokes an intensely personal response from individuals. This intense relation to the individual's experience of his or her own living self through an impassioned response to the fetish object is always *incommensurable* with (whether in a way that reinforces or undercuts) the social value codes within which the fetish holds the status of a material signifier.[23]

---

[21]   Karl Marx, "The Value Form," Appendix to the First German edition of *Capital*, 1, 1867, translated by Mark Roth and Wal Suchting, 1978 from *Capital and Class* 4 (Spring 1978) 130–50. www.marxists.org/archive/marx/works/1867-c1/appendix.htm#n1, 6/20/2009.

[22]   Sigmund Freud, *On Sexuality*, intro. Steven Marcus, trans. and ed. James Strachey (New York: Basic Books, Inc., 1962) 19. He writes, "the normal sexual object is replaced by another which bears some relation to it … What is substituted … is some part of the body … or some inanimate object which bears an assignable relation to the person whom it replaces … Such substitutes are with some justice likened to the fetishes in which savages believe that their gods are embodied." Krips, 6, 7. Most importantly for this inquiry, Freud notes that "the replacement of the [sexual] object by a fetish is determined by a symbolic connection of thought, of which the person concerned is usually not conscious."

[23]   William Pietz, "The Problem of the Fetish," pt. 1, *Res* 9 (Spring 1985), qtd. by Emily Apter, "Introduction," *Fetishism as Cultural Discourse*, 3 (my emphasis).

Pietz summarizes succinctly the interpretive method used for the discussion of *The Hoggarty Diamond* that follows; his methodology focuses on cultural structures and the way individuals either uphold or disavow them through object relations and interactions. We shall interpret the business climate of the 1840s as a starting point from which to explore individual affect.

So powerful are commodity fetishes as cultural symbols that Marx attributes to them the characteristics of gods; they "appear as independent beings endowed with life."[24] Similarly, Thackeray gives the Great Hoggarty Diamond an independent existence and life of its own. Not only does the diamond fetish have a name and a family history as it is "born" into this narrative of its life, it grows in power as it becomes acculturated. Its transformation into a stylish jewel allows it to intercede on Samuel's behalf in business affairs, as it appears to produce credit and profit for its owner, as if by magic. At night, the diamond rests on its own pincushion, specially made by Mary Smith, Samuel's girlfriend. Because Samuel owns the diamond, his faithful friend Gus comes to think of Samuel as "a superior being," as if the symbolic nature of the diamond has metonymically transferred its potent qualities to its owner and wearer. The fetish also shows its supernatural agency for its owner in other specific ways.[25] When Samuel returns to his rural hometown for his wedding, everyone treats him "with marked consideration" (60). As if the diamond offered him a protective shield, a dog that chased him in his youth does "not make the slightest attempt at biting" him now (59). Because his wedding day is "The Happiest Day of [his] … Life," he attributes his good fortune to his fetish, noting, "I wore sparkling in my bosom the GREAT HOGGARTY DIAMOND"[26] (61).

In Thackeray's novella, the diamond is so imbued with supernatural socioeconomic power, that in the moment Samuel receives it from his aunt, he designates the diamond a "machine in … my hands" (5). The "machine" is a label laden with symbolic significance for Victorian readers and for the emplotment of the story. Carlyle had named this period "the Age of Machinery" in his essay "Signs of the Times."[27] The industrial machine itself had just taken on new resonance as a cultural icon in early Victorian times; according to Nancy Armstrong, by the 1840s, "the industrialists … [had] won the intellectual war … to determine the definition of culture itself—as the literate public began regarding resistance to machinery as

---

[24]   Karl Marx, *Capital: A Critique of Political Economy*, ed. Frederick Engels, revised Ernest Untermann, trans. Samuel Moore and Edward Aveling (New York: The Modern Library, 1906) I.I.4, 83.

[25]   Ray B. Browne, "Introduction," *Objects of Special Devotion: Fetishes and Fetishism in Popular Culture*, ed. Ray B. Browne (Bowling Green: Bowling Green University Popular Press, 1982) 1. He defines the term "fetish": "A fetish is … an object, person, concept, theory or philosophy believed to possess extraordinary magical or supernatural power."

[26]   Thackeray's emphasis.

[27]   Thomas Carlyle, "Signs of the Times," *A Carlyle Reader: Selections from the Writings of Thomas Carlyle*, ed. G. B. Tennyson (Cambridge: Cambridge University Press, 1984) 6.

more dangerous than machinery itself."[28] Samuel's diamond fetish has the ability to act as a "machine" in this text, with the power to produce excess wealth far beyond the amount that ordinary human labor could produce. In an alternative, literary definition, Pope had defined the machine as a role played by supernatural beings who intercede to redirect the plot of a literary work. His definition was based, in turn, on the literary device, "deus ex machina," which had been a source of supernatural plot causation in ancient Greek drama.[29]

In Thackeray's work, the diamond fetish appears to exert all these supernatural powers to manage Samuel's career in business. For example, it evinces its agency in a scene in which Samuel and his boss, Mr. Brough, converse about what has caused Samuel's amazing rise within the company's ranks. Mr. Brough attributes Samuel's rise not to his supposed relation to Lady Drum and her family, nor because of his mother's small annuity, nor even because of his aunt's fortune, but because of ... "MY AUNT'S DIAMOND-PIN!" Samuel interrupts naively and spontaneously (55).[30] In the end, the designation of the diamond as a "machine" works in a double capacity as a contemporary economic icon with a supernatural literary agency that can radically influence events. The double source of this label argues for both the diamond's economic power and its power as a fetish to intercede in human affairs.

III. The Diamond's Transformation: From Hair Brooch to Tiepin

In *The Great Hoggarty Diamond*, Samuel Titmarsh engages in business activities that advance him in London society; in the process, he displays all the enthusiastic innocence of a rural youth. His Aunt Hoggarty jumpstarts his career by giving him the heirloom diamond brooch, which the jeweler refashions into a diamond stickpin Samuel can wear to the office and around town. The original setting for the diamond is discarded, because the outlandish image of the brooch conflicts with prevailing taste that values the diamond as a singular stone in a piece of jewelry.

---

[28]   Nancy Armstrong, *Desire and Domestic Fiction: A Political History of the Novel* (New York: Oxford University Press, 1987) 162.

[29]   C. Hugh Holman and William Harmon, *A Handbook to Literature*, 5th edn (New York: Macmillan Publishing Company, 1986) 285–6, 138–9. Edgar F. Harden, *Thackeray's English Humourists and Four Georges* (Newark: University of Delaware Press, 1985) 87. Alexander Pope was one of the featured eighteenth-century writers in Thackeray's subsequent lectures on "The English Humourists." Thackeray thought of Pope as "the greatest literary artist that England has seen," reserving for him the position as "the highest among the English wits and humourists with whom we have to rank him." Harden quoting Thackeray, first published version of the lecture on Pope, 1851. Deus ex machina is defined as "the employment of some unexpected and improbable incident in a story or play to make things turn out right ... It is found most frequently in melodrama."

[30]   Thackeray's emphasis.

The large, hideous old brooch is simply unable to exert any signifying power in the current British cultural setting.[31] Instead, Aunt Hoggarty offers to pay to have the diamond reset as a stickpin for Samuel, for, as he states, "a diamond-pin is a handsome thing, and will give me a *distingué* air."[32] Indeed, the diamond must appear as an updated image in order to function with power as a fetish. Samuel thus takes the diamond brooch to "the great jeweller, Mr. Polonius," who resets the diamond into a new stickpin (7).[33] The diamond within the brooch, which had been shunned and abhorred by Samuel as hopelessly old-fashioned, takes on a new identity as it is reset and transformed by the jeweler into a fashionable jewel that exudes an aura of authentic power within its cultural medium.

Across the narrative trajectory, the Hoggarty diamond materializes as various incarnations that represent values of Victorian culture. It begins as a secondary gem within a larger piece of jewelry, overshadowed by a miniature, hair, and enamel in the brooch. In a parallel manner, diamonds appeared in the early British nineteenth century as one among many gems in a piece of jewelry. Marie-Louise Mastai notes that

> [diamonds] earlier had been simply one of several elements in the composition
> of a jewel, on a par, for instance, with enameling and pearls. But a truly fine

---

[31]   Ginny Redington Dawes and Corinne Davidov, *Victorian Jewelry: Unexplored Treasures* (New York: Abbeville Press Publishers, 1991) 140; Shirley Bury, *Jewellery, 1789–1910, The International Era*, Volume I, 1789–1861 (Woodbridge, Suffolk: Antique Collectors' Club, Ltd., 1991) 67. Concerning the style of the brooch, Dawes and Davidov write that "except for a brief period in 1838 when, for some reason, hair jewelry was reviled, it enjoyed a popularity right up to the last quarter of the century." Since Thackeray published this work in 1841, it is possible that his work reflected this brief fad of reviling hair jewelry. Though Samuel wishes to retain the miniature portrait of his uncle that is contained in the original brooch, he tells the jeweler, "never mind the hair" (II.17). Page 140 also contains an illustration of a "family tree" brooch made of hair: in other words, this kind of brooch featuring hair from different family members was actually made in mid-Victorian times, but the hair is on the reverse side of the decoration, unlike Thackeray's description which places a miniature, the hair, and the diamond all contained on one side of the brooch.

[32]   Peter Hinks, *Nineteenth-Century Jewellery* (London: Faber & Faber, 1975) 73. Though jewelry was generally considered a woman's fashion item, during the Victorian period, men did wear rings, tiepins, and cufflinks—in other words, small pieces of jewelry. Peter Hinks notes that "most men wore tiepins … The most usual designs were of a single pearl or diamond."

[33]   Altick, 583, 214. Altick notes that Mr. Polonius was, in real life, the jeweler, Thomas Hamlet. The connection of "Polonius" and "Hamlet" was sure to be noted by contemporary readers. He also writes that "In the new circumstances of nineteenth-century life, brand names of consumer products and the names of fashionable tradesmen became household words and thus entered the ready vocabulary of fiction depicting contemporary middle-class life with what came to be called 'domestic realism.'"

brilliant-cut diamond pulsates with prismatic radiance ... No longer could such
a gem be regarded as subordinate in design.[34]

Mastai equally attributes this developing trend of wearing the diamond as a sole
gem to advances in the technology of cutting diamonds to create more translucence.
As diamonds increased in value and popularity, they became widely recognized
as iconic symbols of capital; in turn, they also became a singular focal point in
jewelry, displayed as a solitary gem. Capital had become a new basis for upper
class status in the nineteenth century, and the connection made between diamonds,
capital, and class allowed the culture to use this gem to represent to itself the
changing basis of class definitions. The incarnation of the diamond as the sole
gem in a tiepin worn by a businessman thus formed a perfect symbol for the actual
changes occurring within the culture.

Immediately after Samuel receives the diamond from the jeweler in its newly
fashionable form, he experiences a prosperous turn in his socioeconomic fortunes.
These fortunes could be seen as a result of the expanding systems of credit in the
1830s and 1840s, and the power of his fashionable diamond to symbolize wealth.
First, Samuel is claimed as a "cousin" by Lady Drum and is invited to ride in
her carriage in the park. His boss, Mr. Brough, sends him to the tailor for some
expensive clothes, and tells Samuel not to worry about the bill. Business associates
begin to treat him with every possible kindness and respect. He receives so much
income from his job at The West Diddlesex Fire and Life Insurance Company, that
he is able to marry his hometown sweetheart, Mary Smith, whereupon they move
to a house in London. Samuel is the utterly astonished and happy recipient of
profuse good fortune, as beneficial events arise one after another in the narrative.
Indeed, the diamond brings Samuel as close to heaven on earth as he is able to
imagine. As he attributes his fortune to the diamond tiepin, Samuel variously
refers to events surrounding his fetish as "the luck the pin had brought me," "the
magic of the pin," or "the pin that produces wonderful effects" (31, 38, 8).

The plot in this initial section of *The Great Hoggarty Diamond* is fueled by
Samuel's desire to rise within the ranks of society and to succeed in business; he
naturally wishes to receive all the good fortune his society has to offer. Samuel's
aesthetic attraction to the translucent tiepin is at play here: as a symbol of business
success and ever-increasing income, the diamond exemplifies what Thomas
Weiskel conceives as "the aesthetic [which] ... answers, for limited bourgeois,
individualist man, the question, 'What may I hope for?'"[35] To come into a state of
material prosperity as a young adult in this urban society of expanding economic
wellbeing and easy credit may have been a typical aspiration for a young middle

---

[34]   Marie-Louise d'Otrange Mastai, *Jewelry*, ed. Brenda Gilchrist, The Smithsonian
Illustrated Library of Antiques (Cooper-Hewitt Museum: The Smithsonian Institution's
National Museum of Design, 1981) 88.

[35]   Thomas Weiskel, *The Romantic Sublime: Studies in the Structure and Psychology
of Transcendence* (Baltimore: The Johns Hopkins University Press, 1976, 1986) 45.

class man in the early Victorian period—unless, of course, one views the society's goals as tainted, a question that will recur as the work progresses. Though Samuel begins the narrative in a state of rural poverty, he has all the ambition that unfolding business opportunity will allow him to realize; his desire attaches itself to all the jobs, human networks, or commodities other people value. He is naively seduced by whatever *idées reçues* appear advantageous in his society of the 1840s, and his acculturation to the values of capitalism is complete.

In the text, Samuel assimilates the diamond's fetishistic powers to his own economic belief system, while in an exchange, the burden of his desire for financial success is equally appropriated by the diamond. This dynamic of the fetish may "be said to produce for capitalism a desiring subject," as it launches him into a world of capitalist enterprise, investment, and the eros of getting and spending.[36] Here Samuel may encounter a plethora of people, situations, and work demands, but above all Samuel believes in the abstract structure of the business culture, as he builds his identity from business discourses: "premises [that] remain unarticulated, and therefore often unchallenged," both to himself and to the reading audience.[37] It is a clear cultural structure from which a naive character like Samuel can form his identity. Taking the abstraction of the business world as his unified belief system, and projecting it onto the diamond so that the diamond's materiality coincides with its supernatural quality, fetishism can be viewed as "ur-materialism," as John Plotz terms it.[38] The diamond thus acts as a machine that drives Samuel along a chain of desire. Samuel attests to this very dynamic, for at one point in the narrative he summarizes:

> Well, the pin certainly worked wonders: for not content merely with making me a present of a ride in a countess's carriage, of a haunch of venison and two baskets of fruit, and the dinner at Roundhand's … my diamond had other honors in store for me, and procured me the honor of an invitation to the house of our director, Mr. Brough. (33)

These varied commodities and socio-political advantages can be categorized as effects of Samuel's desire. As if to explain, Jean Baudrillard notes that

---

[36]   Redfield, 182.

[37]   Audrey Jaffe, *The Affective Life of the Average Man: The Victorian Novel and the Stock-market Graph*, Victorian Critical Interventions, Donald E. Hall, Series ed. (Columbus: The Ohio State University Press, 2010).

[38]   John Plotz, "'*Victorian Fetishism: Intellectuals and Primitives,*' by Peter Melville Logan," *Victorian Studies* 52.2 (Winter 2010) 284.

> the surface reality of a *desire* … is insatiable because it is founded on a lack. And
> this desire, which can never be satisfied, signifies itself locally in a succession
> of objects and needs.[39]

The original source of the desire is "fixed" in the diamond itself; however, the
fixation modulates into a "consistent displacing of reference," to use Emily Apter's
phrase.[40] More and more material objects circulate through Samuel's fictional life
in the narrative.

Thackeray's work moves between multivalent layers of conscious rationality
and subconscious emotional investment concerning the diamond's fetish value. As
the novel makes its claims for the diamond's magical powers, the text oscillates
between presenting Samuel as a reasonable owner of a diamond, and presenting
him as subconsciously accessible to all its apparent emotive power, responding
to the fetish at a deep psychological level. If the diamond gives an illusion that
it has powers of agency to cause events in business affairs, one could still say
that because its agency informs actual events from Samuel's perspective, he could
experience its power as real.

What does it mean to Samuel as a desiring subject to be caught within this
dynamic of commodity fetishism? If he wishes to ride in a fancy carriage in
the park or furnish a house in London, is he acting individually with agency as
he might think, or is he a mere tool, fatefully framed by his culturally-wrought
desire for commodities? Such questions could be said to situate themselves as
an economic displacement of historically religious concerns over free will versus
predestination.

As narrator, Thackeray couches his own uncertainty in parody, affirming only to
subvert the power of the diamond as a commodity fetish. This process destabilizes
the fetish, effectively calling into question the capitalist enterprise it symbolizes.
In this way, Thackeray reflects a prevailing sentiment of the time that realizes

> the apparent vulnerability of the individual, who seems to need both acuteness
> and a fair share of "rascality" to survive in a world in which older traditions and

---

[39]   Jean Baudrillard, "Consumer Society," *Selected Writings*, ed. and intro. Mark
Poster (Stanford: Stanford University Press, 1988) 45. (Baudrillard's emphasis.)

[40]   Emily Apter, "Introduction," *Fetishism as Cultural Discourse* (Ithaca: Cornell
University Press, 1993) 3. Jacques Lacan, "Agency of the Letter in the Unconscious,"
Ecrits: A Selection, trans. Alan Sheridan (New York: W. W. Norton & Company, 1977)
166–7. Lacan writes: "And the enigmas that desire seems to pose … amount to no other …
instinct than that of being caught in the rails – eternally stretching forth towards the *desire
for something else* – of metonymy. Hence its 'perverse' fixation … and the fascinating
image of the fetish is petrified."

personal relationships have given way to the "cash nexus" of the nineteenth-century economy.[41]

Indeed, the work itself projects a profoundly vexed attitude toward investment and the new power of the business world of the 1840s.

IV. Economic Background

Thackeray's *Great Hoggarty Diamond* lays bare Victorian affective experiences of the newly expanding financial system of the late 1830's and early 1840s, as it narrates the twin stories of Samuel Titmarsh and his diamond fetish. This period featured personal economic crises such as investment fraud and bankruptcy for some, while at the same time it allowed for heady accumulations of profits for others. In *The Great Hoggarty Diamond*, Samuel Titmarsh, along with his diamond fetish, becomes enmeshed in this untamed, unregulated system, experiencing the full range of its financial extremes.

Although investors may have believed in Adam Smith's "invisible hand" to guide business startups toward profit, they also discovered that the hand would lose its grip in certain unfortunate instances.[42] Nicholas Shrimpton informs us that the "commercial crisis of the 1820's ... provided material for literature" and one example he enumerates is Thackeray's *The Great Hoggarty Diamond*. This novella, among other literary works, "reflect[s]" the year 1825, when "it was not one bubble but a thousand; mines by the score ... companies by the hundred; loans to every nation or tribe ... in short, a fever of speculation, and the whole nation raging with it" (Shrimpton, 22, quoting Charles Reade, 188–9.)[43] A. Y. Aytoun, writing in 1849, characterizes investments during the period leading up to Thackeray's drafting of *The Great Hoggarty Diamond* in what may not have been hyperbole:

All kinds of ridiculous schemes found favour in the public eye: nothing was too absurd or preposterous to scare away applicants for shares. Mining,

---

[41]   Barbara Weiss, *The Hell of the English* (Lewisburg: Bucknell University Press, 1986) 67.

[42]   Adam Smith, *An Inquiry into the Nature and Causes of the Wealth of Nations*, 1776, IV, 2. He writes, "Every individual ... generally, indeed, neither intends to promote the public interest, nor knows how much he is promoting it ... By directing that industry in such a manner as its produce may be of the greatest value, he intends only his own gain, and he is in this, as in many other cases, led by an *invisible hand* to promote an end which was no part of his intention."

[43]   Nicholas Shrimpton, "'Even these metallic problems have their melodramatic side': Money in Victorian Literature," in *Victorian Literature and Finance*, ed. Francis O'Gorman (New York: Oxford University Press, 2007) 22.

building, shipping, insurance, railway, colonizing, and washing companies were established: even an association for the making of gold was subscribed for to the full amount, and doubtless a balloon company for lunar purposes would have been equally popular.[44]

Aytoun concludes that "all things are measured by money." However, by the late 1830s and early 1840s, "panic of the middle and upper classes and … anger of the laboring classes over the instability and cruelty of the economy" pervaded the culture, as wild gyrations of profits and losses resulted in emotional states of ecstasy and grief.[45] While "the vision of the nineteenth century *laissez faire* … divorced [the economy] from both psychological and ethical considerations," in contrast, Thackeray represented the emotions of the investment world through the lived experience of the innocent country bumpkin, Samuel Titmarsh.[46]

Two related economic problems are expressed and addressed in *The Great Hoggarty Diamond*: many people had acquired excess capital without an understanding of how to invest it. First, "Britons measured their worth not simply by the acres that surrounded them [their land,] but by [capital,] this immaterial representative of a form of value that was always deferred"[47] (Poovey, "Introduction," 2). The list of abstract numbers on a financial statement had become a key measure of success. The real world context of the plot is a "world that was increasingly filled with objects from all over the globe," and to have the money needed to own and possess these fashionable objects became the ideal of the day. Second, the unfortunate lack of knowledge about investing caused financial distress to most investors: "Britons could not visualize how the market worked … [a circumstance cultivated] by the stockbrokers' desire to control information, [and] … as a result, investors were left to the mercy of the promoters who too often pushed companies only in order to … liquidate them" (4, 18). Like many trusting investors of the period, Samuel Titmarsh does not have a clear idea about how investments work to create profits, and in the cases of fraud and its concomitant secrecy, he would have been the last person to perceive and understand such goings on.

---

[44]   W. E. Aytoun, "The National Debt and the Stock Exchange," *Blackwood's Edinburgh Magazine* 66 (December 1849) in Mary Poovey, ed. and intro., *The Financial System of the British Nineteenth Century* (New York: Oxford University Press, 2003) 144. Eric Hobsbawm, *The Age of Capitalism* (New York: The World Publishing Company, 1962) 45. Hobsbawm notes, "the bulk of the middle classes, who formed the main investing public, were still savers rather than spenders, though by 1840 there are many signs that they felt sufficiently wealthy to spend *as well as* to invest" (Hobsbawm's emphasis).

[45]   Elaine Freedgood, "Banishing Panic," *The New Economic Criticism: Studies at the Intersection of Literature and Economics*, ed. Martha Woodmansee and Mark Osteen (New York: Routledge, 1999) 224.

[46]   Freedgood, 224.

[47]   Poovey, "Introduction," 2.

Unlike economic writers of the period, Thackeray wrote with sympathy for the trusting victims of such scams, and with reproof toward the perpetrators, whom he satirizes and vilifies as behaving unethically. The narrative prompt in this piece was Thackeray's own personal experience of having lost his paternal inheritance through disastrous investments. Although he started with a sizable family inheritance, "gambling was Thackeray's besetting vice ... cards and dice, and until he lost his fortune, he was totally unable to overcome his compulsion to gamble."[48]

The *Great Hoggarty Diamond* exposes and protests widespread contemporary bubbles or pyramid schemes. In these schemes, the insiders who invest first are paid handsomely from the money of those who invest later. Still later investors are largely led on by the example of the first investors' abundant return; their desire for similar profits leads to a belief in the abilities of management to continue to produce such yields on investment. Meanwhile, the managers manage, above all, to make a lavish living. Finally, when new investment money fails to materialize, the "bubble" bursts; the pyramid collapses. Many naive investors were devastated by such schemes in this period; Aytoun wrote that "persons with very little money can speculate ... [and] it is indeed a dangerous game for all concerned, and unless a man plays it with loaded dice he generally loses in the end."[49] Samuel Titmarsh is just such an unlucky fellow, having been lured by the optimism of investment managers.

While Thackeray wrote *The Great Hoggarty Diamond* at a time of extreme personal financial duress, he inscribed his own affective responses to these problems and his experiences into the text. Catherine Peters describes the affect in the work as an "uneasy mixture" of "exuberance and ... sentimental melancholy"; these alternations in tone, as well as "the inexplicable ups and downs of fortune," and the "feeling of helplessness at the vagaries of fate" mar this work, in her estimation.[50] However, historicizing the economic circumstances of the time would prove that this piece is an accurate reflection of some contemporary economic experiences.

------

[48] Ray, 162. Thackeray had lost his entire inheritance within a few years of receiving it in his early twenties. Different biographers have considered various causes: gambling at cards, a failed Indian bank, and two literary newspapers, *The National Standard* and *The Constitutional*. Gordon Ray confirms that Thackeray had been "worth between 15,000 and 20,000 lbs."

[49] David C. Itzkowitz, "Fair Enterprise or Extravagant Speculation," *Victorian Investments: New Perspectives on Finance and Culture*, ed. Nancy Henry and Cannon Schmidt (Bloomington: Indiana University Press, 2009) 99. Writers have defined a difference between gambling and speculating in stocks: even though they seemed somewhat similar, the moral component of Victorian culture, by the end of the nineteenth century, had purged gambling from respectable society as immoral in order to accept financial speculation as a "reputable economic activity."

[50] Catherine Peters, *Thackeray's Universe* (Boston: Faber & Faber, 1987) 98.

V. Heaven and Hell

In the novella's plot, Christian myth transfers its structure to secular values of the business world, as the three-part mythical narrative of paradise, fall, and redemption shapes business events. Christopher Herbert has described this transference as "the inherently contradictory logic of a way of life based, as that of nineteenth-century Britain … on a fusion of the value-systems of capitalism and of puritanical Christianity."[51] Thackeray's narrative takes its hero, Samuel Titmarsh, on a Christian three-part pilgrimage through the business world. After inheriting his family brooch, having the diamond removed from it and reset into a tiepin, Samuel and his new wife Mary first move into a remarkable realm in which they continually satisfy their limitless desires for commodities; their happy economic paradise of getting and spending allows them to accumulate a wealth of objects with which to surround themselves in their daily life.

Then Samuel and Mary undergo financial bankruptcy, or a fall. In this part of the narrative, "fallenness [is] rearticulated to [a] secular … paradigm."[52] Samuel faces extreme depression as he experiences the loss of his house, the household furnishings, incarceration in debtor's prison, and the loss of his wife. Because Samuel's identity arises from his possessions, the loss of these possessions through bankruptcy becomes his loss of identity. Indeed, as Bill Brown notes, "emotions … can be objectified [or] … experienced as objects," so that objects and identity—and their loss—are psychically fused. Samuel tells his story in the first person as an unreliable narrator attempting to be stoic, while the plot itself objectifies, through description of the movement of his possessions, his fluctuations of emotion caused by his economic vicissitudes.

Finally, Samuel and Mary resolve their dilemmas and redeem their life with a financial *modus operandi* characterized by wise moderation.[53] The religious narrative model inscribes personal subjectivity into an economic realm, as individual experiences of the expanding British financial system take on the mythical patterns. Noting the close connection between business events and religious narrative structures—what Peters terms the "inexplicable ups and downs"—becomes nothing short of necessary narrative form in this work. In an all-powerful role as a commodity fetish, the fate of Samuel's diamond reflects this three-part mythical pattern of paradise, fall, and redemption in a fallen financial world. The Hoggarty diamond symbolizes capital and the wealth of objects Samuel

---

[51]   Christopher Herbert, *Culture and Anomie: Ethnographic Imagination in the Nineteenth Century* (Chicago: University of Chicago Press, 1991) 149. See also, Boyd Hilton, *The Age of Atonement: The Influence of Evangelicalism on Social and Economic Thought, 1785–1865* (Oxford: Oxford University Press, 1986).

[52]   Amanda Anderson, *Tainted Souls and Painted Faces: The Rhetoric of Fallenness in Victorian Culture* (Ithaca: Cornell University Press, 1993) 3.

[53]   Ray, 159. In a letter, Thackeray wrote, "better is economy with 500 a year than extravagance with five thousand."

had accumulated, but it becomes inactive, forgotten, hidden, and finally pawned when Samuel has lost everything.

VI. The Gentleman

If the diamond fetish is a "machine" that impels Samuel's rise in socioeconomic realms at the same time that it propels the narrative, then it also locates itself within a cluster of commentary about unstable class constituencies in Victorian England. As well-to-do businessmen and their families pressed upward into the ranks of the upper classes, the hierarchical nature of Victorian classes became destabilized. Moreover, the landed aristocracy began to recognize its need for new capital from the business classes, and accepted the newcomers in order to retain its ascendant position in an age of capitalism. In representing this whole process in an image, what symbol but the diamond could so effectively signify the large surplus of capital required for braving the risks and reaping the rewards of financial investment and gaining admission to the higher classes? The diamond functions as a cross-class sign of upward social mobility in the culture where "money governs."

Samuel aspires to become not only a businessman, but a morally upstanding gentleman, a role outside the power of his diamond fetish to grant. The culture had begun to value—and reward monetarily—personal qualities of performative merit in business, rather than privileging a static realm of inherited leisure of the upper classes. From this moment, a new hybrid role model developed, one that would combine the best of both classes within the cultural imaginary. This personal ideal might typically be thought to have the outer trappings or prestige of the gentry but the inner values of the middling classes, such as honesty, humility, social service, and love of family. Changing class definitions paralleled changing concepts of the gentleman as an ideally acculturated citizen. As Ina Ferris has shown, "the construction of the modern English gentleman served in large part as a response to Britain's shift from a landed to a credit economy with its attendant uncertainties and fluctuations."[54] The early Victorian version of the project of becoming a gentleman is well exemplified in the character of Samuel Titmarsh, who, in *The Great Hoggarty Diamond*, charts a course in which he must earn his title of gentleman on the front lines of business successes and reversals. "Gentlemanly capitalism" is what he practices, a term quoted by Henry and Schmitt, noting that income had to be "compatible with the high ideals of honour and duty."[55]

---

[54]   Ina Ferris, "Thackeray and the Ideology of the Gentleman," *The Columbia History of the British Novel*, ed. John Richetti (New York: Columbia University Press, 1994) 407.

[55]   Nancy Henry and Cannon Schmitt, "Introduction," *Victorian Investments: New Perspectives on Finance and Culture* (Bloomington: *Victorian Studies* and Indiana University Press, 2009) 5 (Henry and Schmitt quoting P. J. Cain and A. G. Hopkins, *British*

The plot of *The Great Hoggarty Diamond* puts into narrative form the ideas that define the gentleman presented in Thackeray's subsequent lecture entitled *George IV*. In the novel, the upwardly mobile young gentleman, Samuel Titmarsh, is contrasted with Edmund Preston, a wealthy member of the gentry who does not have the essential moral spirit to qualify as a gentleman. Thackeray notes in his *George IV* lecture that "heaven made gentlemen."[56] He required a gentleman:

> to have lofty aims, to lead a pure life, to keep ... honour virgin; to have the esteem of ... fellow-citizens, and the love of ... fireside; to bear good fortune meekly; to suffer evil with constancy; and through evil or good to maintain truth always.[57]

In this text, Samuel indeed personifies these ideals. The question of the nature of the gentleman, and the impetus toward sociability that the term implies, are at odds with the notion of individual agency and the autonomous self so highly valued for industrial capitalism.

Therefore Samuel is tested for gentlemanly virtue at the same time that those virtues themselves are tested against business culture. If Samuel is surprised by joy at the happy results of donning his diamond, the joy originates in a substantive core of his gentlemanly innocence that, as we shall see, remains a part of his character through all the caprices of fortune. His aesthetic and emotional tie to his diamond fetish is but one example of this dynamic. His problem is that in a capitalist culture, his purity of vision blinds him to the aggressive, deceptive nature of business behavior represented in the story; his naive honesty does not allow for suspicion of dishonesty in anyone else. Catherine Peters has shown that "young men are, in Thackeray's fiction, impulsive, subject to illusions, easily misled by bad company, but fundamentally innocent."[58] For example, Samuel does not understand that his boss Mr. Brough is engaged in a bubble or pyramid scheme, although, in a display of dramatic irony through much of the work, the text gives the reader many hints about the actual nature of Brough's business activity. We find Brough, for instance, characterizing his dastardly scheme in a rhetoric of self praise:

> I glory in saying that every one of my young friends around me has a father, a brother, a dear relative or friend, who is connected in a similar way with our glorious enterprise; and that not one of them is there but has an interest in procuring, as a liberal commission, other persons to join the ranks of our association. (11)

Imperialism: Innovation and Expansion 1688–1914 (United Kingdom: Longman Group, 1993)).

[56]   Harden, 197.
[57]   Harden, 200.
[58]   Peters, 52.

This deception exemplifies the cheerful face that can mask underhanded business practices such as a bubble or pyramid scheme, and the equally affable manner in which the innocent Samuel is duped. The diamond fetish thus allows Samuel to straddle these two incompatible realms of purity and fraud. As a machine, the diamond commodity fetish works its magical powers both to grant Samuel economic prosperity and then to take it away.

VII. The Fall: the Diamond's Power Eclipsed

While Samuel acts innocently in the fraudulent realm of business, he nevertheless becomes enmeshed in the inevitable financial downfall of the West Diddlesex Company. The plot piles misfortune upon misfortune in this section of the novel. The economic downfall that Samuel and Mary experience takes on aspects of a supernatural fall from grace. Neither the prosperous realm in which they had been living, nor their new world of want and woe are situations of their own making, but are experienced as givens outside their individual human control.[59]

As we have seen, financial vicissitudes marked by wild swings between abundance and want marked many lives in this period. Thackeray instantiates this cultural condition in the text with the description of Samuel's acquaintance, Mr. Tidd, who had once proudly thought of running for parliament and had vied for the hand of Mr. Brough's daughter. Tidd then finds himself in financial ruin after having invested his own inheritance with Mr. Brough. Samuel recounts:

> I pitied poor Tidd, whose 20,000 lbs. were thus gone in a year, and whom I met in the city that day with a most ghastly face. He had 1,000 lbs. of debts, he said, and talked of shooting himself; but he was only arrested and passed a long time in the Fleet. (77)

Mr. Brough himself, however, likes to cite the case of the deceased Mr. Silberschmidt, the "Rothschild of his day," who, "fancying he could not meet his engagements, committed suicide: and had he lived till four o'clock that day, [he] would have known that he was worth 400,000 lbs." (82). The presence of suicide prompted by financial ruin recurs in Victorian literature; Nancy Henry argues that this plot element was incorporated into literature

> when Victorian novelists were compelled to begin incorporating business and finance into literature. Their challenge was to create characters and plots that

---

[59]   Anderson, 3. For Amanda Anderson, "fallenness [is] … a charged site for Victorian concerns with the question of agency itself, ones that include but are not exhausted by apprehension of the power of environment over character."

were at once realistic ... entertaining ... and appropriately moral without being simply didactic.[60]

Thackeray may have been among the earliest of writers to use the plot element of suicide due to financial ruin.

As Samuel is experiencing his own financial breakdown, he is "taken from [his] ... comfortable home and [his] ... dear little wife," to a prison in which there is "a dirty passage and a dirty stair, and from the passage two dirty doors led into two filthy rooms, which had strong bars at the windows and yet withal an air of horrible finery" (85). Images of enclosure, separation, and filth characterize this prison interior that could only be described as Economic Gothic. The surroundings seem sealed away from nature, defined instead by the artificiality of fabricated surfaces: "trumpery pictures in tawdry frames; huge French clocks, vases, and candlesticks; on the sideboards enormous trays of Birmingham plated ware" (85).[61] These commodities have lost their meaning as cultural signs because they rest outside the normal process of market exchange, having been confiscated from debtors. They represent only the death of desire, and they are "goods ... from which value bearing symbolism has leaked away."[62]

In the narrative, these objects have become meaningless, material "things" displaced from their intended cultural roles. They proliferate at the debtors' prison while at the same time Aunt Hoggarty's furnishings at the London House disappear altogether. Samuel's wife Mary relates that back at the house, "horrible men came at four this morning ... to remove the furniture ... I let them carry all ... I was too sad to look" (92). Just as Samuel is repulsed by the overabundance of confiscated commodities piling up at the debtor's prison, Mary is alienated from their "crammed" household furnishings, no longer caring about them as she allows "the horrible men" to take them away.

Then, in relinquishing their desire for commodities, Samuel and Mary purify themselves by placing themselves outside the culture of getting and spending. In this economic scenario of a fallen capitalist world alternatively overstuffed with— or emptied of—meaningless commodities, objects have become superfluous things as desire for them evaporates. Material forms without symbolic significance are all that remain. Such grotesque scenes act as a projection of internal alienation from a

---

[60]   Nancy Henry, "'Rushing into Eternity': Suicide and Finance in Victorian Fiction," *Victorian Investments: New Perspective on Finance and Culture*, ed. Nancy Henry and Cannon Schmitt (Bloomington: Indiana University Press, 2009) 163.

[61]   See Eve Sedgwick, *The Coherence of Gothic Conventions* (New York: Methuen, 1986) 60, 12. In Thackeray's text, characteristics of the Gothic could be defined by some of Sedgwick's categories: for example, in the case of the pawned commodities, "the sign is incapable of knowing what it signifies," or in the case of Samuel, to be in prison is to be "massively blocked off from something to which [he] ought normally to have access," that is, to his wife Mary, his home, and his possessions.

[62]   Herbert, 128.

perceptual realm full of objects; in the text, the superficial presence or the absence of commodities point alike to a refusal of meaning. Samuel and Mary will now reside outside the visual world of consumer culture and the spiral of desire that ensnared them; instead, they live within an internal state of self-determined moral secular election and financial redemption.

Like the furnishings, the diamond has also been transformed into an empty signifier at this point in the narrative. Its role as a commodity fetish is discarded, and Samuel has even forgotten about its existence. It no longer arouses his desire or symbolizes abundant capital. In this incarnation, the diamond is hidden in a desk, forgotten, even lost. It no longer symbolizes the capital which has entirely disappeared; its cultural work as an image appears to be over. Shorn of meaning, it is reduced to its purely physical presence. When Samuel comes across the gem, he pawns it. The family diamond may be reconfigured once again by its next consumer, but in the meantime, it pays for his child's funeral, thus contributing to the end of Samuel's emotional ties to family, business, and the business community. The commodity fetish and the baby born of economic plenitude thus exit the narrative in tandem.

VIII. Redemption

As the power of the fetish to influence Samuel's fate is eclipsed at the pawn shop, the aesthetic meaning he had given it becomes reinvested in Mary, for it is the "good wife," Samuel says, who is "the best diamond a man can wear in his bosom." At this point the text reaches toward allegorical meanings for "diamond." As an agent or a "machine" in the topsy-turvy arena of early capitalism in which Titmarsh feels subject to forces beyond his control, any causal agent can now appear to him as a "diamond."[63]

Left on her own while Samuel is in prison, Mary searches for ways to produce an income, but her sole option is to become a wet nurse.[64] With the money Mary earns as a wet nurse, the couple are able to resume their married life, and Samuel also becomes employed. Between their two jobs, Samuel and Mary are able to live "in prosperity." At her death, Aunt Hoggarty wills Samuel "a very pretty property" consisting of two farms and all her savings. Though Mr. Brough had

---

[63]   Paul de Man, "The Rhetoric of Temporality," *Blindness and Insight: Essays in the Rhetoric of Contemporary Criticism*, 2nd edn, revised, intro. Wlad Godzich, Theory and History of Literature, Volume 7 (Minneapolis: University of Minnesota Press, 1983) 207. De Man defines allegory as "a relation between signs in which the reference to their respective meanings has become of secondary importance." In addition, "a constitutive moral element" is involved which, in narrative, "the allegorical sign refer[s] to another sign that precedes it."

[64]   See George Sussman, *Selling Mothers' Milk: The Wet Nursing Business in France, 1715–1914* (Champaign: University of Illinois Press, 1982).

tried every possible means to get Aunt Hoggarty to invest her fortune with The West Diddlesex Fire and Life Insurance Company, she had been clever enough to resist his advances. The family fortune had been saved. Though Samuel had earned and deserved his aunt's inheritance because of his steadfast personal morality, the realities of the marketplace dictated that he finally receive it only because of her shrewd business sense.

At the time Mary becomes "the best diamond a man can wear in his bosom," she has assumed a new position as a fetish/diamond within Samuel's subjective experience; she has become what Jeff Nunokawa typifies as "secure property available to the bourgeois male, a prospect of property that transcends all tokens and avenues of circulation."[65] Mary is the fixed measure in a set of variables, the constant in a world of (ex)change, in short, Samuel's instrument of economic redemption. Like the diamond, Mary is a "machine" in Samuel's view, for she causes events to happen, and capital to accumulate once again. Just as the diamond had been responsible for the rise in his company position, Mary is now responsible for his entrée to a new job as she regains contact with Lady Drum's daughter. Once Samuel is installed in his new position under Lord Tipton, he and Mary are able to attain middle class financial security. Samuel and Mary have perceived that the business world, rather than responding to personal agency, is one in which a person is subject to forces beyond individual control. Instead, they have retreated to a traditionally structured social position where their security is assured and where they are valued for personal moral qualities.

Yet, in this text about the economic world, Mary's wifely role fills the space of an economic dependent, even as she searches for a position to support herself and her husband after their financial collapse. From the beginning, as she sews a silk purse for Samuel's expected inheritance, and then makes the pincushion for the diamond pin to rest on at night, Mary's role is supportive, always situated in a separate domestic sphere. The question for Thackeray, however, is what a wife does after the "fall." In Thackeray's own life, his wife Isabella Shawe became mentally ill and financially dependent for the rest of her life. In Thackeray's text, however, Mary is the "machine" which starts the family's economic engine once again. Samuel expansively confesses: "I was proud and happy at being able to think that my dear wife should be able to labor and earn bread for me" (109).

---

[65]   Jeff Nunokawa, *The Afterlife of Property* (Princeton: Princeton University Press, 1994) 12. In yet another scenario of wives who experience economic upheaval, Mrs. Brough offers her last savings to her husband to try to stave off disaster. Of course, the disaster is of such a magnitude that her few shillings are powerless to effect the situation for the better. Samuel exclaims: "Brave Mrs. Brough! how she was working for her husband! Good woman, and kind!" (84). Mrs. Brough also shows that a woman's function within capitalism is to legitimize the male position. She kisses her husband's hand in public. Samuel comments, "I felt a liking for that simple woman, and a respect for Brough, too. He *couldn't* be a bad man, whose wife loved him so" (48).

But Mary's new role is a vexed one, to say the least. Her only option for employment in the text is to be a wet nurse, a position tied to her perceived domestic role as producer of children. The text maintains her privatized position in relation to the general economy, even as she earns wages as a laborer in that economy. In the end, one has to question the unnarrated subjectivity of the character of Mary Smith Titmarsh in this work, and imagine that the story she might tell would be troublesome for her husband Samuel's identity as a gentleman. She is given no agency or decision-making power to thwart the initial disaster; neither is she allowed to work as a public person after their financial disaster. Jeff Nunokawa notes that in fiction, such a wife as Mary has "a rhetorical afterlife that arises from the ashes of exchange, and as a narrative whose always anticipated conclusion never comes."[66] Mary's personal narrative remains unspoken in this text, and so her only rhetorical afterlife must exist in the closing paragraphs of critical essays. As she moves from the privatized dependent role of a middle class housewife to assume the fetish value of a diamond, she has also become, like a commodity fetish, a newly-reified object of Samuel's desire.

---

[66] Nunokawa, 14.

Chapter 4

Gift, Theft, and Exchange in *The Moonstone* by Wilkie Collins

Every year, two and half million visitors gain paid admission to the Tower of London to see Britain's most visited heritage attraction, the Crown Jewels. The Keeper of the Jewels attests that managing these tours is a 50 million euro-a-year business. As a result of these crowds, we can assume that millions of people have set eyes on the Queen Mother Elizabeth's crown, made in 1937. This crown does not have the largest gem among the crowns of the Royal Collection, nor did a sovereign ever own it. Yet the crown provides a setting for one of the collection's most famous diamonds in recent centuries. The Kohinoor Diamond, brought to Britain from India in 1850, has been well known throughout the Western world, having been described in both historical accounts and literary texts.[1] This diamond is one of the diamonds on which the fictional Moonstone is modeled in Wilkie Collins's novel, *The Moonstone*.[2] Because the Kohinoor Diamond has been exhibited to the public from the time of the Great Exhibition in 1851 until today, this diamond plays a major role in interpreting Collins's novel *The Moonstone*: Collins uses the dynamic contrast between the history of the Kohinoor Diamond and the fictional Moonstone Diamond to challenge the British cultural practice of building and maintaining empire. The final placement of the two diamonds—the historical Kohinoor Diamond with the British Crown Jewels and the fictional

---

[1]   The Kohinoor Diamond has also been called the "Mountain of Light." For recent nonfictional discussions of the Kohinoor Diamond, see Ian Balfour, *Famous Diamonds*, 5th edn (Antique Collectors Club, 2009) 164–84; Katherine Prior and John Adamson, *Maharajas' Jewels* (New York: The Vendome Press, 2000) 71–4; Kevin Rushby, *Chasing the Mountain of Light: Across India on the Trail of the Kohinoor Diamond* (New York: St. Martin's Press, 2000); Patrick Voillot, *Diamonds and Precious Stones* (New York: Harry N. Abrams, 1998) 32–4. For a transatlantic example in literature, Thoreau counts on his reading audience to know about the Kohinoor Diamond; he refers to it in *Walden* to contrast the translucent gem with nature's translucent waters: "White Pond and Walden are great crystals on the surface of the earth, Lakes of Light. If they were … small enough to be clutched, they would … be carried off by slaves, like precious stones, to adorn the heads of emperors; but being liquid, and ample, and secured to us and our successors forever, we disregard them, and run after the diamond of Kohinoor. They are too pure to have a market value; they contain no muck" (247).

[2]   Wilkie Collins, *The Moonstone*, ed., intro., and notes, J. I. M. Stewart (New York: Penguin Classics, 1966 and 1986). Originally published in 1868.

Moonstone in India in the forehead of the Moon God—reveals the novel's intent to revise history.

I. Fiction Reimagining History

For any reading of *The Moonstone*, the nuanced relation between history and fiction becomes a crucial critical lens, for in this text fiction revises imperial history in order to oppose it. Knowledge of the history of the Kohinoor Diamond allows readers to reimagine the outcome of events that have already occurred so that they unfold according to an alternative moral ideal.

In his "Preface to the First Edition," Collins presents two historical diamonds only to fictionalize them by combining their identities to form the Moonstone Diamond as a centerpiece of the novel. As he implements his textual vision, Collins explains his creation of the fictional Moonstone Diamond with these remarks:[3]

> With reference to the story of the diamond, as here set forth, I have to acknowledge that it is founded, in some important particulars, on the stories of two of the royal diamonds of Europe. The magnificent stone which adorns the top of the Russian Imperial Sceptre, was once the eye of an Indian idol. The famous Koh-i-noor is also supposed to have been one of the sacred gems of India; and more than this, to have been the subject of a prediction, which prophesied certain misfortune to the persons who should divert it from its ancient uses. (27)

Collins had read C. W. King's *The Natural History, Ancient and Modern, of Precious Stones and Gems, and of Precious Metals* (1865), published three years before *The Moonstone*.[4] This contemporary sourcebook discusses three diamonds, presenting them as parallel in either history or appearance. For instance, King

---

[3] The Moonstone diamond in the novel thus derives its name from its ultimate narrative end where it is placed in the Moon God statue's forehead, not from the type of stone. Moonstone gems and Collins's Moonstone Diamond in the novel are two different categories of stone. C. W. King describes the actual moonstone gem as "extremely soft" and quotes Pliny as reporting that "within the center shines a star with the light of the full moon." He notes that "the Indian sort [of moonstone] is incomparably superior to the European, and ... presents upon its silver-grey surface that softly lustrous and full orb comparable to nothing except the luminary from whence comes its name" (C. W. King, *The Natural History, of Ancient and Modern Precious Stones and Gems, and of The Precious Metals* (London: Bell and Daldy, 1865) 91). On the other hand, Collins explains in the Prologue to *The Moonstone* that the Moonstone is a "yellow diamond" that was originally placed in the forehead of a Hindu religious statue in Somnauth, and was later removed to a new shrine in Benares where it resided in the forehead of the Moon God. Vishnu, the Preserver "breathed the breath of his divinity on the Diamond in the forehead of the god."

[4] William Baker, "Wilkie Collins's Notes for *The Moonstone*," *Victorians Institute Journal* 31 (2003) 190, 193.

notes that the history of the Kohinoor Diamond is "often confounded" with the Mogul Diamond. Furthermore, the Orloff and the Mogul Diamonds "resemble" each other "in form and cutting ... in the newly-invented European pattern, the Rose." The Mogul Diamond, once shown to the seventeenth-century French trader Tavernier, had "one little flaw inside," an important feature Collins gives to the fictional Moonstone.[5]

With this comprehensive source at his fingertips, it is easy to understand how Collins seized on all this information, and by combining the real-life "famous" diamonds into a composite diamond-idea called the Moonstone, used their merged exotic allure, as described by King, as a centerpiece for his novel.[6] Collins also combines two actual histories to form the fictional Moonstone: the history of the Kohinoor Diamond, set in India's northwest state of Punjab, and the history of the Battle at Seringapatam set in the southern state of Mysore. Of first importance is the fact that the Kohinoor had been taken among the spoils of victory by military troops of the British East India Company in Punjab, and given to the queen in 1850. A parallel of this historical fact emerges in the section of *The Moonstone*'s plot, in which Uncle Herncastle gives the Moonstone Diamond to "Queen Rachel." Both gifts of diamonds—to Queen Victoria and "Queen Rachel"—attempt to legitimize what could have been deemed a theft.

Second, the Battle of Seringapatam's history in the south and the events leading up to it played a foundational role in the British Indian Empire's history, while it equally sets the narrative in motion in the novel's preface. In 1799, the British East India Company's soldiers stormed Seringapatam, killing the defiant and unfortunate Tipu, the maharaja often called "the Tiger of Mysore." Tipu had tried to arrange an alliance with the French to fight British troops, but the anticipated French aid never materialized. The 1799 battle at Seringapatam served as a founding event for the British Indian Empire because it ended French presence on the Indian subcontinent and secured British control of the only area still in the hands of Mughal rulers. Collins begins his revision of the British imperial project in the novel's opening pages, where he depicts the Battle of Seringapatam as a scene of outrageous British bloodshed and uncontrollable greed rather than as the officially sanctioned historical version of the battle, namely, a victorious event that achieved British hegemony in India.

During the actual battle, the soldiers stormed the palace, plundering the magnificent gem collection. A British military committee then formed to distribute

---

[5]   King, 35. King notes that the "Orloff Diamond, weight 193 carats, [is] set in the top of the Russian Imperial scepter."

[6]   Although C. W. King mentions nothing about a prophesy of misfortune in connection with any of these diamonds, it is known that the Timur Ruby, a spinel, accompanied the Kohinoor, producing a like biography. In fact, it was also given to Queen Victoria and made into a necklace in 1853 (Prior and Adamson, 70–1). According to Patrick Voillot, "sovereigns wore [rubies] because of their prophetic power: they were said to announce evil omens by suddenly turning from pure red to black" (25).

the huge collection in an orderly fashion. Prior and Adamson relate the fate of the gems of Mysore this way:

> There were ... many acts of officially sanctioned vandalism, such as the breaking up of Tipu's gold and gem-studded tiger throne to provide prize money for the troops. The largest tiger head from the throne was salvaged for presentation to the directors of the East India Company; in 1831 the Company gave it to King William IV and it remains in the British Royal Collection at Windsor today, along with almost two dozen other souvenirs of Tipu's fall.

Divided up among the British soldiers employed by the East India Company, the jewels were sold or brought home as prize souvenirs for the female members of the soldiers' families.[7] Tipu's jewels, in Barry Milligan's words, "mirror the collective terms of a desiring England and a desired India," and, indeed, the fictional Moonstone embodies the desires of the novel's characters, too.[8] The actual history thus parallels the fictional Uncle Herncastle's gory seizure of the Moonstone at the Siege of Seringapatam and his subsequent gift of the Moonstone to Rachel. Here, "desire knows nothing of [economic] exchange—it only knows gift and theft," in Constantin Boundas's words, a comment most clearly applicable to Herncastle's experience represented in the text.[9] Seductive values and practices of empire—symbolized for the British by the gems—included political power, notions of racial superiority, the call of a moral mission, and increased wealth from trade.

II. Diamonds and Gems of India and Britain: the Seventeenth to Nineteenth Centuries

In a reading of *The Moonstone*, exploring the historical background of diamonds and gems in India and Britain broadens critical perceptions. While it has been valuable to understand the history of how Indian diamonds became acculturated in Europe in the early modern period as noted in Chapter 3, it is also essential to know about the later history of Indian gems, leading up to the Kohinoor Diamond's

---

[7]   Prior and Adamson, 68. Captain Cochrane received diamonds, turquoise, and gold from the royal turban ornaments and had three necklaces with matching brooches made for his three daughters. David Price, *Memoirs of the Early Life and Service of a Field Officer* (London: Wm. H. Allen & Co., 1839) 434–43. Denys Forrest, *Tiger of Mysore: The Life and Death of Tipu Sultan* (London: Chatto and Windus, 1970) 354.

[8]   Barry Milligan, *Pleasures and Pains: Opium and the Orient in Nineteenth-Century British Culture* (Charlottesville: University Press of Virginia, 1995) 72.

[9]   Constantin Boundas, "Gift, Theft, and Apology: Editorial Introduction," *Angelaki: Journal of the Theoretical Humanities* 6.2 (August 2001) 4.

story in the nineteenth century, for it is this story around which the novel largely revolves.

The metonymic linkage of fabulous gems to political power in India was a connection not lost on the British as they built their trading relation with India. For centuries, Europeans had been aware of the rich caches of gems that lay to the East in India, but they had not been able to trade for any of the larger jewels. By the sixteenth century, the Mughal Empire controlled the Indian subcontinent except the southern tip, and Indians along the coast barely tolerated English traders. Furthermore, English and Dutch traders vied with the Portuguese for trade agreements with Indian rulers.

In the early seventeenth century, Jahangir, a grandson of the Mughal conqueror Timur, underscored the political importance of gems by amassing every jewel he could find through extortion, invading neighboring territories, and plundering defeated maharajas' gems. William Hawkins, a British traveler to the court, reported that Jahangir owned 82 pounds of diamonds, "none smaller than two carats," half a ton of pearls, almost a quarter ton of emeralds, and 100 pounds of rubies, to mention just a portion of the loose stones. In addition, Jahangir owned thousands of jewel-encrusted horse saddles, swords, and daggers. Thrones sparkled with ornaments as did court umbrellas. Later, during the eighteenth century, India's many kingdoms fought among themselves, with the victors looting their enemies' treasuries, securing the glittering symbols of power into their own possession.

The British monarchy and the newly rich upper classes of Victorian culture were fascinated with this material sign of Indian power and prestige, and were quick to adopt it as their own. The fact that diamonds became so prominent in the Victorian era can be traced in part to these customs of India and the reflexive influence that British colonial endeavors in India exerted upon Victorian domestic culture. In the process of integrating the diamond from Indian culture to European culture, Europeans refashioned this religious, political, and talismanic Indian icon into a marketable commodity produced for economic exchange as a recognized sign of fashion, class, and wealth. Bernard Cohn tells us that "it was the British who, in the nineteenth century, defined in an authoritative and effective fashion how the value and meaning of the objects produced or found in India were determined. It was the patrons who created a system of classification which determined what was valuable."[10] In its cross-cultural adaptation, the diamond became a valuable commodity, with a radically transformed appearance and altered cultural meaning.

The diamond in India and the diamond of Europe in the modern period may have been the same category of stone, yet their contrasting cultural interpretations were as divergent as their continents were distant. In the global culture of the nineteenth-century Empire, the British held the power to define the symbolic meanings of diamonds: while their Western heritage had changed the appearance and distribution of diamonds through cutting and commodification, the British

---

[10]   Bernard Cohn, *Colonialism and Its Forms of Knowledge: The British in India* (Princeton: Princeton University Press, 1996) 77.

retained readings of prestige and power in the diamond, from previous Indian eras.

III. The Kohinoor Diamond's Transculturation

While political power and gems were practically synonymous, the largest gems had absorbed and projected the most significance in the eyes of the maharajas. Igor Kopytoff explains that "power often asserts itself symbolically precisely by insisting on its right to singularize an object." Acting as singularized conduits of power, the largest stones were passed down from father to son as symbols of a family's dynastic political power.[11] Such was the case with the Kohinoor Diamond.

To best appreciate Collins's crafting of the fictional Moonstone Diamond as based on the Kohinoor Diamond's history, we must first appreciate the transfiguration of the Kohinoor Diamond from Indian culture to British Victorian culture. The story, or "biography," of this single stone reveals the way the diamond was manipulated and how its symbolic meaning changed in the process of cross-cultural adaptation. Indeed, Igor Kopytoff convincingly argues that

> biographies of things can make salient what might otherwise remain obscure … in situations of culture contact, they can show what anthropologists have so often stressed: that what is significant about the adoption of alien objects—as of alien ideas—is not the fact that they are adopted, but the way they are culturally redefined and put to use. (67)

In the nineteenth century, the Kohinoor Diamond inhabited the very center of colonial relations between Britain and India, and its singular fate reveals the changing geopolitical balance of power around the globe.

One history dates the Kohinoor Diamond to 3000 BC, at which time it was lodged in the forehead of a statue of a Hindu god; other histories date the jewel to around AD 1300. Whatever the reaches of its antiquity, most historians agree the Kohinoor Diamond was inventoried in the gem collections of Mughal rulers beginning in the fifteenth century. In the eighteenth century, Nader Shah of Persia conquered Delhi and, although he knew of the stone's existence, he could not find it among the spoils of victory, for the defeated ruler had hidden the jewel in his turban. But with luck on the side of the victor, Nader Shah honored the vanquished with a customary feast at which the two exchanged their turbans as tokens of peace. Here Nader Shah finally gained the prized Kohinoor Diamond.

The diamond was eventually passed down as an inheritance to the Nader Shah's son, and later, Afghan rulers and the Sikhs of Punjab possessed it. In 1849,

---

[11]   Igor Kopytoff, "The Cultural Biography of Things: Commoditization as Process," *The Social Life of Things: Commodities in Cultural Perspective*, ed. Arjun Appadurai (New York: Cambridge University Press, 1986) 73.

British soldiers employed by the East India Company invaded and annexed the politically unstable state of Punjab and removed the 11-year-old maharaja, Dalip Singh, from his throne in Lahore. According to Indian custom, the British victors could take possession of the maharaja's jewels of state, which they did. While these soldiers left some jewels to Singh, they auctioned others, but not the grand prize, the Kohinoor Diamond. The British East India Company offered it as a gift to Queen Victoria to commemorate the Company's 250th anniversary in 1850. The timing was perfect: the queen wore the diamond to the grand opening celebration of the Great Exhibition of 1851, after which it was displayed in the Exhibition's famed Crystal Palace.

In 1852, Victoria and Albert ordered the diamond to be cut, because the Indian style cutting had appeared "crude," and "probably suppressed rather than enhanced its brilliance."[12] The Indian Kohinoor Diamond thus underwent a physical and cultural transformation at the request of the British monarchy. The diamond weighed 186 carats when it was first presented at Court, cut "attractively in 'old Indian' style," according to historian Emily Hahn. Victoria's court historian gives the official version of the diamond's cutting at the hands of the British monarchy:

> in consequence of the keen interest evidenced by Her Most Gracious Majesty the Queen and the late Prince Consort in the manipulation of this wonderful gem, Messrs. Garrard, the Queen's jewellers, at their instance, had a room specially fitted up at their present establishment in the Haymarket, where Her Majesty herself, and nearly all the members of the royal family, personally assisted at putting on the facets, which for perfection are unequalled, the Duke of Wellington personally putting on the first.[13]

Moreover, Prince Consort Albert "spent hours and hours ... assisting in the cutting of the Kohinoor," with the result that today it weighs but 106 of its original 186 carats.[14] Here the diamond and its symbolic meaning was, in the words of Homi Bhabha, "translated, rehistoricized, and read anew."[15]

In an opposing historical interpretation, however, Charles W. King (1865) asserts that the cutting of the Kohinoor was

---

[12]   Dena K. Tarshis, "The Koh-I-noor Diamond and its Glass Replica at the Crystal Palace Exhibition," *Journal of Glass Studies* 42 (2000) 138.

[13]   Emily Hahn, *Diamond: The Spectacular Story of Earth's Rarest Treasure and Man's Greatest Greed* (Garden City: Doubleday & Company, Inc., 1956) 201. Hahn quotes Atkinson (no notation).

[14]   According to the 1875 *Ure Dictionary of the Arts* II.24, "The value of a cut diamond is esteemed equal to that of a similar rough diamond of double weight."

[15]   Homi Bhabha, *The Location of Culture* (New York: Routledge, 1994) 37. Bhabha argues that "meaning and symbols of culture have no primordial ... fixity."

a most ill-advised proceeding, which has deprived the stone of all its historical and mineralogical value; for as a specimen of a monster diamond whose native weight and form (186 carats) had been as little as possible diminished by art (for the grand object of the Hindoo lapidary is to preserve the weight), it was unrivalled in Europe; and giving in their stead a bad-shaped, shallow brilliant, of but inferior water, and only 102 ½ carats weight.[16]

As we shall see in the following discussion, fictional characters express subjective and highly symbolic experiences through their reactions to and manipulation of the diamond; however, the most public of historical personages, Victoria and Albert, constituted a true to life model for these symbolic interactions with jewels.

Figure 4.1 The Duke of Wellington placing the Kohinoor Diamond on the scaife for the cutting of the first facet, July 16, 1852, *Illustrated London News*

---

[16]   King, 36; see also Balfour, 170. King's measurements of the Kohinoor's final weight differ from other sources. Ian Balfour presents the final cut diamond as 108.93 metric carats "which represented a loss of weight of just under 43 per cent. There is no doubt that such a substantial reduction in the gem's weight came as a disappointment to many, not least to the Prince Consort who voiced his views on the matter in no uncertain terms" (170).

THE POOR OLD KOH-I-NOOR AGAIN !

1. THE KOH-I-NOOR.
2 2. THE DUTCH ARTISTS.
3 3 3. THE REQUISITE MACHINERY.

4. THE "DOOK" MANIFESTING GREAT INTEREST IN THE PRECIOUS GEM.
5 5 5. EMINENT SCIENTIFIC MEN WATCHING PROCEEDINGS.

Figure 4.2 The Kohinoor cutting in a contrasting artistic version, July 31, 1852, *Punch*

As Albert and the royal jewelers restyled the diamond's physical appearance with their own hands, they enacted symbolically Britain's imperial dominance over India. The cutting of the Kohinoor thus parallels the fate of the exchange of British and Indian political power on the subcontinent, and across geographic and cultural boundaries; now the history and fiction we shall compare combine to reveal a confrontational set of meanings about the empire for the historical Kohinoor and the fictional Moonstone Diamond.

IV. *The Moonstone*'s Domestic Colonialism

The Moonstone (1868) centers on a "yellow deep" Indian diamond, a gem that represents British imperialism as it returns upon itself to destabilize domestic British culture.[17] Within the narrative, the Moonstone's presence on British soil

---

[17]   My statement could be thought to parallel one of Nayder's chapter titles, "Reverse Colonization." Critics have discussed a range of critical viewpoints in books about Collins and about *The Moonstone*: for example, some edited volumes of essays: Maria K. Bachman, ed., *The Woman in White/Wilkie Collins* (Peterborough, ON: Broadview, 2006), and Maria K. Bachman and Don Richard Cox, *Reality's Dark Light: The Sensational Wilkie Collins*, Tennessee Studies in Literature, Volume 41 (Knoxville: University of Tennessee Press, 2003); Lyn Pykett, ed., *Wilkie Collins: Contemporary Critical Essays* (New York:

provokes the troubled discourses by which post-Mutiny Britain attempts to justify its presence in India. In the novel, the diamond's catalytic role is its gift as a bequest, but a series of subsequent thefts complete its fate.[18] At the moment of its giving, the diamond's dense materiality attracts the aesthetic focus of readers and characters alike, yet never again does the diamond appear as a material object in the narrative until the final scene. With the exception of these two framing scenes—the diamond's transfer of ownership as a gift near the novel's beginning and its location in the forehead of the Indian Moon God at the end—the absence of the material diamond allows the narrative to focus instead on the diamond's immaterial, culturally-symbolic meaning as each narrator-character discusses its status as a gift and its thefts.[19] The novel charts the British spectrum of affects in the period following the Mutiny of 1857 across all classes of British domestic culture as the diamond's representation of colonialism invades mind, body, and experience of the novel's characters.[20]

Initial reviews and critical reception of *The Moonstone* (1868) were lukewarm at best, a reception that reveals ideological underpinnings of imperialism in the domestic culture. In an unsigned review in the *Spectator* (July, 1868), a critic notes that "in the Moonstone ... we have no person who can in any way be described as a character, no one who interests us, no one who is human enough to excite even a faint emotion of dull curiosity as to his or her fate." In other reviews, the characters are similarly described as "ingenious pieces of mechanism," "mere puppets," "merely conventional figures," and "secondary to the circumstances."[21]

St. Martin's Press, 1998); literary biography in the historical context: Lillian Nayder, *Wilkie Collins* (New York: Twayne Publishers, Twayne's English Author Series, ed. Herbert Sussman, 1997); nationalism: Cannon Schmitt, *Alien Nation: Nineteenth-Century Fictions and English Nationalism* (Philadelphia: University of Pennsylvania Press, 1997); British use of opium: Milligan, as cited above; Tamar Heller, *Dead Secrets: Wilkie Collins and the Female Gothic* (New Haven: Yale University Press, 1992); detective fiction: D. A. Miller, *The Novel and the Police* (Berkeley: University of California Press, 1988).

[18]   Kopytoff. See also Alana Blumberg, "Collins's *Moonstone*: The Victorian Novel as Sacrifice, Theft, Gift, and Debt," *Studies in the Novel* 37.2 (Summer 2005) 163, 183. I agree with Ilana Blumberg that Collins's "Moonstone ... fantastically embodies a history of theft and gift," and that "the identity of a circulating object is not stable, that it takes its identity in exchange."

[19]   The theft of the diamond by Uncle Herncastle in the novel's foreword is actually outside the narrative.

[20]   For extensive discussion of some Mutiny novels, see, for example, Jenny Sharpe, *Allegories of Empire: The Figure of Woman in the Colonial Text* (Minneapolis: University of Minnesota Press, 1993) Chapter 3, "The Civilizing Mission Disfigured." See also Patrick Brantlinger, *Rule of Darkness: British Literature and Imperialism, 1830–1914* (Ithaca: Cornell University Press, 1988). Chapter 7 presents history of the Mutiny, "The Well at Cawnpore: Literary Representations of the Indian Mutiny of 1857."

[21]   Norman Page, ed., *Wilkie Collins: The Critical Heritage* (Boston: Routledge & Kegan Paul, 1974) 172, 174.

Since the characters of the novel seem so boringly predictable to its contemporary audience, the characters for all appearances occupy subject positions of culture-wide typicality rather than individuality; in this typicality, the characters represent various roles informed by colonialism in the domestic Victorian society of the text. Indeed, the contemporary reception of the novel indicates the depth to which the colonial mindset had taken root in British domestic culture: as Ian Duncan explains, "empire appears nowhere because it is everywhere."[22] Not only does the novel represent this colonial mindset, but it exposes the negative influences of empire on domestic culture, raising this account to the level of leitmotif.

Through the diamond's emblematic role, Victorian subjective experience of colonialism in British domestic culture is revealed, including the aesthetic attraction to gems, the harmful yet widespread use of opium, and the organization of society through coercive race, class, and gender hierarchies. Readers see that the values that sustain the empire abroad also structure home life, as colonialism resonates deeply with the British domestic population; the empire invades the private lives of those who, at first glance, are not involved with overseas colonial practices. For example, Melissa Free writes that "To 'be' English in the nineteenth century was to be of, and hence constituted by, (the British) empire, to claim the summary position not only of Britishness but of empire itself."[23] Furthermore, Tricia Lootens calls attention to "the Victorians' assumption of an intrinsic connection between the values of domestic sanctity and of imperial domination."[24]

The characters' experiences at the country manor setting reveal the connection between the empire's foreign political and military service and domestic households of Britain. The text argues convincingly that a parallel exists between colonial practices abroad and domestic hierarchical practices at home as Gabriel constructs his own perceptual grid for managing the manor through continual consultation with the text of *Robinson Crusoe*. When he becomes confused and needs a moment of "conversion," he consults this handbook of colonialism—in the same manner that St. Augustine consults his Bible—by opening to a random

---

[22] Ian Duncan, "*The Moonstone,* the Victorian Novel, and Imperialist Panic," *Modern Language Quarterly* 55.3 (September 1994) 298.

[23] Melissa Free, "'Dirty Linen': Legacies of Empire in Wilkie Collins's *The Moonstone*," *Texas Studies in Literature and Language* 48.4 (Winter 2006) 340. Duncan, 298.

[24] Tricia Lootens, "Hemans and Home: Victorianism, Feminine 'Internal Enemies' and the Domestication of National Identity," *PMLA* 109.2 (March 1994) 239. Based on Hazlitt's ideas, Lootens notes that Hemans anticipates "Victorians' intrinsic connection between the values of domestic sanctity and of imperial domination." Nayder, *Wilkie Collins* 118. Nayder also agrees that "throughout the novel, Collins combines his interest in domestic 'sensation' with his interest in imperial relations developing the tie between the rape of India and the symbolic violation of Rachel Verinder."

page and accepting its wisdom as predestined. "I never fail to obey the secret Dictate," Gabriel says in one of his perplexed moments (460).[25]

The connection between the domestic household and the British nation-state also proves to be very tight, with the manor functioning as synecdoche for the island of Britain. Gabriel Betteredge evinces the textual connection between national politics and the politics of domesticity when, for example, he gives a pointedly satirical speech to the kitchen servants before Rachel's birthday dinner:

> I follow the plan adopted by the Queen in opening Parliament—namely, the plan of saying much the same thing regularly every year. Before it is delivered, my speech (like the Queen's) is looked for as eagerly as if nothing of the kind had ever been heard before. When it is delivered, and turned out not to be the novelty anticipated, though they grumble a little, they look forward hopefully to something newer next year. An easy people to govern, in the Parliament and in the Kitchen—that's the moral of it. (93)

Intensifying the novel's connection between the organization of the household and the political structure of the state, the Verinder family, ruled by the regal Lady Verinder and by Rachel, "queen of the day," reflects the model upheld by Queen Victoria as both sovereign and dedicated wife and mother.[26] Moreover, like a prime minister of state, Head Servant Betteredge reproduces the values underlying colonial administration on a global level as coercion in class and gender hierarchies in the domestic household (100). The smug complacency of Gabriel's "moral" that the English are "an easy people to govern" awakens readerly awareness to the power politics at work in the domestic culture, replicated as the society of the manor (93).

V. Giving and Receiving Gifts

The giving of a gift forms *The Moonstone*'s catalytic episode from which the remaining narrative action springs: Uncle Herncastle bequeaths the Moonstone Diamond to Rachel, his niece, on her birthday. A gift in its most literal sense is a material object passed from one person to another, yet here the gift endlessly proliferates with questions about the cultural context in which it is given, for it symbolizes the relationship between the giver and receiver—Uncle Herncastle and Rachel Verinder.

---

[25]   For an example of Defoe's *Robinson Crusoe* interpreted as an imperialist text see, for instance, Diana Loxley, *Problematic Shores: The Literature of Islands* (New York: St. Martin's Press, 1991).

[26]   Sharon Aronovsky Weltmann, "'Be no more housewives, but Queens': Queen Victoria and Ruskin's Domestic Mythology," *Remaking Queen Victoria*, ed. Margaret Homans and Adrienne Munich (New York: Cambridge University Press, 1997) 105–22.

As a basis for critical analysis of culture and its texts, the significance of the idea of the gift first emerged in Marcel Mauss's foundational essay *The Gift*, originally published in 1925, and ideas concerning gifts have been an area of scholarly interest ever since.[27] Mauss's vision of the gift in "archaic ... societies" develops around the idea that a culture elicits three obligations concerning gifts: "to give, to receive, and to reciprocate." Mauss then asks this question with emphasis, *"What power resides in the object given that causes its recipient to pay it back?"*[28] Mauss argues that the gift cannot be perceived as a single object, nor can its giving be considered as occurring in a single moment; its diffuse ontology exists as a nexus within a web of interpersonal relations and across time as a token of future reciprocity.

Indeed, in Collins's work, the prismatic transparency of the diamond embodies the idea of the gift, for, in *The Moonstone*, the gift is at once visible and invisible; a material object and an exchange of power; an ordinary gesture and a risk as it symbolizes and transfers values that bind the society in which it is given. What makes the diamond so valuable as a gift to be given and received makes it equally valuable as an object to be taken by others for whom the gift was never intended. In this way, gift giving and theft create value reciprocally.

Gift giving and theft involve a change in the possession of a material object and, as such, are both exchanges, albeit of different kinds. If giving and taking are parallel actions insofar as a material object passes from one person to another, how exactly do gift and theft differ with regard to the object's transfer of ownership? What do the discourses about giving and taking tell us about *The Moonstone* and the problems of imperialism in Victorian culture the novel addresses? Answering

---

[27]   Insightful critiques of the gift have recently come forth to complicate and validate Mauss's conception of the gift; these discussions prove that a gift forms a vital function in the ongoing structure of cultures. See Alan Schrift, *The Logic of the Gift: Toward an Ethic of Generosity* (New York: Routledge, 1997) 4. Schrift writes, for example, that "Mauss's *The Gift* is without doubt the text that initiates the modern reflections on gifts and gift giving." For a survey of some ideas about gift giving, see Chapter 2 in this work. Also see Mark Osteen, ed., *The Question of the Gift: Essays Across Disciplines*, Routledge Studies in Anthropology (New York: Routledge, 2002). Also see the special issue on the gift in *Angelaki: Journal of Theoretical Humanities* 6.2 (August 2001), which contains cultural critiques on the gift. Marcel Mauss's, *The Gift: The Form and Reason for Exchange in Archaic Societies*, trans. W. D. Halls, foreword Mary Douglas (New York and London: W. W. Norton, 1990) was originally published as *Essai sur le Don*, L'annee sociologique, new series, 1 (1925) and was reprinted by Presses Universitaires de France, 1950. For some anthropological discussions, see Lewis Hyde, *The Gift: Imagination and the Erotic Life of Property* (New York: Vintage Books, 1979) reprinted in 1980 and 1983; Annette B. Weiner, *Inalienable Possessions: The Paradox of Keeping-While-Giving* (Berkeley: University of California Press, 1992); Maurice Godelier, *The Enigma of the Gift*, trans. Nora Scott (Chicago: Polity Press and the University of Chicago Press, 1999) originally published as *L'enigma du don*, Librairie Artheme Fayard, 1996.

[28]   Mauss, 3, 13, 3.

these questions involves uncovering the novel's narrative structure, discovering that it depends on gift, theft, and exchange.

Like many other scenarios in *The Moonstone*, Uncle Herncastle's desire to give the diamond to someone in the Verinder family reflects historical precedent: we recall that, in 1831, the British East India Company had given King William the jeweled tiger's head from Tipu's throne; in following this precedent, the company celebrated its 250th anniversary in 1850 with a gift of the Kohinoor Diamond to Queen Victoria. Royal support for the British East India Company's military actions in India was at stake in these exchanges.[29] By accepting the gems, the British throne signaled that it supported the company's military and commercial actions in India and approved the looting of the Indian gems. With the monarchy's acceptance of these glittering gifts, the gems could be seen as symbolizing the power of the British throne, just as the acceptance of such tributes had at one time augmented the Indian maharajas' power. This former Indian practice of giving gifts as tributes, "constitute[d] … [a] case of upward, one-way giving."[30]

However, as Mauss notes, a gift always commands a reciprocal gift. Were these gifts simple tributes to the British throne's power with no need for reciprocation? Or did these gifts elicit a reciprocal response legitimating the East India Company's military actions? While the British monarchy wanted to add to its own collection of gems, the British East India military had also adopted two Indian customs at once: the looting of treasure and the giving of gifts to superiors.[31] *The Moonstone* (1868) thus questions with post-Mutiny hindsight the wisdom of the monarchy's past acceptance of gifts of Indian gems and its support for the

---

[29]   The East India Company's trading ventures began in 1600, when Elizabeth I, on the last day of the year, granted a charter to a "Company of Merchants trading into the East Indies." Over the next two to three centuries, government support of the East India Company continually expanded, punctuated with the following significant events. In 1757 the East India Company's military forces overran Bengal. Then in 1773, parliament passes The Regulation Act to rescue the East India Company from bankruptcy brought on by military expenditures. The bill puts India under the rule of a Governor-General. In 1799, the Company's military defeats Tipu, Sultan of Mysore, giving Britain administrative power over all of India. In 1857, the Mutiny occurs. In 1858, the East India Company was dissolved, and the administration of India became the responsibility of the Crown.

[30]   Yuxiang Yan, "Unbalanced Reciprocity: Asymmetrical Giving and Social Hierarchy in Rural China," *The Question of the Gift: Essays Across Disciplines*, ed. Mark Osteen (New York: Routledge, 2002) 67–84, 81.

[31]   Ashish Roy, "The Fabulous Imperialist Semiotic of Wilkie Collins's *The Moonstone*," *New Literary History* 24.3 (Summer 1993) 657; *Literature Resource Center*, 9. Roy notes that "Following Crown rule, an important resolution of the problem [of governing India] was to adopt Moghul court procedures involving prestation objects like precious gems, robes of honor, ceremonial swords, as well as gold and silver;" however this rule came after the "Sack of … Seringapatam."

East India Company's actions in India.[32] By having Lady Verinder reject and turn away Uncle Herncastle and his gift, the novel argues against the British throne's acceptance of the East India Company's Indian diamonds and, in so doing, it also argues against royal support of the company's actions in India. Lady Verinder judges Uncle Herncastle's actions in India by British domestic moral precepts, refusing to accept the gift of the diamond because "he had got possession of his Indian jewel by means which ... he didn't dare acknowledge" (63).

Collins poses a question about the possibility of Lady Verinder accepting the gift in this way: "Was the legacy of the Moonstone a proof that [Lady Verinder] had treated her brother with cruel injustice? or was it a proof that he was worse than the worst she had ever thought of him? Serious questions those for my lady to determine" (96). These questions highlight the rupture between Uncle Herncastle and Lady Verinder, between gift giver and intended recipient, as Collins represents the cross-cultural, transoceanic moral divide as a non-negotiable frontier. Readers learn in the novel's preface that the East India Company's military adhered to different moralities in India than they did in Britain, and, as a result, the novel notes that "the Colonel's life ... outlawed him ... among his own people. The men wouldn't let him into their clubs; the women—more than one—whom he wanted to marry, refused him; friends and relations got too near-sighted to see him in the street" (64). Christopher Herbert considers the moral question this way:

> could it be that savage excesses on the part of the British forces in this war were not, after all, momentary aberrations committed in the fury of war but signals of essential characteristics? Did the circumstances of the Mutiny simply afford an opportunity for a strain of devilish cruelty *native to the British character* to cast off its garment of Christian piety and humanitarian sentiment and reveal itself in plain view?[33]

In *The Moonstone*, Uncle Herncastle had crossed over the moral divide and would not be forgiven nor allowed to return to respectable English society.

Lady Verinder's refusal to accept her brother's gift of the diamond highlights the tensions involved in gift giving and receiving. Mauss explains that "the gift is ... at one and the same time what should be done, what should be received, and yet what is dangerous to take" (59). This danger represented as Lady Verinder's rejection of Uncle Herncastle's gift of the diamond, and hence her symbolic rejection of the national mission of empire building, becomes a key element in interpreting the points the text makes about imperial morality through its focus on the Moonstone gem.

---

[32]   Jaya Mehta, "English Romance; Indian Violence," *The Centennial Review* 39.3 (1995) 617.

[33]   Christopher Herbert, *War of No Pity: The Indian Mutiny and Victorian Trauma* (Princeton: Princeton University Press, 2008) 38.

While in the text Lady Verinder has applied her British ethical standards on a global setting, historical records show that looting was customary in India throughout the eighteenth century, as political turmoil enveloped the many small provinces and kingdoms. The kingdoms of India had been fighting among themselves, and the victors commonly looted their enemies' treasuries of gems to possess these symbols of power. Prior and Adamson tell us that "a strong ruler amassed jewels; a weak ruler lost them." In fact, the word "loot" had come into common use in English in the eighteenth century, adapted from the Hindi verb *lutna*, meaning "to rob," or "to plunder." Gems flourished as a sign of wealth and power, yet, as chattel, they were easily transferable through gift and theft in an age of unstable political structures. Prior and Adamson explain: "the fate of India's royal jewels was intimately bound up with ... political upheavals."[34] Here we might speculate about the complicity of political power and jewels: could the gems containing the political power the Indians read into them have been one cause of the geopolitical instability of India?

Collins's novel thus raises the question, *what ethical standards are applicable in the cross-cultural conditions of building empire*? Is looting the prerogative of victory, or is it theft? There seem to be no definitive answers to these regrettably rhetorical questions. If we historicize and relativize Herncastle's actions, knowing that sanctioned looting was the norm throughout India, can we successfully apply moral standards from British culture and make subsequent judgments about the events embedded in a different culture, one with different standards, half a world away? Or, as Collins seems to suggest, are Lady Verinder and the British correct in ideally insisting on a cross-cultural moral equivalent, disowning alternative practices committed by the British in India, and barring those associated with them from returning to influence British domestic culture?[35] Again, can a person in the military fighting overseas separate the moral tenets of the home culture from the actions performed abroad? The novel argues against this geopolitical separation of standards, evinced in the contrast between Lady Verinder's rejection of the gift of the diamond, and in her daughter Rachel's subsequent acceptance and unhappy ownership of it.

Despite Lady Verinder's refusal of the gift, Uncle Herncastle ultimately achieves his goal of giving the diamond to the Verinder family by earmarking it as an inheritance for Lady Verinder's daughter, Rachel. In so doing, he attempts to be perceived by the Verinder family as a magnanimous gift-giver, looking out for the inheritance of the cultural household, rather than as a murdering plunderer, bringing the danger of mutiny and death to those who must oversee the empire he helped found. If he succeeds in leaving the diamond to Rachel as her

---

[34]   Prior and Adamson, 62.

[35]   See also the narrative end of Joseph Conrad's *Heart of Darkness*, in which malevolent practices of empire in the distant jungle are hidden from people residing in the domestic culture, a problem which Conrad also takes up in *Lord Jim*.

inheritance, he appears heroic in the view of the Victorian household society, even if posthumously, and he appears to live up to the duty of every English gentleman.

Because the text presents Rachel, a member of the next generation, as "innocent" of all knowledge," the novel marks the bloody military history of empire-building in the very process of deletion. Rachel does not understand the circumstances under which her uncle gained possession of the diamond, so that his negative truths are bypassed and forgotten; like a palimpsest, a new, less violent history writes over and erases what had been experienced and known before. Alert to the problem that historical erasure could replace Uncle Herncastle's personal memory, Franklin Blake suggests with urgency: "Betteredge … we must face the question of the Colonel's motive in leaving the legacy to his niece" (74).

In contrast to her mother, Rachel's primary role in the text is to accept the jewel and consequently validate the actions of empire. In the text, Rachel's role and experience thus prompt the question of whether the children inherit the sins of the father, and, more generally, whether all citizens bear guilt arising from the actions of the state. The question that surrounds and plagues the text is this: given the fear and doubt arising from the contemporary cultural experience of the Mutiny, is England to accept gratefully the legacy of empire it has inherited from previous generations, or should England feel the moral weight of its actions in India as "worse than the worst?" (96). To the extent that colonial British culture had to construct a narrative with idealistic reasons to support its ongoing colonial projects, it also had to dissimulate the immoral nature of its own history in India: after all, "getting its history wrong is part of being a nation," Hobsbawm notes.[36]

In *The Moonstone*, Herncastle's life as an empire builder is legitimated through Rachel's acceptance and ownership of the symbolic Diamond, in the same way that the military actions of the East India Company are legitimated through Queen Victoria's acceptance of the Kohinoor Diamond. The diamond's durability implies the power of this single material object to convey history, cultural identity, and political legitimacy. But this effect is not the only outcome Herncastle's legacy produces. Annette Weiner, author of *Inalienable Possessions: The Paradox of Keeping-While-Giving*, would appear to explain the nature of Herncastle's ultimate achievement in giving the Moonstone to Rachel, for the inherited gifts "succeed

---

[36]   E. J. Hobsbawm, *Nations and Nationalism Since 1780: Programme, Myth, Reality* (Cambridge: Cambridge University Press, 1990) qtg. Renan, *Qu'est que c'est une nation?*, 7–8. The actions of an individual on behalf of national endeavors such as colonialism or war become morally problematic if, as Hobsbawm writes, "nations as a natural, God-given way of classifying men, as an inherent … political destiny, are a myth" (9–10) See also Bhabha, 37. From the beginning of *The Moonstone*, the narration plays out what Bhabha terms the "ambivalence in the act of interpretation" which "challenges our sense of the historical identity of culture as a homogenizing, unifying force."

their owners through time," both transferring and preserving the values of empire the diamond represents.[37]

Because Victoria accepted the gift of the Kohinoor Diamond, an object whose transfer of possession symbolized the subsumption of India into the British Empire, the post-Mutiny British government's obligation to reciprocate the East India Company's gift was established: by involving the government in the administration of India, in support of the company's colonial trade, the queen reciprocates the gift, as she accepts the title of "Empress of India" in 1877, nine years after the publication of *The Moonstone*. Here the gift has become a temporal token, the acceptance of which is a guarantee of commitment for the foreseeable future. We can note that

> until the Indian Mutiny ... Victoria had taken relatively little interest in foreign affairs outside Europe. But the Mutiny awoke her with a jolt to her imperial responsibilities, and as her reign wore on they took up more and more of her attention. In December 1879 she recorded "a long talk with Ld Beaconsfield, after tea, about India and Affghanistan [*sic*] and the necessity for our becoming Masters of the country and holding it" ... In July 1880, she was "urg[ing] strongly on the Govt, to do all in their power to uphold the safety and honour of the Empire." "To protect the poor natives and to advance civilization," she told Lord Derby in 1884, was to her mind "the mission of Great Britain."[38]

In the novel, Rachel experiences remorse and hysteria after accepting the Moonstone; these affects could be said to represent Queen Victoria's problems that would arise from the government's administration of the empire in the post-Mutiny period. Gabriel Betteredge could thus be heard quoting from his reference source for colonialism, *Robinson Crusoe*: "Now I saw, though too late, the Folly of beginning a Work before we count the Cost, and before we judge rightly of our own Strength to go through with it" (39). With these words, *The Moonstone* uses the story of the symbolic gem to challenge British colonialism to the core.

---

[37] Weiner, 11, 33. An inheritance is what Weiner terms "the representation of how social identities are reconstituted through time." She describes inalienable, or permanent, possessions—in this case, the historical and fictional diamonds—as having "unique, subjective identity [that] gives them absolute value placing them above the exchangeability of one thing for another."

[38] Niall Ferguson, *Empire: The Rise and Demise of the British World Order and the Lessons for Global Power* (New York: Basic Books, 2002). The important dates would appear like this over a 27-year period: 1850, the East India Company gives the Kohinoor Diamond to Victoria; 1851 the Great Exhibition, where the diamond is displayed; 1852 the cutting of the diamond; 1857 Mutiny; 1868 publication of *The Moonstone*; 1877, Victoria is named "Empress of India"; 1879–80, Victoria becomes committed to ruling the Indian Empire, as noted in the statement above.

Rachel is positioned, like Queen Victoria, at the center of a narrative about empire: one fictional, the other historical. Like the queen, Rachel engages in silence about negative events concerning the empire and her domestic love relation. These two themes go hand-in-hand: as Mehta notes, "the novel counterposes colonial terror to domestic romance," for acts of colonialism abroad feed the unhappiness involved in domestic romance.[39] Rachel's love relation, Franklin Blake, supports the empire through such actions as safekeeping, giving, and even unconsciously stealing the diamond, but his support for the colonial enterprise distances him from Rachel, causing her hysterical and emotional distress. Yet even "Queen Rachel" is not blame-free: when she desires and accepts the Moonstone Diamond from Uncle Herncastle, she also assumes a role of complicity in promoting the inevitably negative practices of empire.[40]

Although Rachel and Franklin begin the narrative as "innocent," they become emotionally ruined through interaction with the empire's diamond. Rachel's acceptance of this symbolic gift leads to her own hysteria and Franklin's breakdown. Evelyn Ender defines hysteria as the "pathological expression of the impossible" and Rachel's pathological hysteria arises from the impossible role of silent complicity the culture would have her assume in its colonial agenda, and from the vexed love relation with Franklin Blake, who has stolen the symbolic diamond in a drugged state brought on by the ingestion of opium imported from the empire (29).[41] While Rachel actually sees Franklin steal the diamond from her Indian cabinet, Ezra Jennings notes, "we can hardly blame her for believing [Franklin] to be guilty, on the evidence of her own senses" (404–5). To protect Franklin, however, she remains silent. Therefore, though Rachel is at the center of the action in *The Moonstone*, she has no narrative in this text so replete with other characters' narratives. It is clear, however, that on a culture-wide level, Rachel operates, in essence, as an alibi for Uncle Herncastle: his actions are redeemed if she accepts them—and the diamond—even if she does so without accurate knowledge of their precise nature.

Despite her relative silence, the diamond's status as a symbol of India and as a gift that demands reciprocity is delineated in the text, for the novel rejects the idea of acculturating the diamond as an economic commodity for monetary exchange. For example, Gabriel Betteredge notes that even "the questions of accurately valuing it

---

[39]   Mehta, 612.

[40]   James Buzard, "Victorian Women and the Implication of Empire," *Victorian Studies* 36.4 (Summer 1993) 443–53. See this essay for a wide range of critical commentary on the roles of women in empire as seen by critics.

[41]   Evelyn Ender, *Sexing the Mind: Nineteenth-Century Fictions of Hysteria* (Ithaca: Cornell University Press, 1995) 29. Ender cites Monique David-Menard, "How the Mystery of Conversion is Constructed," *Hysteria from Freud to Lacan: Body and Language in Psychoanalysis*, trans. Catherine Porter (Ithaca: Cornell University Press, 1989) 47–63. Ender further notes that, "in its textualized form, hysteria … finds, in its figures and intensities, a language that reveals the presence of something that is unpresentable" (17).

present ... some serious difficulties" (70). The discussion between Gabriel Betteredge and Franklin Blake about turning the diamond into a commodity proves what Alain Caille suggests, namely that we cannot understand what gift "reciprocity" means until we *contrast* the gift with economism.[42] Here we are concerned with thinking about the gift of the Moonstone Diamond to Rachel in far more complicated terms, and until we think about reciprocity in terms other than "book-balancing equivalence," we cannot begin to know its role in cultural cohesion.[43]

Yet, the diamond's original value for the domestic culture rests upon the *possibility* of its monetary value, and Betteredge and Blake must note this option for the novel's reading audience. However, the text's ultimate refusal to allow the diamond's economic circulation with a designated monetary worth instead leads the characters into a realm of aesthetic, political, and moral interpretation of the diamond. The dark, inaccessible location of the Moonstone in the bank's "strong" box during much of the narrative, in addition to its shrouded history, allows its intangible meanings to circulate freely among the novel's characters. What is at stake, then, is the characters' competing interpretations of the symbolic diamond. If Uncle Herncastle's diamond is an artifact taken from the East India Company's military engagement in a decisive battle in India, Rachel is primarily attracted to the Moonstone's aesthetic appearance, as a piece of jewelry. She appears at the dinner party with the diamond as a brooch in her dress, in the same manner that Queen Victoria posed, wearing the Kohinoor Diamond in her portrait by Winterhalter, in 1856, 12 years before the publication of *The Moonstone*.

Rejecting the diamond as a commodity for trade, the text also emphasizes what Mauss would refer to as "*hau*," or the spirit of the gift. In Mauss's view, "the *hau* follows after anyone possessing the thing ... and the thing itself possesses a soul. Finally, the thing given is not inactive. Invested with life, often possessing individuality, it seeks to return to ... its place of origin" (12–13). Mauss's early twentieth-century discourse on the gift bears an uncanny relevance to the plot of *The Moonstone*, for the diamond comes with a curse: "The Moonstone will have its vengeance yet on you and yours!" (37) Collins privileges Indian interpretations of the diamond as a political or sacred symbol to remain intact to the narrative end, as it "return[s] to its place of origin," in Mauss's words.

As the narrative unfolds, the British and Indians in the text are locked in a life-or-death battle over possession of the diamond. For the British characters and Indians alike, power to interpret this symbol also implies the power to form a national identity and to rule India. However, for the British, the flaw in the diamond could be interpreted as the flaw in colonialism, which is its coercive cross-cultural imposition of political, military, and economic rule most brutally manifest in events such as the Collins's version of the Storming of Seringapatam. As the plot

---

[42]   Osteen, 230. He paraphrases Kopytoff, noting that "commodity status is not permanent for most objects; rather, the term may accurately name only one phase of an objects 'career'."

[43]   Osteen, "Introduction," 7, quoting Alain Caille.

moves toward its concluding scenes, the diamond is returned to India and placed in the forehead of the Moon God. In contrast to the historical Kohinoor Diamond resting among the Crown Jewels, the fictional Moonstone's final placement in India becomes the novel's argument against the practice of colonialism in defining the British nation-state.

Figure 4.3 Queen Victoria, painted by Winterhalter, 1856, wearing
Kohinoor Diamond brooch

Source: The Royal Collection (© 2010, Her Majesty Queen Elizabeth II)

VI. The Politics of Speaking

Other parallels also tie text to historical cultural context through emotion and affect surrounding the gift of the diamond. The text presents Rachel's birthday dinner-party as a parallel to post-Mutiny contemporary concerns, as Mrs. Threadgall—a version of Queen Victoria—can only talk of her husband, assuming that "every able-bodied adult in England ought to know" of her husband's death. When one of the other guests does not know about his death, Mrs. Threadgall can only mourn, "My husband is no more ... My beloved husband is no more," she repeats (103). Her single focus and emphasis on this one event would certainly have reminded contemporary readers of the Queen's many years of mourning over Prince Albert's death in 1861, seven years before the publication of *The Moonstone*.

Yet Mrs. Threadgall's mourning persists after "ten years!"—the amount of time that has passed between the Mutiny of 1857 and the publication of *The Moonstone*. Jaya Mehta notes that "The Mutiny, simultaneously absent and present, inhabits *The Moonstone* as a powerful yet invisible undertow."[44] In the same way that Collins mixes historical and fictional diamonds, here he has mixed deathly national events: the death of Prince Albert and the Mutiny of 1857. The habitual mourning of Prince Albert's death carries over into mourning the dark days of the empire brought on by the Mutiny, since the "cursed Diamond ... cast a blight on the whole company" (101). Fear and mourning take over the birthday celebration, as the British characters' anxiety for their own physical safety surfaces and the "quiet English house [is] suddenly invaded" by the diamond (36).

Post-Mutiny fears thus saturate the text. In the dinner party scene, Mr. Murthwaite acknowledges this fear as a result of the Mutiny when he tells Rachel, who is wearing the Moonstone, of the "danger in India ... Dressed as you are now, your life would not be worth five minutes' purchase" there (101). While the Moonstone exudes a malevolent agency that wreaks havoc for the characters in the text, it is probable that the Kohinoor Diamond—the "allegorical emblem of India as a jewel in the British Crown," in Jenny Sharpe's words—had similar harmful effects within domestic culture. Fearful emotions had replaced complacent desire in Britain when, during the year following the 1857 Mutiny, "the end of British rule appeared imminent, [so that] ... to be a European [living in India] meant almost certain death."[45]

Yet when "queen of the day," Rachel, accepts this symbol of empire, thereby validating its aims, the occasion of its presentation in the text contains a countervailing rhetoric that denies the diamond's attractions and calls attention to its "flaw." The novel presents the diamond's flaw as the empire's adverse effects on the dinner guests of the domestic culture, too. The celebratory birthday dinner that re-enacts a state occasion becomes instead the site of the diamond's curse; fissures

---

[44]   Mehta, 617.

[45]   Sharpe, 149, 58; Mehta, 620. Mehta notes that "Newspapers were drawing attention to the tenth anniversary of the Mutiny."

of silence and contradiction erupt in the dinner conversation. Communication breaks down; the society fragments. Language's meaning becomes obscured when used for immoral reasons, where what can and what cannot be said aloud are so narrowly configured: in this society, fear of speaking trumps freedom of expression or truth. Michel Foucault argues against this condition of constrained speech in a culture that suppresses dissent. He writes:

> There is no binary division to be made between what one says and what one does not say; we must try to determine the different ways of not saying such things, how those who can and those who cannot speak of them are distributed, which type of discourse is authorized, or which form of discretion is required in either case. There is not one but many silences, and they are an integral part of the strategies that under lie and permeate discourses.[46]

In applying Foucault's observations specifically to the historical context represented in the novel, we could note that Victorian historians of the Mutiny regarded atrocities committed by the British as "*unspeakable.*" Christopher Herbert quotes a military officer: "You in England will not hear the worst [about the rebels' atrocities], for the truth is so awful that the newspapers dare not publish it."[47]

Therefore, the citizens of the novel's cultural household fall silent at the mention of death as they are rendered "speechless" and "blank." In the text of the novel, "Gaps of silence" alternate with "unfortunate" expressions and "worst possible" intents. "When they ... speak, they [are] perpetually at cross-purposes," and "when they ought to have spoken, they [do not] speak" (103). The dinner-party conversations generally lack "smoothness;" one guest "burst[s] out," and another "terrifies the company with outbreaks." Franklin Blake and Mr. Candy fall into a "dispute" in which they "hit back smartly," "cut and thrust," and "lose ... self-control." In sum, according to Betteredge, "the Devil (or the Diamond) possessed that dinner-party" (105). The presence of the Moonstone—the possession of empire—has fragmented Victorian society into factions, imposed silence among them, and changed their language into incommunicative garble. Unhappily, it is the discourse of war and domination that characterizes the society of the dinner table, as the citizens' inner voice is censored. A crisis of representation—as a submerged knowledge existing only as a lack—portends the mystery to come. The language and emotional tone of the dinner party scene reaffirm the status of the Moonstone Diamond as a symbol of an empire forebodingly troubled, for the dinner guests are unable to articulate the unspeakable negative truth that informs their communal experience.

With the politics of language swirling around the diamond, which we must remember was a gift, we have perhaps realized Marcel Mauss's ultimate hope in

---

[46] Michel Foucault, "The Repressive Hypothesis," in *The Foucault Reader*, ed. Paul Rabinow (New York: Pantheon Books, 1984) 309.

[47] Herbert, 139, quoting Charles Ball, *History of the Indian Mutiny* (1860–1) 1:97.

analyzing the gift in several cultures: to "throw … a little light upon the path that our nations must follow, both in their morality and in their economy" (78). Indeed, Collins's *The Moonstone* harbors these ambitions.

VII. Theft

Earlier in the chapter, the reciprocal relationship between gift giving and theft was noted, while exploring the meaning of the Moonstone in its role as gift. We now turn to explore the meaning of the diamond's theft more fully. The novel's storyline, involving the Moonstone's repeated thefts one after another, and hence the gem's symbolic redefinition, conveys the Victorians' splintered opinions about imperialism. Franklin Blake becomes embroiled in the empire's ethos the minute he becomes involved with the diamond. Because he facilitates the diamond's integration into British society by acting as its guardian and courier, he is guilty of abetting the empire's cultural growth, for he later steals it, in a drug-induced sleep. Ablewhite steals the diamond, too, and, for him, ownership of the diamond means a paradox consisting of his wish to spread the Christian moral word with a missionary zeal, while also solving his financial problems; he aims to enlarge his sphere of action in the world and his own importance to the domestic culture. Finally, at the novel's end, readers may assume that Indians have killed Ablewhite, stolen the diamond he had stolen, and returned it to its place of origin in the statue of a religious idol in India. In this way, each theft makes its own political statement.

From a purely biographical standpoint, Collins harbored deep anxieties about the Indian Mutiny; not only had he written essays and a play about the mutiny prior to publication of *The Moonstone*, but he also was a heavy user of opium imported from the empire. Heller points out that, in the novel, "Collins writes himself into the role of Blake, who stole the Moonstone in a drugged trance."[48] Indeed, Blake steals the diamond as he sleepwalks, because the empire's opium has invaded his body with his ingestion of "Godfrey's cordial" and ruled his behavior from an unconscious realm. It is a tricky labyrinth of reasoning in the text: if ocular proof of his theft of the diamond attests to his complicity with the aims of empire, he is also represented as innocent of the crime of endorsing the empire because he remains "innocent of all knowledge" of his actions (96).[49] He is an innocent hero duped by his own colonial culture. Although the opium experiment will prove him "guiltless, morally speaking, of the theft of the Diamond," Franklin comments as he finds his own paint-stained nightgown, "I had discovered Myself as the Thief" (441, 359). The "abominable impossibility which, nevertheless, confronts [him] as undeniable fact," arouses his deepest anxieties. After Franklin Blake's discovery

---

[48]   Heller, 162.

[49]   This phrase is used for Rachel when she accepts the diamond, but I use it here to show Franklin Blake's equally ambivalent position, and their equally ironic positions in regard to moral action within the domestic sphere of British imperial culture.

of imperialism's insidious division of his own subjectivity and the reunification of the "I" with "Myself" through his newly acquired knowledge of the psychic polarity of colonialism, he falls into "complete bodily and mental prostration," an example of the emotional toll arising from practices of empire in the novel (360).

In essence, the text calls into question Victorian imperial aims as it evinces the ultimate cost of constructing a pervasive colonial cultural subjectivity: an inability to unify consciousness and survive. The empire either separates private moral consciousness from public self if the subject adheres to the culture's praxis, or else it radically separates a person with integrity from the culture at large if the subject refuses to believe in or engage in imperial practices. In such a culture, to set aside this doubleness and work for a unification of moral conscience, while rejecting a separation of public and private conscience, can only produce hysteria and violence. Because Rachel and Rosanna understand the truth of empire as an evil about which they cannot speak, they suffer its effects through their hysteria: Rachel is always ill in her room, whereas Rosanna must live with "one shoulder bigger than the other," ultimately dying in the Shivering Sand (55). For Franklin, it takes the form of "bodily and mental prostration."

When the text reveals who stole the diamond, Ablewhite's death is the inevitable outcome. It is a death caused by the reader's new knowledge of the nature of colonial praxis in the culture, and a resulting impulse to eradicate from the text the colonialism embodied in the hypocritical Ablewhite. Godfrey Ablewhite, who embodies cultural ideals of Victorian England—religion, chivalrous assistance to women, philanthropic endeavors, an irresistible personal style and public speaking ability, and, as his family name represents, the ability to carry "the white man's burden"—is, in the end, a personification of his first name, an amoral "God-free" person. His internal identity emerges through his ministrations of "Godfrey's Cordial," the palliating opiate for the sensitive non-imperialist, to Franklin Blake. Godfrey Ablewhite becomes the imperial nation-state's victim of homicide in the omniscient narrator's statement of retribution against the practices of empire in the culture. The only way for Victorian England to have escaped these inevitable pathologies of empire might have been for Rachel to have rejected Uncle Herncastle's symbolic gift of the Moonstone like her mother before her, thereby saving the culture from the diamond's "flaw," the evils of empire.

The question remains: can a person give what has been taken? Can Herncastle give Rachel the diamond he had stolen in bloody battle? A positive response to these questions might rely on the fact that Herncastle, filled with desire for India and its gems, had only engaged in the kind of political behavior that Indians themselves had practiced. However, at the end, the Indians' reciprocal theft of the stone from Godfrey Ablewhite completes a cycle, which is ended when the Indians place the stone in its sacred and authentic position in the forehead of the Moon God's statue; the text's placement suggests that the diamond was never Herncastle's to give. John Reed points out that, at the end of the novel, "Murthwaite's letter, describing the safe return of the Moonstone to its proper home in India is, of course, dated 1850. The significant relationship of dates and events is too obviously ironic to be coincidental."[50] We recall the contrasting action in 1850 when the East India Company had given the Kohinoor Diamond to Queen Victoria. In the novel, with the Indians' return of the stone as a gift to the Moon God, fiction's revision of history prevails and is still valid today in a fantasy of imperial reversal; the fictional Moonstone ends up in India, unlike the historical Kohinoor which to this day resides with the British Crown Jewels in London.[51]

Figure 4.4 The Kohinoor Diamond set in the 1937 crown made for Her Majesty, Queen Elizabeth, the Queen Mother. This is now in the Jewel House at the Tower of London

Source: Crown © The Royal Collection. © HM The Queen

---

[50] John R. Reed, "English Imperialism and the Unacknowledged Crime of *The Moonstone*," *Clio* 2 (1973) 287.

[51] Patrick Voillot, *Diamonds and Precious Stones* (New York: Harry N. Abrams, Inc., Discoveries, 1998) 33.

Chapter 5
Cameo Appearances:
Aesthetics and Gender in *Middlemarch*

In recent times, the covert yet insistent relation between aesthetics and political economy has claimed significant critical focus, for these two discourses have implicated and complicated each other in puzzling ways.[1] In offering some background to this perplexing relation, Mary Poovey has traced the modern history of aesthetics and political economy to a common origin within the eighteenth-century field of moral philosophy.[2] As a study in search of cultural cohesion, moral philosophy drew together a wide-ranging set of critiques including ethics, aesthetics, economics, and government. Then, in the second half of the eighteenth century, the field branched, Poovey tells us, shaping new categories of knowledge through such works as Edmund Burke's *Enquiry* (1757) on aesthetics and Adam Smith's *Wealth of Nations* (1776) on political economy. As these divisions in knowledge became further refined through discursive practice in the Victorian Age, aesthetics and political economy appeared to have little to do with each other; however, Poovey argues that "one way to remember the originary relationship between these two discourses—and to measure the toll exacted by their division— is to tease from each its past and present entanglements with gender."[3] I take up her call by examining the relation between aesthetics and political economy, as they inscribe their mediations on gender roles in George Eliot's *Middlemarch*. While I note that differing gender roles attach themselves to images of specific jewelry

---

[1]   I consider "aesthetics" and "political economy" to function as systems of meaning circulating in Victorian culture and refer here to the notion often formulated as "aesthetic ideology," which has occasioned criticism by Eagleton, Levine, de Man, and Redfield, for example. The political effects of Victorian economic practices on gender have been discussed by Armstrong and Poovey. Discussion of the culture interpreted through the economic commodity can be found in writings by Appadurai, Richards, Nunokawa, and Miller, for example.

[2]   Mary Poovey, "Aesthetics and Political Economy in the Eighteenth Century: The Place of Gender in the Social Construction of Knowledge," *Aesthetics and Ideology*, ed. George Levine (New Brunswick: Rutgers University Press, 1994) 79–105. In a more detailed explanation, Poovey argues that "the generic continuity of political economy and aesthetics underwrites the persistence in one discourse of concerns and metaphors that increasingly seemed to belong to the other … Once they are consolidated as generically discrete, each discourse continues to make visible issues and formulations that are still active but no longer definitive in what was once its other half" (82).

[3]   Poovey, 8.

in the text, the interpretation of jewelry as a vigorous system of interactive signs also uncovers textual commentary on the relation between Victorian aesthetics and political economy as they work together to effect gender definition.

I. Political Economy: "Reading Adam Smith"

I begin here with a close reading of some opening passages of *Middlemarch* to look at how the text lays out the problem. As the plot unfolds, Dorothea Brooke experiences the constraints of political and economic practices that partition Victorians into separate gendered spheres and hierarchical power relations; however, she continually privileges the aesthetic allure of a possible ultimate meaning arising from that same set of cultural practices that subordinate her.[4] The text introduces her troubled dilemma within this knot of discourses when, in a performative remark meant to reinforce separate gender roles, Uncle Brooke comments to Casaubon, "Young ladies don't understand political economy, you know ... I remember when we were all reading Adam Smith. *There* is a book now" (12; bk. 1, ch. 2). Mapping the terms of the debate still further, the narrative then discloses Dorothea's silent point of view about aesthetics and political economy as they differ from her uncle's assertion and relate to her future marriage with the scholar, Casaubon:

> To reconstruct a past world, doubtless with a view to the highest purposes of truth—what a work to be in any way present at, to assist in, though only as a lamp-holder! This elevating thought lifted her above her annoyance at being twitted with her ignorance of political economy, that never-explained science which was thrust as an extinguisher over all her lights. (13; bk. 1, ch. 2)

Through a web of metaphors based on light, the text consistently marks a personally-defined aesthetic ideal of ultimate meaning as an ideological balm for gender subordination. While Dorothea desires to hold the lamp of learning, the text ironically deconstructs her aesthetic dream of access to Casaubon's "attractively labyrinthine" knowledge: not much light emanates from this source.[5] She will have to pursue the "provinces of masculine knowledge" with her lamp set at "Lowick," in the company of a man with a "smile like pale wintry sunshine" (17, 47, 19;

---

    [4]   Nancy Armstrong, *Desire and Domestic Fiction: A Political History of the Novel* (New York: Oxford University Press, 1987) 8–9. For example, Armstrong notes that "the entire surface of [Victorian] social experience had come to mirror ... the existing field of social information as contrasting masculine and feminine spheres."

    [5]   The idea of education as a location of the aesthetic derives from Schiller's *On the Aesthetic Education of Man*, first published in German in 1801, translated into English in 1845; it was one of the first influential German works Eliot read. I will return to a consideration of "aesthetic education," or *Bildung*.

bk. 1, ch. 3, 7). Pursuing the ideal of ultimate meaning equally subordinates her politically, for her Victorian belief in a hierarchy of ideas ranging from the "trivial" to "the greatest things" also stamps its form on other, political facets of her life. When she marries Casaubon to gain access to his knowledge, his valued "standing-ground from which all truth could be seen more truly" will prove to be inaccessible to her because it is a product of the same structures of stratification that dictate her dependent status in the male-dominated political economy (47; bk. 1, ch. 7). The interdependence of all these practices is hidden from Dorothea because "political economy [is] ... never explained." *Middlemarch* thus presents an opportunity to examine this continuum of discourses as they cluster and conflict within the microcosmic range presented as her affective experience.

II. Aesthetics: "Fragments of Heaven"

This textual confrontation between aesthetics and political economy in gender formation also reveals itself through jewelry, a class of objects well suited to interpretations of woman's role because of its nearly exclusive use by women in the Victorian Age. In another early scene, Dorothea and her sister Celia consider the family's collection of amethysts, emeralds, and diamonds, as they form another focal point for aesthetic thought. Although Dorothea finds that an amethyst necklace harbors "complete unfitness ... from all points of view," by contrast, she desires a ring and bracelet made of emeralds and diamonds. Here the text alludes to the ability of jewelry to figure aesthetic and religious meanings as the sunlight emerges from its cloud cover to send "a bright gleam over the table":

> "How very beautiful these gems are!" said Dorothea, under a new current of feeling, as sudden as the gleam. "It is strange how deeply colours seem to penetrate one, like scent. I suppose that is the reason why gems are used as spiritual emblems in the Revelation of St. John. They look like fragments of heaven. I think that emerald is more beautiful than any of them."

> "They are lovely," said Dorothea, slipping the ring and bracelet on her finely-turned finger and wrist, and holding them towards the window on a level with her eyes. All the while her thought was trying to justify her delight in the colours by merging them in her mystic religious joy.

> "Yes! I will keep these — this ring and bracelet," said Dorothea. Then, letting her hand fall on the table, she said in another tone — "Yet what miserable men find such things, and work at them, and sell them!" (10; bk. 1, ch. 1)

As the "fragments of heaven" captivate Dorothea's imagination, transporting her into an aesthetic reverie of sensual and spiritual free play, their beauty functions as a source of affective power that also suggests higher religious meaning. Then, as she places the bracelet on her wrist to look at it—actually wearing it in its traditional way—she disengages mentally from the body part the jewelry touches by "letting her hand fall on the table, exclaiming, '... what miserable men ... !"[6] Her delight in the beauty of the jewels, and her recoil at their inevitable association with materiality, money, and male economic practices, reveal the jewelry's power to signify contradictory discourses. In fact, the text reveals its own preoccupation with diverse sign meanings as it explains, "signs are small measurable things, but interpretations are illimitable" (18; bk. 1, ch. 3). As Dorothea considers the family jewelry, she instinctively grasps its twinned aesthetic and economic implications. However, even after she disdainfully acknowledges the economic source of the gleaming emeralds, she keeps them; for, across the plot's trajectory, she will consistently embrace belief systems grounded in aesthetic values. As a result, she also makes decisions which, by default, espouse political or economic positions that ultimately consign her to a subordinate gender role. Her grand mistake in marrying Casaubon, for example, rests upon her ignorance of the material questions of political economy. The disjunction between her uplifting aesthetic view of education and her downgraded political position as Victorian wife allows the text to focus upon this discursive conflict. The plot thus reveals Dorothea's growing understanding of the relation between aesthetic and political or economic forces that trouble her identity as a woman.

I will relate the dynamic tension that enlivens the association between aesthetics and political economy emanating from these early passages of *Middlemarch* to later passages within *Middlemarch* and to Victorian culture outside the text. The instability of this association will become inscribed in the text as a confrontation between a miniature, which embodies a version of aesthetic female *Bildung* and its opposite, a cameo bracelet, which delineates traditional Victorian female gender definition formed by structures of the political economy.

III. Talking Cameos

In *Middlemarch*, Dorothea's aversion to those who "find ... work ... and sell" jewelry highlights its status as a product of the political economy. As an economic commodity, jewelry carries political as well as economic significance. Behind the

---

[6]   Jacques Lacan, *Ecrits: A Selection*, trans. Alan Sheridan (New York: W.W. Norton, 1977) 11. Wilfried Ver Eecke, *Interpreting Lacan*, ed. Joseph H. Smith and William Kerrigan, *Psychiatry and the Humanities*, 6, 113–138 (New Haven: Yale University Press, 1987) 119. *Lacan* discusses "*imagos of the fragmented body*" as forms of aggressivity (Lacan's emphasis). They are "mental phenomena"—images that "represent ... aggressive intentions." In this case, Dorothea experiences an image of "dismemberment" as she thinks aggressively about the economic enterprise that mines and manufactures the emerald bracelet on her wrist. Ver Eecke further explains: "Lacan makes the fantasy of dismemberment function as a reminder that our bodily unity is a psychological achievement."

scenes of the novel, economic practices coalesce with political force, appearing as a unified discourse of political economy that affects Dorothea's material circumstances. In the context of Victorian culture at large, industrial development had ensconced middle class women in discrete domesticity while dispatching men to work in the factory or office. It has been well-documented that, as men and women became radically separated by their designated work roles, middle class women also experienced subordinated status in all aspects of public life from which they were barred: production of goods for sale, ownership of capital, legal rights to custody of children and property, participation in political processes, education. The economic system thus imposed its negative political consequences on the subjective experience of individual women, so that in *Middlemarch*, Dorothea could, by mental association, connect the politically oppressive economic system that produces jewelry with the same gleaming emeralds and diamonds she admires for their aesthetic qualities. She therefore finds that she has momentary misgivings about the jewelry because of its manufacture by "miserable men [who] find such things, and work at them and sell them."

As aesthetics and political economy permeate nineteenth-century British culture as separate discourses, they reveal their unstable yet ongoing relation at the gendered site of Victorian fashion, where rhetorical invocations to beauty collide yet collude with economic motives. Gilles Lipovetsky has argued that "no system of fashion exists without the conjunction of two logical systems: the system of ephemera," such as all the commodities produced by Victorian industry and trade, "and the system of aesthetic fantasy," such as Dorothea Brooke displays in the previously cited passages.[7] If fashion must have both its material products and its aesthetic fantasy, it participates in an innately Victorian realism, described by Richard Stein as a "double vision that sense of what we can and cannot see, can and cannot represent directly"[8] (251). Products of fashion perform as a visual language to be read in the newly expanding city as a method for conceptually processing crowds of strangers at a glance. Victorian fashion arises as a phenomenon resulting from overlapping cultural trends toward capitalism, industrialization, the growth of cities, the spectacle of marketing the commodity, aesthetics, and separate gendered spheres.

The Great Exhibition of 1851 had "conjured up a vision of commodities and banished from sight the reality of their exchange" (38). This interpretation equally describes Dorothea's attitude toward the emerald and diamond bracelet: the text emphasizes Dorothea's response to the spectacle of the gleaming light shining on its facets, until her rapture over their beauty is given full play; then only

---

[7]   Gilles Lipovetsky, *The Empire of Fashion: Dressing Modern Democracy*, trans. Catherine Porter, foreword Richard Sennett (Princeton: Princeton University Press, 1994) 25.

[8]   Richard Stein, "Street Figures: Victorian Urban Iconography," *Victorian Literature and the Victorian Visual Imagination*, ed. Carol T. Christ and John O. Jordan (Berkeley: University of California Press, 1995) 251.

briefly does she acknowledge the source of their economic production. Here the aesthetic quality of the commodity sustains its attractive power only insofar as the economic and political considerations to which the object owes its existence have been ignored or bypassed in favor of its aesthetic appearance.

The cameo comfortably resides within this Victorian fashion framework containing clothing, commodities, and jewelry. The iconic images on cameos circulated through Victorian culture as a spectacle of everyday fashion, their chiseled heads adorning bracelets, brooches, pendants, necklaces, and earrings. Like other jewelry, a cameo had the ability to function as a visual language, such that a number of cultural interpretations could have presented themselves to viewer and wearer alike. As a memento of travel to Italy, for example, cameos could have functioned doubly as a sign of monetary or class status. However, as a graphic representation with classical lines, a cameo may have suggested history, tradition, or ideals of womanhood.

Figure 5.1 A three-layered carved cameo representation of a Victorian lady dressed ornately, covered with garlands of roses, with earrings, a tendril of hair on the neck, and a peacock, c.1850

Source: © Anita Arnold (2010), courtesy of MaryAnn-tiques

To interpret the role of jewelry in *Middlemarch* as an imagistic language is also to imply meanings this language conveyed to Victorian readers. Here a brief background that traces how cameos became a commonly recognizable object suffused with meaning specific to the culture would serve also to establish further the connective link between text and context. In Western Europe, cameos had circulated as a cultural artifact since Roman times, yet this jewelry enjoyed a resurgent popularity in the Victorian era. The "craze for cameos" began in Northern Europe with the [French] Italian campaign of 1796. In response to a treaty obligation, the Pope used Vatican jewels to pay for the upkeep of French troops in Italy, and, as a result, "many fine cameos must have been sent to France," Peter Hinks surmises.[9] Napoleon admired the cameos, founded a school for engraving gems, and had his own bust portrayed on cameos, in the style of a Roman Statesman. As the nineteenth century progressed, and the fad of cameos was imported to England, the male face on the cameo gave way to female images, a small fashion detail that replicated the gender separation of Victorian culture. Thereafter, feminine faces evolved over a period of more than 50 years from "a light downward tilt ... [and] an expression of coy modesty" to a type that "looks us boldly in the face," according to Dora Jane Janson. By 1880,

> the ideal self that women chose to recognize in these little images had undergone a remarkable change: from a lovely but lifeless chimera, to a saccharine fairytale personage ... through a brief period of calm self-awareness in the beginning of the second half of the century, which shortly gave way to a more agitated, and finally to a downright self-pitying image at the point where the evolution of the cameo as a popular genre comes to a halt.[10]

A historical progression of cameos constitutes a perfect medium for imaging the evolution of women's cultural roles and their attendant subjectivities throughout the Victorian period. Even more significantly, the cameo's changing image suggests that its corresponding cultural image could also be reinvented, and therefore, arbitrarily constructed.[11]

---

[9]   Peter Hinks, *Nineteenth Century Jewellery* (London: Faber & Faber, 1975) 19.

[10]   Dora Jane Janson, *From Slave to Siren: The Victorian Woman and Her Jewelry from Neoclassic to Art Nouveau* (Durham, NC: The Duke University Museum of Art, 1971) 3.

[11]   For additional nineteenth-century history and description, see C. W. King, "Cameo Engravings," *Antique Gems: Origins, Uses, and Value as Interpreters of Ancient History; and as Illustrative of Ancient Art: with Hints to Gem Collectors* (London: John Murray, 1860) 181–200, and S. M. Burnham, *Precious Stones: In Nature, Art, and Literature* (Boston: Bradlee Whidden, 1886) 156–9.

IV. Gender Criticism

The dilemmas of female subjectivity are conceptualized within a historical setting in *Middlemarch*, which was written with a backward glance from about 1870 to 1829. Although Eliot's historical setting creates an effective site for safe comment on contemporary gender problems, her novel also harbors historical fiction's inherent ambivalence which logically subverts its polemic: the cultural context of the earlier period tends to be rewritten to address problems that concern the later period, when cultural perception of women's problems had shifted. "The Woman Question" had intensified into a vigorous debate around the time Eliot was writing this text, so that her impulse to narrate women's problems of the 1830s was created by perceived difficulties of the middle to late Victorian era. An 1864 essay in the *Westminster Review* reports that

> The greatest social difficulty in England today is the relationship between men and women. The principal difference between ourselves and our ancestors is that they took society as they found it while we are self-conscious and perplexed. The institution of marriage might almost seem just now to be upon trial.[12]

The statement carries resonance for historical fiction's inevitable process of re-visioning, in which current problems are read into fictional scenarios of the past.[13] However, just as Eliot writes about female roles of the 1830s from the standpoint of vexed gender relations of the 1870s, contemporary feminist criticism has also read Eliot's feminism of the 1870s from a contemporary vantage; it has rigorously, and effectively, called into question Eliot's practice of reproducing patriarchal social structures that wield coercive power, leading her to uphold and extend narrow Victorian gender roles.[14]

---

[12]   Justin M'Carthy, Untitled Essay, *Westminster Review* (July 1864), *Norton Anthology of English Literature*, ed. M. H. Abrams, 5th edn, Volume 2 (New York: W. W. Norton & Company, 1986) 1635–6.

[13]   Hayden White, *The Content of the Form: Narrative Discourse and Historical Representation* (Baltimore: The Johns Hopkins University Press, 1987) 150. Acknowledging White's discussion of history as a written text with a political agenda, historical fiction would then be considered doubly written. White writes that revision of history serves revolutionary causes: "willing backward occurs when we rearrange accounts of events in the past that have been emplotted in a given way, in order to endow them with a different meaning or to draw from the new reasons for acting differently in the future from the way we have become accustomed to acting in our present ... events formerly regarded as unimportant are now redescribed as anticipations or prefigurations of the new society to be created by revolutionary action." On this basis, feminism's method of reading present perceptions of problematic gender relations into historical texts is supported.

[14]   Bonnie Zimmerman, "George Eliot and Feminism: The Case of *Daniel Deronda*," *Nineteenth-Century Women Writers of the English Speaking World*, ed. Rhoda B. Nathan (New York: Greenwood Press, 1986) 231; Sandra M. Gilbert and Susan Gubar, *The Madwoman in*

In sum, both Eliot and contemporary critics have used the past—whether historical or fictional—to argue a position that concerns contemporary problems. A feature of this transhistorical method is that it essentializes gender as it elides perceptions of gender roles across changing historical periods. I would emphasize that because gender is a cultural convention superimposed upon sexual difference, it is a role that can vary radically between cultures and through history. Gender definition is always open to revision. To conceptualize the ground for this analysis, I foreground Eliot's topic of *Bildung*, and recast the feminist analysis both as historical, and as primarily concerned with a woman as an individual rather than as a category; this analysis is further symbolized as the painting of an individual on a miniature rather than the standard representation of a woman on a cameo. Upon this ground, my particular analysis historicizes Eliot's feminism, as it recognizes that, within the context of her time and place, she stands at the forward edge of change.

In historicizing Eliot's feminism in *Middlemarch*, one site of analysis immediately presents itself with an alternative interpretation: the novel's problematic ending. It is commonly noticed that, in the process of recounting her heroine's gender troubles, the narrator does not allow Dorothea to reach the final resolution she leads her readers to hope for at the outset; instead, the narrator takes perverse pleasure in enumerating Dorothea's "unhistoric acts," "hidden life," and "strength spent in channels which had no great name on the earth." This overdetermination of Dorothea's abjection works to formulate negative reader reaction against the imposed scenario in both the text and the culture from which the text arises. One must then account for the possibility that Eliot harbored a purposefully ironic stance toward this narrative ending. Narrative resolution can hardly be willed into framing culturally revisionary notions because it must be commensurate with established social structures of a work's reading public. Indeed, one could even say of the narrative ending that it is "greatly determined by what lies outside it," as Eliot characterizes Dorothea's fate (612).[15] It begs to be historicized. While the text itself dutifully moves from its narrative conflicts over gender roles toward a placating conclusion that reflects a status quo acceptable to the reading public, a space opens up between the revisionary author and the

---

the Attic: The Woman Writer and the Nineteenth-Century Imagination (New Haven: Yale University Press, 1979) 466; Jacqueline Rose, *Sexuality in the Field of Vision* (New York: Verso, 1986) 120. In discussing Showalter's article, "Feminist Criticism in the Wilderness," Rose notes Showalter's point "that there is a danger of complicity between a strategy of reading which identifies these instances of disturbance [against repression of women] and a damaging image of femininity itself." However, Rose rereads this point as "a type of crisis in feminist criticism which looks to women's writing for the signs of a revolt against this condition (the assertion of another femininity) or else can only repeat that [repressive] condition as a truth about women of which the wider culture is then accused" (120).

[15]   Rosemary Bodenheimer, *The Real Life of Mary Ann Evans: George Eliot, Her Letters and Fiction* (Ithaca: Cornell University Press, 1994) 44–5. Bodenheimer discusses Eliot's "hyperconsciousness of audience."

conforming narrator as their purposes diverge. The irony written into Dorothea's abjection thus enables the text to argue normally unacceptable counter-discourses about gender roles. In sum, because *Middlemarch* rereads the past from 1870 to 1830, it enables a revolutionary narrative by situating commentary on gender roles outside its contemporary culture; the ending, however, necessarily abandons inspired deliberation about a range of gender roles to mirror the established cultural standards of the contemporary reading audience. As Eliot achieves a precocious argument for Victorian woman's self-development, the narrative ending is but one more example of how a resolutely patriarchal culture inscribes its conventions on female gender definition.

In taking a cursory glance at some other aspects of Eliot's feminism in its time and place, one also notes that as a narrator she can only talk about women's roles at all when her assumptions are based upon a conception of an organically whole culture in which those roles repeat themselves throughout, as a matter of discursive practice. Such phrases as "we Middlemarchers" (130; bk. 2, ch. 18), "Middlemarch institutions" (135; bk. 2, ch. 18), "good Middlemarch society" (117; bk. 2, ch. 16), or "Middlemarch perception" (337; bk. 5, ch. 46) mark normative behavior for all characters in the text as an oppositional community against which Will, Dorothea, Lydgate, and other characters must model an authentic individual self. The initial presentation of the community as an attractive haven of mutually affirming, fun loving citizens lures the reader into happy complacency which then becomes radically disturbed when the town imposes its rigid standards for conformity, and the characters' troubles mount. One could assume that this tightly knit society, produced in the text to present the drawbacks of constrictive mores, projected behavior patterns recognizable to the reading public. Finally, in a literal image of this organically whole culture as a horticultural backdrop, Will Ladislaw, the rebel against the status quo, first appears as "a figure, conspicuous on a dark background of evergreens," while Casaubon, the epitome of patriarchy, is presented with "no bloom that could be thrown into relief by that background" (58, 54; bk.1, ch. 9).[16]

Inasmuch as this well-regulated society of Middlemarch flourishes in the text as a reflection of Victorian culture, it draws its structure from the general practices of capitalism. The text assumes a totality of middle class values and addresses itself toward a middle or upper class audience, such that the whole issue of woman's work is presented with an assumption of moneyed leisure that was unavailable to an underclass of servants and laborers. While Dorothea thus finds that, as its mistress, "there was nothing for her to do in Lowick," the text, with heavy irony, has Casaubon comment that "each position has its corresponding duties;" her duty, of course, is to do nothing, a sign that shows the Casaubons' wealth and class (57; bk. 1, ch. 9). The class-based nature of the text is further revealed when at the

---

[16]   Alison Booth, *Greatness Engendered: George Eliot and Virginia Woolf*, Reading Women Writing (Ithaca: Cornell University Press, 1992) 48. She writes, Eliot is "drawn to what for convenience I will call horticultural imagery. We might consider these images as a literalization of the metaphor of culture."

end Dorothea and Will decide to marry; Dorothea foresees that her consequent descent from the moneyed ranks of society will mean that she must literally and figuratively "learn what everything costs" (594; bk. 8, ch. 83). Eliot's feminism thus arises from middle class issues masquerading as monolithic cultural issues, with few exceptions. As her treatment of feminine problems appears essentialized across time in this historical fiction, it also presents itself as essentialized across the space of class lines. Oddly enough, these totalizing and essentialist perceptions of gender and class exist side by side with a Victorian belief in progress, such that change toward "the growing good of the world" could animate the idea of the future (613; bk. 8, Finale).

V. Gender and *Bildung*

Within the defining terms of this inconsistency between class and gender stasis and cultural change, the female *Bildungsroman* carves out its conflicted discursive space. No aspect of reading this novel within its historical period is more important than recognizing the influence of *Bildung*, which traces its source to German aesthetic thought. The project of *Bildung* involves autoproduction of a unique and autonomous self, a process which also structures narrative in the *Bildungsroman*. The self as uniquely produced has been described as a "historically-situated norm."[17] In very broad terms, this norm attempted to integrate the Self of the Romantic era into the needs of the subsequent Victorian culture of industry and empire. In his idealized description of *Bildung*, Moretti notes that it offered "one of the most harmonious solutions" to the "dilemma of modern bourgeois civilization: the conflict between the ideal of 'self-determination' and the just as imperious demands of 'socialization.'"[18] Yet if Dorothea carries a "desire to make her life greatly effective," and a "passion ... transfused through a mind struggling towards an ideal life" toward which *Bildung* strives, she engages in a speculative project of a radical nature for her time: she must transgress inflexible gender boundaries if she is to succeed (20, 32).

Dorothea's problems with *Bildung* arise from a culture at odds with itself as *Bildung*'s ideology intersects with questions of gender definition. For men in Victorian society, patriarchal capitalism and German idealism were unified discourses in their valuation of individual agency. Both the individual of capitalism and the Schillerian Personality of German idealism were concepts of a personal transcendental identity that existed in a realm unaffected by everyday exigencies, and would permit an individual to impose ideas and views upon the

[17]   Irving Howe, "The Self in Literature," *Constructions of the Self*, ed. George Levine (New Brunswick: Rutgers University Press, 1992) 249–67, 251.

[18]   Franco Moretti, "The Comforts of Civilization," *Representations* 12 (Fall 1985) 115.

social environment.[19] Yet the agency that informs this valued individual's actions is one that was denied to Victorian women. As cultural practices such as education, work, and dress divided themselves into distinctly gendered realms, the capitalist economy and German idealist philosophy rested alike on assumptions that divided males from females. In practice, the ideologies of *Bildung* had been produced by males, and applied to males only.

It would be impossible to analyze *Middlemarch* as a female *Bildungsroman*, however, if one were to pay strict heed to the critical commentary of Esther Kleinbord Labovitz who describes the female *Bildungsroman* as "a twentieth-century genre 'made possible only when *Bildung* became a reality for women'" (background qtg. Labovitz, 2–3). On the contrary, I would maintain that it was Eliot's particular project to use an ideal of *Bildung* to question Victorian female gender conventions. As Eliot conceptualizes her feminist project in terms of *Bildung*, her works also "provide us with a literary interrogation of aesthetics ... engaged with the Schillerian tradition," as Marc Redfield has shown (49).[20] The ideas of *Bildung* circulated in English intellectual circles of the 1870s; Carlyle had written a *Life of Schiller* in the 1820s, and Eliot had begun her German readings with Schiller's works.[21] As we shall see, aesthetic judgment as it was envisioned as a moral project by Schiller, and Kant before him, illuminates oppositional discourse about gender roles in *Middlemarch*. Yet the female *Bildungsroman* is so vexed a genre in this instance that its irony is impossible to avoid, for it promotes the impossible task of free female self-formulation as a dream that cannot be realized in a culture that only allows males to engage in such practices. Showing its nature as *Bildungsroman*—described as a genre featuring "failure or loss"—the text notes

---

[19]   Ian Watt, *The Rise of the Novel: Studies in Defoe, Richardson, and Fielding* (Berkeley: University of California Press, 1957); Friedrich Schiller, *On the Aesthetic Education of Man: In a Series of Letters* (Oxford: Clarendon Press, 1967) 12.4, 81; 13.3, 87. Watt defines the individual of this period in economic terms: "he alone was primarily responsible for determining his own economic, social, political and religious roles" (61). Schiller defined the Person as "an absolute and indivisible unity ... the more power and depth the Personality achieves, and the more freedom reason attains, so much more world does man comprehend, and all the more form does he create outside of himself."

[20]   Marc Redfield, *Phantom Formations: Aesthetic Ideology and the* Bildungsroman (Ithaca: Cornell University Press, 1996) 49. He writes that "Schiller's *On the Aesthetic Education of Man* ... is arguably the most influential text on the notion of aesthetic pedagogy to come out of Germany during this period."

[21]   Rosemary Ashton, *The German Idea: Four English Writers and the Reception of German Thought, 1800–1860* (New York: Cambridge University Press, 1980) 91–2, 147. Deborah Guth, "George Eliot and Schiller: Narrative Ambivalence in *Middlemarch* and *Felix Holt*," *Modern Language Review* 94.4 (October 1999) 913, 915; she writes, "Schiller's reputation and popularity during the first half of the nineteenth century was enormous and is well documented," and "Schiller fired [Eliot] with a devotion to lofty feeling" (Guth quoting Donald Stone, *The Romantic Impulse in Victorian Fiction* (Cambridge, MA: Harvard University Press, 1980) 188).

that Dorothea "always wanted things that wouldn't be."[22] In *Middlemarch*, the narrator inserts wisely disapproving editorial comments about Dorothea's naive perceptions of gender relations, so that the tension between narrator and heroine in *Middlemarch* often takes the form of an oscillation between the argued ideal of *Bildung* and its inevitable failure. The text fluctuates between Dorothea's "desire to make her life greatly effective," and her realization that she "never could do anything that [she] liked," nor had "carried out any plan yet" (20; bk. 1, ch. 3; 600; bk. 8, ch. 84).

Eliot thus carves out a site of her own feminist concerns as she plots a trajectory of Dorothea's expanding understanding about woman's roles. Yet Dorothea's ultimate understanding becomes her ironic aesthetic education attained through an unsuccessful attempt at *Bildung*. The Victorian capacity to conceptualize the culture as an "age of transition" offered Eliot a ground from which to imagine female *Bildung* as a wider cultural change toward empowerment of women as autonomous individuals.[23] The narrative impulse behind this novel, I suggest, remains the author's concern to imagine the actualization of an ideal of specifically female *Bildung*, for, when her heroine's sense of individual self is at stake, Eliot's feminism is of a "nature altogether ardent" (21; bk. 1, ch. 3).

VI. Sculpture, Cameos, and Women's Roles

In the interests of bringing to light the opposition between female *Bildung*, or self-development, and narrow Victorian imperatives for women, I present scenes featuring sculpture, an art form that enriches a critique of cameo jewelry and the iconic representation of woman in *Middlemarch*. For cameos are miniature pieces of sculpture immersed in the domestic space of the home where they project carved images to women within everyday life. In *Middlemarch*, the chiseled outlines of both sculpture and cameos construct a series of visual representations that project meanings separate from the words of the text. Yet whether the characters' discussions feature sculpture, jewelry, or painting, the inescapable intentionality of the text of *Middlemarch* to present an expansive array of commentary on various art forms reflects the degree to which Victorians are preoccupied with aesthetics. Eliot had indeed read Ruskin's *Modern Painters* and allowed—even endeavored—to let Ruskin's aesthetics and realism influence her own writing.[24]

After I offer an interpretive view of textual sculpture, I analyze passages from *Middlemarch* that feature cameos and a miniature representation. In all these scenes that contain art and jewelry, the characters' aesthetic judgments emerge

---

[22]   Redfield, 135; Eliot, *Middlemarch*, 600, bk. 8, ch. 84.

[23]   John Stuart Mill, "The Spirit of the Age," *Essays on Politics and Culture*, ed. Gertrude Himmelfarb (Garden City: Doubleday, 1962) 2.

[24]   Gordon Haight, *George Eliot: A Biography* (New York: Penguin Books, 1968) 197, 201. Haight quotes George Eliot: "I think [Ruskin] is the finest writer living" (204).

as crucially important political and economic statements. For example, when Dorothea points out to Uncle Brooke that his "simpering" artwork paints a false picture of the real conditions under which laborers live, he asserts his upper class interests by countering, "we do not like our pictures and statues being found fault with" (285; bk. 4, ch. 39).

The text also integrates its artwork into issues of gender definition. Even Dorothea herself is presented as a work of art, though a cautionary irony always plays around the edges of her many images, troubling the view of her as an aesthetic object. In fact, when Dorothea Brooke and Edward Casaubon take their wedding journey from Middlemarch to Rome, the reader is treated to a veritable catalog of perspectives of Dorothea. One of these views is set in the Hall of Statues of the Vatican Museum, where Dorothea is imaged as "a breathing, blooming girl … in Quakerish grey drapery" as she stands "against a pedestal." Dorothea fixes her eyes "dreamily [on a] streak of sunlight," for she has become "a brooding abstraction … inwardly seeing the light of years to come in her own home" where her role is "not so clear to her" (140; bk. 2, ch. 15; 151; bk. 2, ch. 20). Assuming a fixed, statuesque pose herself, she stands next to the marble statue of the reclining Ariadne, so that the text features Dorothea in a tableau that likens her to a work of sculpture. Indeed, in playing her culturally assigned role as mistress of Lowick, Dorothea becomes as immobilized as a work of sculpture, and equally removed from the energies of cultural life as a statue obscurely installed in a museum. As a "locus of aesthetic embodiment," Dorothea's image as Ariadne conflates with the other textual images of sculpture and cameos, which accumulate to represent a woman's loss of movement or personal freedom to build an ideal life.[25] As the plot subjects Dorothea to Casaubon's coercive power, sculpture functions in the text as a visual representation of the narrow lines of convention that reify her as a subordinate partner in her marriage. Indeed, the continuities of allusion generated by the sculptural image throughout the text form a cohesive discourse against the constraints of Victorian gender practices.[26]

As a figure of mythical resonance, the statue of Ariadne would have had deep narrative and ideological significance for Victorian readers. Ariadne's story features her involvement with two lovers, the first unhappy relation with Theseus evolving into a rapturous second relationship with Bacchus. Ariadne's two affairs roughly parallel Dorothea Brooke's love relationships in the novel. Small figures of Ariadne could often be found in Victorian parlors. While the textual presence of Ariadne underwrites the importance of Dorothea's female consciousness, the statue also represents a figure of desire, according to Abigail S. Rischin, or "a triadic mother-maid-daughter" figure, according to Nina Nichols.[27] However, in the text, one could

---

[25]   Redfield, 148.

[26]   See 396, bk. 6, ch. 54; 461, 464, bk. 6, ch. 62 for additional scenes that compare Dorothea to sculpture.

[27]   Abigail S. Rischin, "Beside the Reclining Statue: Ekphrasis, Narrative, and Desire in *Middlemarch*," *PMLA* 111 (1996) 1129; Nina DaVinci Nichols, *Ariadne's Lives*

say that Ariadne sets the terms of the debate by embodying and valorizing female consciousness. In this mythic representation, the individual self immersed in a historical time and place is overlooked in favor of a timeless essence, for Ariadne's accession to male-dominated culture through marriage sculpts her into a role defined only by its relation to the male. As opposed to the scene where Dorothea poses with Ariadne, it will remain Eliot's priority to explore the possibilities of acceding to a realm of individuality for her heroine within a Victorian time and place. This exploration will privilege *Bildung*, process, and becoming, rather than preconceived gender roles, stasis, and preserving the status quo.

Showing that Dorothea's pose is remarkable, the text enlarges the scene's frame to show two male characters, Naumann and Ladislaw, looking on with interest. The overdetermined, precisely-arranged tableau functions in this text as "a lure ... to attract the notice of readers," just as it attracts the male characters.[28] While the male gaze at Dorothea objectifies her into their perceptions of her role within the male ordered culture, the reader imaging the males gazing at Dorothea gains an even wider perspective into the political power of this determining male gaze, which presupposes Dorothea as a "privileged object of investigation and control."[29] Viewing males viewing a woman in this instance serves to destabilize the Victorian male view of women as the text ironically deconstructs the process of stereotyping at the very moment of its enactment. Here one sees the process by which Dorothea is turned to marble rather than the timeless image of the female marble statue itself.

Accordingly, in other passages describing the journey to Rome, Dorothea is variously labeled by Will Ladislaw and Naumann as "a happy wife," "Mrs. Second-Cousin," a "perfect young Madonna," a "Christian Antigone," an "English lady," "Mrs. Casaubon," "a benignant matron," "an angel beguiled," "the beautiful bride," "the gracious lady," "the lady-wife," and, even, "a woman [not] to be spoken of as other women were" (160–1; bk. 2, ch. 22). While the men verbalize their categories for Dorothea in ways that relegate her to various positions within patriarchal culture, the narrator presents a far different, internal psychological picture of Dorothea. Here she is variously described as "in a fit of weeping," or "sobbing bitterly;" because she has an "ardent nature ... quick emotions," and a "mind [that is] ... continually sliding into inward fits of anger and repulsion," she experiences a "faintness of heart at the new real future," and a "dream-like strangeness [to] her bridal life" (bk. 2, ch. 20). Like the span of a circular theater, the views of Dorothea come from opposite directions simultaneously, to form a disjunctive concept of her identity. As the men's categories and the formal sculptural conventions impose a static, definitive perception of Dorothea from an external, culturally-wrought vantage, her own subjective experience chafes at

---

(Madison: Fairleigh Dickinson University Press, 1995) 24.

[28]   Michael Riffaterre, "How Do Images Signify?" *Diacritics: A Review of Contemporary Criticism* 24 (Spring 1994) 11.

[29]   Rose, 113.

such formulaic outlines. Indeed, the narrator editorializes that "it is a narrow mind which cannot look at a subject from various points of view," for, in the end, one would hope that "we ... can be seen and judged in the wholeness of our character" (49, bk. 1, ch. 7; 558, bk. 8, ch. 76).

The chapters that feature the Casaubon's wedding journey to Rome thus present the opposition as it is figured in this museum scene: the cultural concept of a woman's gender role crafted by a Western patriarchal tradition versus an internal concept of identity formation, or the self-realization involved in *Bildung*. As Dorothea walks with her new husband through "the stony avenue of inscriptions" at the Vatican, it is she who is becoming inscribed with the imposing tradition of Victorian patriarchy; the passage infers that social structures are inscribed upon women with a coercive force similar to the manner in which a sculptor shapes inert material into a form. This sort of analogy is not without precedent. Schiller's *On the Aesthetic Education of Man* argues that "when the artisan lays hands upon the formless mass in order to shape it to his ends, he has no scruple in doing it violence; for the natural material he is working merits no respect for itself."[30] By substituting "woman" for "mass" or "material" in this passage, the textual analogy between aesthetic sculptural form and the politics of gender formation becomes clear. The sculptural images at the Vatican museum suggest similarities between the process of carving sculpture and the process of inscribing Victorian woman's gender roles in the new bride, both of which are achieved by carving away and discarding unwanted parts of the original form.

Most importantly for this study, the spectacle of sculpture in Eliot's narrative then transfers its meanings of patriarchal constraint to the classical carved heads on cameos. The disinterested ideal of human beauty had led the German idealist, Schiller, to emulate the Greeks for their classical art; in *Aesthetic Education*, he writes, "We perceive eternally in them that which we have not but which we continually strive after ... the archetype of a human being."[31] For Eliot—who had read Schiller—a paragon of applied aesthetics would rightly have been these cameos of classical design. In a scene in the Casaubon's Roman apartment, Dorothea and Will discuss the aesthetic merits of cameos, for which they must develop their own "critiques of judgment;" for Kant states that "rule and precept are incapable of serving as ... [a] standard for aesthetic finality in fine art."[32] Later, Goethe had written that

> the subject of engraved gems could always be introduced as an excellent intermediary whenever the conversation threatened to flag ... The amateur who, having procured such treasures, shall desire to raise his acquisitions to the rank of a respectable cabinet, must ... call external proofs to his assistance; a thing

---

[30]   Schiller, 4.4.19; 316.

[31]   Schiller, 4.2, 17.

[32]   Immanuel Kant, *Critique of Judgment*, trans. James Creed Meredith (Oxford: Clarendon Press, 1952), I.57.1, 212.

which must be excessively difficult for one who is not himself a practical artist in the same department.[33]

The context for this handy advice from Goethe is an actual conversation between Goethe and Princess Galitzin, in which they attempt to apply their aesthetic judgment to the Princess's antique cameo collection. Here Eliot equates Dorothea to the Princess and Ladislaw to Goethe.[34] As they replay the scene as it was described by Goethe, they model their behavior after esteemed people of "high culture," acting out the Victorian version of today's media celebrities. As Dorothea and Will interact to form aesthetic norms, their self-generated good taste allows them to act as role models for the novel's reading audience.

In the scene, Dorothea has bought a souvenir cameo bracelet she plans to take home to her sister Celia, and as she attempts to assess the cameos aesthetically, Will comes to visit her in her Roman apartment. The scene has as its point of reference the earlier scene in which Dorothea assumes her statuesque pose beside the Ariadne in the Vatican sculptural tableau. This apartment scene concerning cameos supersedes the earlier one: whereas the earlier scene presents a still, silent image of Dorothea as woman perceived from a male point of view, the latter scene features Dorothea and Will in a contrapuntal debate over the sculpted image of woman. Words now intervene in the interpretation to alter the image of woman, so that passive acceptance of the image becomes revisionary critical analysis instead. While the terms of the debate are couched in aesthetic language, it becomes clear that the underlying politics of gender definition are stake.

As Dorothea and Will converse about the cameo bracelet, eight different judgments about cameos and "art generally" are pronounced in rapid-fire succession; this textual overdetermination about opinions of cameos points toward their function as signs, though Will and Dorothea say that they are of little importance. As Will disdains them as "little Homeric bits," he still finds them "exquisitely neat" (162). Although he feels that they would "suit" Dorothea, she counters that they are only for her sister. As Will notes that Dorothea "seem[s] not to care about cameos," she agrees that she does not "think them a great object in life;" yet they have made her "uneasy." Finally, Will states, "I fear you are a heretic about art generally." Will's choice of the word "heretic" implies that art imposes belief upon its viewers; this political twist to aesthetic theory, lightly tinged with inquisitional rhetoric, inhabits the center of Dorothea and Will's discussion. In his *Critique of Judgment*, Kant claims that "judgements of taste ... must have ... universal validity" (I.20; 82). Under these precepts, if aesthetic taste is not shared with those who generally have the power to determine it, then "heresy" would be the designated result. While such agreement could be a positive source of social

---

[33]   C. W. King, "Introduction," *Antique Gems*, xxvi–xxviii.

[34]   Guth, 914. Guth notes that Eliot had traveled to Germany at least eight times with George Henry Lewes, and had collaborated with Lewes on Goethe's biography, published in 1855. She was well-versed in German language, literature, and ideas.

cohesion under ideal circumstances of mutual consent, the effect could also impose an unwelcome orthodoxy from the point of view of someone like Dorothea who does not identify with cultural givens, and who would prefer to engage in *Bildung*. Dorothea is not in sympathy with the ideological messages that emanate from the cameos, or "art generally." In fact, she judges the tradition of Italian art as a "consecration of ugliness rather than beauty" (163; bk. 2, ch. 22).

Figure 5.2 Cameo conch shell bracelet, 1840–60. Seven oval disks carved from a queen conch shell with high three-dimensional relief, and set in gilded gold over silver. Seven Victorian ladies with differing hairdos. While right-handed carvers made left-facing relief profiles, left-handed carvers made right-facing profiles. This bracelet, however, features profiles that face in both directions, divided in the middle

Source: © Anita Arnold (2010), courtesy of MaryAnn-tiques

Figure 5.3 Cameo bracelet, c.1850 carved from lava in a variety of darker colours. Darker colours were often used for male profiles. Lava jewelry was in vogue because of archaeological digs going on at Pompeii

Source: © Anita Arnold (2010), courtesy of MaryAnn-tiques

After Will has identified Dorothea as a "heretic," he asks, "how is this?" and then voices his own assumption: "I should have expected you to be very sensitive to the beautiful everywhere" (162; bk. 2, ch. 22). This seemingly complimentary statement again has undertones of gender politics. Moritz, a German idealist, offers an explanation; he puts forth in his essay "On the Creative Imitation of the Beautiful" the following idea of gender relations:

> Man ... is a microcosm--the Universe on a small scale. Effectiveness is given to this congruity of Man with the Universe by two complimentary faculties; the "formative" and "sensitive" powers (*Bildungskraft, Empfindungskraft*), the first being related to the second as activity to passivity, male to female. Both powers ... have a biological basis in "the finer tissue of our organism." They are both directed toward the harmonious organization of the universe. The "sensitive" power" receives its impress, the "formative power" reproduces its structure.[35]

Indeed, Dorothea experiences this exact "impression" in Rome, as "her husband's way of commenting on the strangely impressive objects around them had begun to affect her with a sort of mental shiver" (146; Bk. 2, ch. 20). When Will says that he expects Dorothea to be "sensitive to the beautiful everywhere," his thought implies that he has expected her to typify *Empfindungskraft*, a sensitive passivity characterized as feminine. In being sensitive to the beautiful she would "receive the impress" of the "universe" formed by the male. But Dorothea replies, "I suppose I am dull about many things." Under the guise of modesty, or a ploy of ignorance, or a simple lack of interest or response, Dorothea rejects the role of aesthetic appreciation, because at the same time it values "sensitive" powers, it also entails attesting to an orthodox female passivity. While earlier in the stay in Rome Dorothea had found the art works "strangely impressive," she can now say in relation to the cameos that she is "dull" about "many things" (162; bk. 2, ch. 22). Dorothea has indeed undergone a change; no longer "impressed," she is now positively and intentionally dull as a mode of resistance to the art work that projects male cultural authority. In response to this view, one can understand why in this scene Dorothea greets Will at the door of her Roman apartment with the cameo bracelet in her hand, yet she never puts it on.

Following Will's statement that he would presume Dorothea's sensitivity to the beautiful everywhere, Dorothea replies, "I should like to make life beautiful—I mean everybody's life." This statement attests to Dorothea's interest in *Bildung*, as well as to the fact that it is problematic for woman. The hiatus in her remark reveals an anxious hesitancy as she superimposes opposite meaning on her original statement: she knows that she cannot make her own life aesthetically beautiful at the same time that she fulfills the cultural ideals of adaptability and submission in married women. For above all, the process of *Bildung* must build a life "free of

---

[35]   Katherine Everett Gilbert and Helmut Kuhn, *A History of Esthetics* (New York: Macmillan, 1939) 319.

conflict" and Dorothea's "formation as an individual in and for herself does [not] coincide ... with [her] social integration as a ... part of the whole."[36]

In this novel, the cameo bracelet projects the ideal image of woman to be read as a reinforcement of established Victorian gender roles.[37] The classical image in any cameo is non-individualized, and it could therefore function as a prime vessel for a viewer's assumptions about ideal beauty. As the Victorian era popularized Kant and Schiller's aesthetics, ideal beauty became defined as moral; as a result, judgments of ideal beauty related to perceptions about ideal social behavior. Because the established morality of this strong patriarchal society was necessarily dictated from a male subject position, it imposed its political values and practices upon its judgment of beauty in females. So conceived, the cameo then becomes an image which projects a political view of gender roles conveyed under the seemingly quietist guise of ideal beauty, a process which equally has the effect of naturalizing moral precepts for women, putting those precepts beyond question. The connection between an aesthetics that privileges classical lines and capitalism's need to see all women homogeneously thus becomes clear: in classical aesthetics and in capitalism, ideal images collapse individual distinctions in women, for in a developing industrial economy that separates genders, the need is to perceive all women as naturally performing the same domestic functions in all homes.

Aesthetic theory, then, through Kant and Schiller, has become anthropocentric. The moral ideal was an important link between theory and practice, and the practice of *Bildung* to form an archetypal, ideal everyday life was the result of this ethos—for males. In *Middlemarch*, this illusory ideal of a unity of self-development and morality can last only until Dorothea's marriage. The text reveals that before marriage, "Dorothea's passion was transfused through a mind struggling towards an ideal life" (32; bk.1, ch. 5). After the marriage, she must qualify her statement; she must decide to make "everybody's life beautiful," instead of her own life. It becomes apparent to her that her personal development and her moral duty can never be united. To live by the female moral standard of unselfishness means to give up personal agency, to practice what the narrator terms at first "the freedom of voluntary submission," and later, "resolved submission" and, finally, "the

---

36   Moretti, 122, 116.

37   This discussion of *Bildung* and its bases in aesthetic theory situates itself within a conceptual context of the nineteenth century in which the male/female sexual differences were naturalized into rigid gender definitions within the society, and in which an originating monadic consciousness was a given. These beliefs are of course posited in contrast to current concepts of both female agency and flexible gender perceptions, and of psychoanalytic theory which situates the ego relationally. In the conclusion, however, Eliot actually moves to the concept of a relational ego as she writes of Dorothea's fate and failure of her female *Bildung*: "there is no creature whose inward being is so strong that it is not greatly determined by what lies outside it" (612).

retrospect of painful subjection to a husband" (21, bk. 1, ch. 3; 312, bk. 4, ch. 42; 362, bk. 5, ch. 50).

VII. *Bildung* and the Miniature

When Dorothea is prevented from making her unique life "beautiful," the grounds of her perception of the everyday undergo a radical shift. The journey to Rome represents in the text "a suppressed transition which unite[s ... the] contrast" between Dorothea's premarital belief that she can actualize a beautiful personal life and her postmarital realization of the impossibility of this dream (143; bk. 2, ch. 20). The shift has import for the reading of *Middlemarch* after Dorothea's marriage, when she finds that she is not in a position to determine cultural discourses but only to be determined by them. The text presents Dorothea's subjective perception of this change as "the vividness with which we all remember epochs in our experience when some dear expectation dies, or some new motive is born" (156; bk. 2, ch. 21). In enacting her "new motive," Dorothea operates in a realm of the political as personal rather than in a realm of ideally designed aesthetic activity. Her frontier, or march, shifts from a horizon of abstracted aesthetic ideals to a march in the middle of the culture: a daily negotiation along the boundaries between power and submission. This change in the narrative argues that aesthetic interpretations are ultimately grounded in the political. As a site of aesthetic possibility, the nineteenth-century female *Bildungsroman*, then, seems doomed to failure. The text explains that the "determining acts of [Dorothea's] life are not ideally beautiful;" "feelings" are nothing but "error;" "noble impulse[s]" become "mixed results;" and "faith" becomes "illusion." In the end Dorothea must sacrifice her personal development to a male designated agenda: she will "give ... wifely help ... live faithfully a hidden life, and rest in [an] unvisited tomb" (612, 611, 613; bk. 8, Finale).

However, if the cameos in *Middlemarch* embody an ethos of male dominance that Dorothea rejects, then the opposing miniature of Will's grandmother conveys a message of woman's autonomy, which Dorothea espouses. These two types of jewelry that feature facial images are locked in combative strategies in the text. Whereas the cameo bracelet portrays women as ideal icons, the miniature foregrounds individual difference: it portrays a woman with unique features that image the autonomous self of *Bildung*.[38] The miniature features a picture of Edward Casaubon's aunt—Will's grandmother—Aunt Julia, who is described as having made a "*mesalliancé*." Having then been disowned by the family, her inheritance was handed down to Edward Casaubon rather than to his cousin, Will Ladislaw.

---

[38] A miniature is a jewel-sized painted portrait of an individual, usually round or oval, worn as a brooch or in a bracelet. Often used as mourning jewelry, and present in the culture before the widespread use of photography, the intent of the miniature was to show particular characteristics of the featured person in order to serve the memory.

Aunt Julia's painted miniature becomes, for Dorothea, the object upon which all her ideals are projected: "many fresh images had gathered round ... Aunt Julia, the presence of the delicate miniature, so like a living face that she knew, helping to concentrate her feeling" (272; bk. 4, ch. 37). Unlike the bracelet of cameos which collapses the distinctions among women as they appear as interchangeable types all in a row, the description of Aunt Julia's miniature shows her singularly distinctive characteristics: "a peculiar face ... those deep gray eyes rather near together—and the delicate irregular nose with a sort of ripple in it—all the powdered curls hanging backward" (55; bk. 1, ch. 9). As if to show the connection between Will and his grandmother, the text describes Will as having similar "grey eyes rather near together, a delicate irregular nose with a little ripple in it, and hair falling backward; but there was a mouth and chin of a more prominent, threatening aspect than belonged to the type of the grandmother's miniature" (58; bk. 1, ch. 9). The single miniature is an aesthetic object which appeals to Dorothea because of its individualized facial features and its affective connection to her own life and knowledge:

> [Dorothea] kept it before her, liking to blend the woman who had been too hardly judged with the grandson whom her own heart and judgment defended. Can any one who has rejoiced in woman's tenderness think it a reproach to her that she took the little oval picture in her palm and made a bed for it there, and leaned her cheek upon it, as if that would soothe the creatures who had suffered unjust condemnation? She did not know then that it was Love who had come to her briefly. (399; bk. 6, ch. 55)

Because "images are the brood of desire," Dorothea directs her desire toward Will through the miniature which represents his whole family line of rebels against the wrongfully legitimated heirs of authority, Casaubon's family (237; bk. 4, ch. 34). While the miniature may represent Will as a symbol of empowerment for Dorothea because of her affective reactions to it, it also combats the proscriptive ideas about gender roles projected by the cameos.

Throughout the text, spatial placement of jeweled images will function as a key to reading its visual messages, such that when it is worn in a customary fashion, jewelry can be read as a symbol of Victorian male power within the status quo. By contrast, the textual jewelry imaged outside its traditional placement on the body indicates a departure from that status quo. For instance, as Celia and Dorothea contemplate the cameo bracelet—each holding it in her hand in a different scene, yet not wearing it, contemplating woman's traditional role—they have different reactions to it. Celia follows her passive, wordless contemplation of the bracelet with a happy announcement of her engagement to Sir James; however, Dorothea shows through critical discussion that she does "not ... care for cameos." Finally, the miniature, which was normally worn in Victorian times in bracelets, pendants, and brooches, appears removed from public view, hanging on the wall of Dorothea's boudoir. Removed from circulation and from view, it instead comes to rest in

Dorothea's hand and against her cheek. The placement of the jewelry throughout the text shows such allusive power, that it can hardly be read as random; rather, its overdetermined arrangement, and the reactions of the characters to it through their aesthetic judgments, present a seamless portrayal of the power of an object like jewelry as a commodity, and an artistic image to communicate important invisible meanings. In affirming all these connections, we could note that if Dorothea reacts with sympathy toward a single female image on the miniature, while rejecting the sequence of images on the cameo bracelet, the cause of her choice must be the meanings these two imagistic types of jewelry convey.

Figure 5.4 Small miniature of Victorian lady (two inches in diameter) with powdered wig hairdo, in a setting of silver and miniature pearls

Source: © Anita Arnold (2010), courtesy of MaryAnn-tiques

Figure 5.5 Miniature of Victorian lady, set in a gold frame. Miniatures were
normally made to be worn either as a brooch or pendant

Source: © Anita Arnold (2010), courtesy of MaryAnn-tiques

VIII. "I should like to make life beautiful"

The process of aesthetic judgment in *Middlemarch* raises larger questions about the
value of the aesthetic realm as a source of meaning for individual Victorians. Here
I would refer to George Levine's wide-ranging discussion of the aesthetic, which
argues for the reconsideration of an illuminated space—the dazzle—of aesthetic
experience, as it gives rise to "a rare if not unique place for almost free play"
outside the realm of politics and cultural pressures.[39] One could ask if the Victorian
reader would consider the "mystic" gleam of emeralds as a meaningful experience

[39]   George Levine, "Introduction: Reclaiming the Aesthetic," *Aesthetics and Ideology*,
ed. George Levine (New Brunswick: Rutgers University Press, 1994) 17.

for Dorothea, when she is equally aware that the jewels are mined and marketed by "miserable" people whose main motive is monetary profit. This opening passage in *Middlemarch* exemplifies the way the text continually questions and coaxes aesthetic affect and aesthetic judgment into an experience of political economy—to the point that one begins to see these two aspects of experience as inextricably joined even as their association creates anxiety and perceptual discontinuity. Defining themselves by their separation from each other, aesthetic and political forms of knowledge thus permeate the text. The disjunction forces this kind of question: does Dorothea attain an aesthetic ideal by marrying Casaubon for access to his educated knowledge? Or can Dorothea, in the end, attain an aesthetic realm by marrying Will Ladislaw for love? Dorothea acts on the belief that a woman can have access to these valued meanings of aesthetic experience only if she ignores her connections with the political economy. Here she engages in a self-deceiving and ultimately self-defeating activity because of her subordinate gender position. In *Middlemarch*, the text continually advocates the aesthetic realm of *Bildung*, only to equivocate its validity for women by destabilizing its real foundations based in political questions of gender formation. The uneasy relation between these two perceptual realms thus forms a basis for conflict in the novel.

Yet the text ultimately validates—within a discrete space—the meanings of aesthetic experience; it validates the attempt at *Bildung*, a process that unifies all Dorothea's diverse endeavors. In the plot, Dorothea marries Casaubon for access to ultimate "truth," wanting to be his "lamp-holder," and she decides to marry Will because of her wonder and belief in him expressed through her fondness for the miniature, whose "vivid presentation came like a pleasant glow to [her]" (13, bk. 1, ch. 2; 203, bk. 3, ch. 28). The textual fact of her marriage to Will attests that she believes their relation will redeem her existence. Is valorizing this aesthetic experience of love the final goal of the text? While Dorothea thus appears to have fallen prey to the ideological "sentimentalization of marriage," the equivocal text has Dorothea say, "I will learn what everything costs," for even in the euphoria of her second marriage, she will have to live a "hidden life"[40] (594, bk. 8, ch. 83; 613, Finale).

However, the fact remains: aesthetic beliefs are the driving force, the ultimate arbiter of Dorothea's existence, regardless of political "cost." Here is where the separation of aesthetics and political economy imposes its negative consequences on women, and an understanding of this dynamic is what distances the narrator from Dorothea. Yet the narrator indeed valorizes moments of aesthetic transcendence: "we mortals have our divine moments," she explains; "Let the music which can take possession of our frame and fill the air with joy for us, sound once more," she intones (462, bk. 6, ch. 62; 266, bk. 4, ch. 37). In forming aesthetic judgments, whether they be on art, cameos, *Bildung*, or love relationships, the narrator of *Middlemarch* argues that aesthetics and political economy should balance and

---

40   Adrienne Munich, *Andromeda's Chains: Gender and Interpretation in Victorian Literature and Art* (New York: Columbia University Press, 1989) 33.

inform one another, as they once did in what Mary Poovey terms their "originary relationship."[41]

In the novel as a whole, the two types of pictorial Victorian jewelry thus image the textual opposition: cameos impose identical roles upon women, whereas the single miniature celebrates a woman's individuality that would permit the project of *Bildung* to go forward. The text attempts to imagine ways in which a woman can adjust to Victorian culture without being tied to normative gender roles. Eliot constructs a proleptic ground for feminism, as her narrative protests rigid gender roles that do not allow for individual difference, preference, or agency in woman's self-definition. The iconic female images of sculpture and jewelry in *Middlemarch* thus become encoded as sides of the debate between these opposing views concerning gender definition in Victorian culture. The ideal of *Bildung*, embodied in the individualized representation of the miniature, is opposed to the ideal beautiful woman who reflects the appearance of the cameo and who is relegated to making, in the culture, a cameo appearance.

---

[41]   Poovey, 98.

Chapter 6

Tactics and "Strate-Gems":
Jewelry, Gender, and the Law in Trollope's
The Eustace Diamonds

A tactic is determined by the absence of power, just as a strategy is organized by
the postulation of power.

—Michel de Certeau[1]

…the futility of possession accrues new pathos [and] like the diamonds themselves,
the self becomes fugitive.

—Andrew H. Miller[2]

In previous chapters, discussions of jewels in fiction have ranged from the
commodity fetish, and the dynamics of the cross-cultural artifact as a gift, to
aesthetics and gender relations. After focusing on these culturally symbolic
meanings of diamonds, turquoise, and cameos represented by Thackeray, Collins,
and Eliot, we turn now to Trollope's *The Eustace Diamonds* in which possession of
a diamond necklace forms a crucial role in the process of Lizzie Eustace's identity
construction.[3] Lizzie cultivates her identity through an affective relation with her
necklace-fetish, as she interacts with it day and night, holding, hiding, carrying,
and sleeping with it. Her emotional interactions with her fetish echo Thackeray's
narrative about *The Hoggarty Diamond* previously discussed in Chapter 3. Yet,
whereas Samuel Titmarsh's relation with his diamond-fetish tiepin assists him in
building his identity as an accepted member of the business community, Lizzie's
relation with her necklace-fetish sabotages her attempts at identity formation
within her cultural context. Divergent gender roles for Victorian men and women
underscore and inform the differences in these two plots, as Lizzie's willful
possession of her diamonds is challenged by public opinion and traditional gender
roles backed by the law.[4] Her determined possession of the diamond necklace

---

[1]   Michel De Certeau, *The Practice of Everyday Life*, trans. Steven Randall (Berkeley:
University of California Press, 1984) 38.

[2]   Andrew H. Miller, *Novels Behind Glass: Commodity Culture and Victorian
Narrative* (Cambridge: Cambridge University Press, 1995) 12.

[3]   Anthony Trollope, *The Eustace Diamonds*, ed. Stephen Gill and John Sutherland
(New York: Penguin Books, 1969).

[4]   See Dagni Bredesen, "What's a Woman to Do? Managing Money and Manipulating
Fictions in Trollope's *Can You Forgive Her?* and *The Eustace Diamonds*," *Victorian Review*

allows the novel to highlight for contemporary readers existing laws concerning a widow's possession of property, in contrast to laws denying married women's possession of property.

At the time *The Eustace Diamonds* was published in 1873, laws concerning women's property rights gave widows an advantage over married women. Victorian writer Barbara Bodichon explains that "a widow has a right to a third of her husband's lands and tenements for her life," so that, in the novel, the widow Lizzie Eustace has economic power because of her personal control over real property and its sizable income of £4,000 a year.[5] According to Alan Roth, "this income was enough to maintain [Portray] castle, rent a house in London, and keep servants, horses, and all other accoutrements of the era's fashionable aristocracy."[6] As Trollope imaginatively explores the possibilities of social and financial privilege for the widow Eustace, he creates one of Victorian fiction's finest arguments for changing the law to benefit married women, too.[7]

In the novel, Lizzie employs her feminine "tactics" concerning her diamond necklace to form her personal identity in conflict with the nineteenth-century legal convention concerning married women and involving the principle of coverture, in which the husband owns and controls all of a married couple's property.[8] The necklace thus occupies a contested space in the intersection of private and public meanings: through her possession of the necklace, Lizzie creates her personal meaning for the jewelry in conflict with the public values of patrilineal succession for the jewelry as voiced by the Eustace family lawyer, Mr. Camperdown. This intersection of private and public meanings is equally a confrontation about gender roles, for Lizzie must use "tactics" to retain her necklace, whereas Mr. Camperdown formulates "strategies" as he argues from a position of established authority within his legal profession.

Tactics and strategies are opposing styles of social interaction within a hierarchy. For those who could be defined as powerless, achieving any advantage at all must come from the use of tactics. Defined by Michel de Certeau as an "art

---

31.2 (2005), for a sensitive discussion of this issue of public opinion, truth, and the law.

[5]	Barbara Leigh Smith Bodichon, "A brief summary, in plain language of the most important laws concerning women: together with a few observations thereon," 1854, Appendix One, in Tim Dolin, *Mistress of the House: Women of Property in the Victorian Novel* (Brookfield: Ashgate Publishing Company, 1997) 128.

[6]	Alan Roth, "He Thought He was Right (But Wasn't): Property Law in Anthony Trollope's *The Eustace Diamonds*," *Stanford Law Review* 44.879 (April 1992) 13 fn10.

[7]	While my critique of *The Eustace Diamonds* centers on the novel's historical context concerning the debates over women's property rights and ownership of land, estates, and jewels, another promising historical sub-context concerns the question of ownership of objects or jewels taken in India in the course of building the empire. The problem of ownership is also discussed in Chapter 4 on *The Moonstone*. See *The Eustace Diamonds*, 98–9, in the chapter entitled "Mr. Burke's Speeches."

[8]	Bredesen, 99–102.

of the weak," performed "within the enemy's field of vision," a tactic is a response to given conditions created by those in power; a tactician like Lizzie must depend upon tactical and conditional behavior, being "without any base where [she] could stockpile [her] winnings."[9] On the other hand, a character such as Mr. Camperdown forms strategies from an established place of power within the culture, a practice suggested by his name. While the strategist relies on his status or place within the society, the tactician must rely on timing, circumstance, and wit. As Mr. Camperdown operates from the established power base of a legal practitioner to formulate his "strate-gems" concerning the necklace, Lizzie operates on the run, as it were, evading surveillance, and adapting her use of language to fit her needs, for the content of her speech is determined by the strategist's system of power, even as she tests its boundaries.

I. Criticism

In recent times, critics have perceived *The Eustace Diamonds* through a variety of important critical lenses: legal, economic, gender, and Freudian criticisms have built rich and wide-ranging insights into this text.[10] While D. A. Miller looked at the novel as an example of police surveillance in the late Victorian Age of "social control" and "discipline," Alan Roth researched the background cases that the character Mr. Dove researches in the novel, to find that Mr. Dove "was not the lawyer Trollope made him out to be" and that his thoughts are "legally ... amateurish."[11] These two critiques began a tradition of legal analysis of the novel, and in the 1990s Dolin added gender analysis to the legal critical lens in his *Mistress of the House*. Also in the 1990s, commodity analysis emerged with Andrew Miller's *Novels Behind Glass* as he interprets Lizzie's diamond necklace as an economic commodity circulating with powerful effects in Victorian culture. The 1990s also saw a turn toward sexual scandal and gender analysis in Cohen's and Psomiades's work, respectively. After the turn of the century, Yishai and Bredesen wrote about epistemology and the law of the 1870s as shown in *The Eustace Diamonds*. More recently still, Plotz's *Portable Property* argues that personal objects—chattel—are

---

[9] De Certeau, 37.

[10] For example, see D. A. Miller, *The Novel and the Police* (Berkeley: University of California Press, 1988); Alan Roth, as cited above; Miller, *Novels Behind Glass*; William A. Cohen, *Sex Scandal: The Private Parts of Victorian Fiction* (Durham, NC: Duke University Press, 1996); Tim Dolin, as cited above; Kathy Alexis Psomiades, "Heterosexual Exchange and Other Victorian Fictions: *The Eustace Diamonds* and Victorian Anthropology," *Novel: A Forum on Fiction* 33.1 (Fall 1999) 92–118; Dagni Bredesen, as cited above, 99–122; Ayelet Ben-Yishai, "The Fact of a Rumor: Anthony Trollope's *The Eustace Diamonds*," *Nineteenth-Century Literature* 62.1 (2007) 88–120; John Plotz, *Portable Property: Victorian Culture on the Move* (Princeton: Princeton University Press, 2008).

[11] Roth, 9.

psychically important for Victorians to carry along as they build their global empire. The book might be considered a response to current discussions about objects and things, with the addition of the significance of their portability. In the introduction, Plotz refers to Lizzie's "extreme, and extremely physicalized attachment to the jewels," as she carries them with her wherever she goes. I would certainly agree with Plotz's assessment that she has "fallen under an object's thrall," a condition that perfectly describes the interaction of characters with their fetishes.[12] If, as Henry Krips argues, the fetish substitutes for a lack—"that which is and must remain repressed"—the question then becomes what might that lack be?[13] While William Cohen's Freudian analysis sees this lack in the novel as repression arising from the unspeakability of sexuality in 1870s fiction except through processes of symbolization, I would argue that the lack embodied in Lizzie's fetish could be identified historically as the practice of coverture, the legal convention that did not allow married women to own property. If, as a married woman, Lizzie had not owned property, as a widow, here was her chance to redeem that legislated lack by maintaining possession of the diamond necklace.

II. The Law

Coverture turns out to be an important concept for this argument, because it is the legal convention against which the novel argues. Bredesen points to a "serious rupture between social reality and the legal ideal of coverture," thereby labeling coverture as a "legal fiction." She explains:

> Institutionalized in British common law, the doctrine ... placed a married woman under the covering, or "the guardianship" of her husband ... Based on the notion that in marriage a husband and wife become one person, this doctrine of marital unity deemed a wife incapable of managing her own property or of having a will of her own ... distinct from her husband's.[14]

Although a wife was not responsible for debts she incurred, neither could she own property or make contracts. By contrast, the widow Lizzie, legally speaking, is a *feme discoverte*, a *feme sole*, who manages her own money, property, and possessions.[15] Her struggles in managing her wealth in a male-dominated society and legal system cause her to challenge the status quo; she must resort to lies, avoidances, and underhanded tactics in order to retain possession of her fetish-necklace—a difficult goal, given her social disadvantage as a female. She is continually trying to find a male who will protect her from the onslaught of

---

12   Plotz, 35, 36.
13   Henry Krips, *Fetish: An Erotics of Culture* (Ithaca: Cornell University Press, 1999) 7.
14   Bredesen, 99.
15   Bredesen, 100; Dolin, 99.

lawyers, courts, and police. Questions about laws concerning inheritance and gender therefore configure the events and character interactions in the novel, and ultimately, "the widow Eustace's proficiency in evading the law ... calls the idea of law itself into question."[16]

Therefore, *The Eustace Diamonds* is not unlike a legal case study of the conflict between two antagonists. At the age of 22, the lovely, newly widowed Lizzie Eustace desires to keep possession of her diamond necklace worth £10,000, while Mr. Camperdown, the lawyer who looks after the Eustace family's estate, wishes to wrest the diamonds from Lizzie's possession in order to establish their ownership for the Eustace heir, Lizzie's very own infant son.[17] Readers learn that Lizzie has "done well for herself ... as an independent young woman, [and] she was perhaps one of the richest" (56). She has attained her wealth through her "splendid match" with Sir Florian Eustace. As the author's succinct description puts it, "Twelve months since she had hardly known the man who was to be her husband. Now she was a widow – a widow very richly endowed – and she bore beneath her bosom the fruit of her husband's love" (47). Lizzie thus summarizes her view of the circumstances for her cousin, Frank Greystock: "My husband gave me the necklace, and they want me to give it back." Choosing to keep the diamonds, she protests to Miss McNulty, "Though I am only a woman I have an idea of my own rights, and will defend them as far as they go" (76, 321). Unlike Camperdown, Lizzie does not refer to the necklace in accordance with the novel's title, the "Eustace Diamonds," but as "my diamonds" (536).

On behalf of the opposition led by Mr. Camperdown, Lizzie's Aunt Lady Linlithglow proclaims, "They are family diamonds, Eustace diamonds, heirlooms – old property belonging to the Eustaces, just like their estates" (89–90). She can argue this position because, historically, "the key characteristic of an heirloom was its customary attachment to a real property inheritance ... to symbolically or legally confer legitimacy." Lady Linlithglow argues in essence that the necklace is a part of the Eustace hereditary estate, for "heirlooms were a way for the aristocracy to extend restraints on alienation from real property to chattels."[18] Keeping the inheritance all together was the rule of survival for the upper class, following the mandates of primogeniture, and jewels that held monetary value were no exception.

---

[16]   Bredesen, 118.

[17]   Roth, n3, 13. Roth writes, "in 1840, commodities were relatively much more expensive while labor was much cheaper. A fair approximation might be that a £10,000 necklace would not be worth less than $500,000 today." However, see also www. measuringworth.com: using the Retail Price Index in Great Britain, the relative worth of £10,000 sterling in 1840 would make the necklace worth approximately £636,000 sterling in 2005. The latter source would put the value of the necklace somewhere between $500,000 and $1 million; any accuracy of value in today's currency is elusive at best.

[18]   Roth, 4, 3.

In the novel, Mr. Camperdown thus assumes and acts on the belief that the law and the patriarchal line of heredity are two vital institutions to uphold, each one supporting the other; along this line of reasoning, the necklace named "The Eustace Diamonds" belongs not to the widow Lizzie Eustace, but to her deceased husband's family. For widows, however, the law entertains some doubt about the ownership of chattel, so that Mr. Camperdown is disconcerted to find that "in a country which boasts of its laws, and of the execution of its laws, such an impostor as this widow should be able to lay her dirty, grasping fingers on so great an amount of property, and that there should be no means of punishing her" (289). The law, as practiced assertively by Mr. Camperdown, is in direct opposition to Lizzie's fragile position: she occupies an ambiguous gap between class privilege and gender disadvantage. Taking the opposite view from Mr. Camperdown and Lady Linlithglow, Lady Glencora, who "like[s Lizzie] for wearing [her diamonds]" states that Lizzie is a "victim" at the same time that she "stood too high among her set to be subject to that obedience which restrains others—too high, also for others to resist her leading" (195, 531).

Lizzie's untidy predicament leads readers to question the existence of two different laws for married and widowed women in the age of gender debates and the New Woman. The source of the confrontation over the necklace resides in its unusual monetary value, a value that had escalated exponentially as diamonds had become an icon of desire and a symbol of wealth over the course of the nineteenth century. The narrative itself centers on the necklace and its proliferating interpretations, as they develop into legal battles that destabilize gender roles in late Victorian culture.

III. Aesthetics

An aesthetic magnetism toward the diamond necklace enlivens and informs both Lizzie and Mr. Camperdown's narrative trajectories in *The Eustace Diamonds*, even though their aesthetics arise from opposing interests. For purposes of discussion here, I would define aesthetics as an emotional and contemplative realm where the political and the ideological are bypassed in order to experience the beautiful: a realm where identity, loyalty, and unconditional belief are located.[19] Lizzie values aesthetic experience that includes personal beauty, poetry, love, wealth,

---

[19]   George Levine, "Introduction: Reclaiming the Aesthetic," *Aesthetics and Ideology*, ed. George Levine (New Brunswick: Rutgers University Press, 1994). Levine wishes to resurrect consideration of the role of the aesthetic in its "rare ... place for almost free play," whereas 10 years earlier, Paul de Man had noted that the "partly shorted circuited" politics of aesthetics should be a focus of analysis. Paul de Man, *The Rhetoric of Romanticism* (New York: Columbia University Press, 1984). De Man writes that "it is as a political force that the aesthetic still concerns us as one of the most powerful ideological drives to act upon the reality of history" (264).

wit, and imagination: for her, "poetry was life and life was poetry" (526). The diamonds become an integral part and material symbol of this value system. In a stunning passage, the aesthetic appeal of the diamonds allows Lizzie to stage a striking image as she enters an evening party at Lady Glencora's. For one fine moment, Lizzie makes a personal fashion statement in high society, as she takes full advantage of the diamonds' ability to display her self-importance:

> The [diamonds] were very beautiful, and seemed ... to outshine all other jewellery in the room. And Lady Eustace was a woman of whom it might almost be said that she ought to wear diamonds. She was made to sparkle, to be bright with outside garniture – to shine and glitter, and be rich in apparel. (195)

This passage anticipates Georg Simmel's late Victorian sociological statement that jewelry contributes to this enlargement of self:

> in the *adorned* body, we possess *more* ... we are masters over more and nobler things ... It is ... deeply significant that bodily adornment becomes private property above all; it expands the ego and enlarges the sphere around us which is filled with our personality and which consists in the pleasure and the attention of our environment.[20]

If, as the narrator notes, Lizzie "ought to wear diamonds," he also notes that "She liked jewels. She liked admiration. She liked the power of being arrogant to those around her" (51). Lizzie's desire to test the lawyers about the ownership and possession of the diamonds requires an attitude of arrogance for a project that includes a confrontational attitude with legally-established, patriarchal power of the era. As Christoph Lindner observes, "Lizzie undermines the smooth running of the patrilineal process."[21]

Interpretations of the gems proliferate when Lizzie appears in high society at Lady Glencora's soiree. Rumors about the necklace have preceded Lizzie: "the subject had been discussed [so] that the blaze of the stones immediately brought

---

[20]   *The Sociology of Georg Simmel*, trans., ed., and intro. Kurt H. Wolff (New York: The Free Press, 1950) Part IV, Chapter 3, 344. Originally published as *Soziologie, Untersuchungen uber die Formen der Vergesellschaftung, 1908*. Kurt H. Wolff writes in his introduction, "Simmel's relation to things –'things,' 'objects,' ... occupied him in many of his writings" (xx). Simmel's late Victorian descriptions of the personal dynamics of wearing jewelry is corroborated in current times by Gilles Lipovetsky, *The Empire of Fashion: Dressing Modern Democracy*, trans. Catherine Porter, New French Thought (Princeton: Princeton University Press, 1994) 46. Lipovetsky writes that haute couture reflects an "exaltation of human uniqueness and its complement, the social promotion of signs of personal difference."

[21]   Christoph Lindner, *Fictions of Commodity Culture: From the Victorian to the Postmodern* (Burlington: Ashgate, 2003) 85.

it to the minds of men and women." One of the gossiping bystanders doubles the actual value of the diamonds, pointing out, "There she is, with poor Eustace's twenty thousand pounds round her neck ... and there is Lord Fawn going to look after them" (194). Lord Fawn, who is engaged to be married to Lizzie, is made to feel uncomfortable in escorting her around the room; after all, the diamonds belong, in his view, to her previous husband's family. Because Lizzie will not give up the necklace, it becomes a "bone of contention" between Lizzie and Lord Fawn, who supports Mr. Camperdown's position; eventually, the disagreement precipitates a rupture in their plans to marry.

If Lizzie is attracted to her diamonds by their aesthetic sparkle, Mr. Camperdown's aestheticism takes a far different tack: he has a reverence for the practice of law, although "it could not be said of him that he was a learned lawyer." The narrator explains that, in the branch of law Camperdown practices as a solicitor, he is fortunate that "experience goes further than learning" (291). As Lizzie's opponent in the struggle over possession and ownership of the diamonds, he is described as "handsome, healthy, somewhat florid and carrying in his face and person external signs of prosperity and that kind of self assertion which prosperity always produces" (290). Here the aesthetics play out: if Lizzie adorns her body with diamonds to "expand her ego," Camperdown practices law to assert himself and expand his ego. Opposing identities with large egos and self-defining aesthetic beliefs are at stake in this confrontation over the jewels.

The source of Camperdown's attachment to the law resides in Mr. Dove's legal mind; the two men "share a poetic and mystical notion of the law" (82). When the erudite Mr. Dove holds forth his legal opinions, Camperdown listens with "undoubting reverence," experiencing a "poetic spirit in his bosom. He would think of these speeches afterwards, and would entertain high but somewhat cloudy ideas of the beauty and the majesty of law" (297). It is perhaps unusual to find a legal opinion in a literary text, but the legal opinion in this text serves as a vital part of what Camperdown considers "the majesty of the law." Edlin notes that, in common law theory, "we cannot fully apprehend the meaning of a legal rule without also contemplating the reasons for that legal rule;" theorists such as Mr. Dove therefore "examine the scope of precedent by asking when and why cases are relevantly like prior decisions so that analogical reasoning may be deemed an appropriate method for understanding a later case in light of an earlier one."[22] Ultimately, according to Edlin, "public explanations and justifications demonstrate, or attempt to demonstrate, to the public and to the government the law's claims of legitimacy and authority" (3). The legal opinion in the text is thus a part and process of Camperdown's aesthetic values and his identity as a practitioner of the law.

However, Dove's opinion proceeds in the text with irony as it incorporates elevated language, legal terminology, and impressive Latin usages into the

---

[22]   Douglas E. Edlin, *Common Law Theory* (Cambridge: Cambridge University Press, 2007) 7, 2–3.

discussion of such mundane, low-value objects as heirlooms, chattels, and paraphernalia. Having grown up around the legal profession, and having sat in his father's law chambers, Trollope would have known much about the law, and it has been verified that his friend, barrister Charles Merewether, actually wrote the novel's legal opinion on the necklace.[23] This delivery of the researched legal opinion takes on a humorous turn in Trollope's text, after Mr. Dove has meticulously cited past court cases: "Pusey v. Pusey ... Carr v. Lord Errol ... and Rowland v. Morgan." The reader is led through this lackluster list to arrive at the following analogy:

> Lord Hardwick ... decided that Mrs. Northey was entitled to wear jewels to the
> value of 3,000 lbs – saying that value made no difference; but seems to have
> limited the nature of her possession in the jewels by declaring her to wear them
> only when full-dressed. (263)

This final example leads the reader into a realm of absurdity, suggesting that the text harbors a good-natured mockery for high-flown legal opinions and the law, as they concern jewelry, gender, and the law.

Ultimately, Mr. Dove concludes that Lizzie is entitled to the diamond necklace as "a piece of 'paraphernalia' belonging to her station" (265).[24] Camperdown is outraged. Dove's conclusion shows that the law is outdated, for diamonds circulating through late nineteenth-century culture hold much more monetary value than they do in any of the case analogies Mr. Dove presents. This problem locates itself within a "recurring common law dilemma: How can the law remain stable and yet not stand still?"[25] The undecidable legal dilemmas that exist between a long-standing, established law and evolving cultural practices form the discursive space where Lizzie Eustace chooses to locate herself and her necklace. No appropriate precedent or analogy can guide Dove in his legal opinions nor can Camperdown call on any precedent or analogy to bolster his efforts to retrieve the necklace.

In the end, Mr. Dove asks the rhetorical question: "Would the Law do a service, do you think, if it lent its authority to the special preservation in special hands of trinkets only to be used for vanity and ornament?" (295). The inheritance of land remains under law, because the land is "fixed and known. A string of pearls is ... alterable ... and cannot easily be traced," Dove explains. Valuable chattel in the form of a diamond necklace worth £10,000 is a new phenomenon in Victorian culture, and the £10,000 value placed on the Eustace diamonds reveals the inadequacy of the analogies in Mr. Dove's legal opinion. This top-heavy valuation

---

[23] Rowland McMaster, *Trollope and the Law* (New York: St. Martin's Press, 1986) 79, fn165.

[24] Bodichon, 128. Bodichon writes, "A wife's paraphernalia (i.e., her clothes and ornaments) which her husband owns during his lifetime, and which his creditors can seize for his debts, becomes her property on his death."

[25] Edlin, 8.

also signifies that changing membership in the upper classes in late Victorian times was not solely a matter of inherited lands and privileged titles: instead, membership in this class could very well be defined by anything that could be given monetary value, whether it is land, castles, stock, buildings, businesses, or very valuable jewels.

IV. Surveillance

In *The Eustace Diamonds*, the pervasive threat of a lawsuit is associated with ongoing surveillance by lawyers, plainclothesmen, and police to form much of the narrative tension. When Lady Linlithglow first visits Lizzie on behalf of Mr. Camperdown, she delivers this warning:

> If you don't take care, you'll find yourself brought into a court of law, my dear, and a jury will say [that you must give up the diamonds]. That's what it will come to. What good will they do you? You can't sell them; – and as a widow, you can't wear 'em. If you marry again, you wouldn't disgrace your husband by going about showing off the Eustace diamonds! … As you are my niece, I have undertaken to come to you and to tell you that if you don't give 'em up within a week from this time, they'll proceed against you for – stealing 'em. (90)

Because Lizzie's identity is associated with the diamonds—"few days passed on which she did not handle them and gaze at them"—she will not give back the diamonds: "I did not steal them," she replies, "My husband gave them to me with his own hands" (435, 91). Mr. Camperdown will never be able to determine whether this assertion is fact or lie, and therein lies the ambiguity of his project of retrieving the diamonds.

If the twin ghosts of the law and male prerogative formulate disciplinary authority in the culture, then Lizzie, as a woman outside the power structure, is the target and victim of surveillance. As D. A. Miller describes it, "Lizzie's desires are at once the effect of the power she withstands and the cause of its intensified operation."[26] The omniscient narrator, seeming to watch Lizzie like the rest of her world, explains, "she would carry on the battle, using every will she knew, straining every nerve to be victorious, encountering any and all dangers, yet she had no definite aim before her" (212). Indeed, her aim cannot be defined, for she has no model or cultural ideal that she can aspire to as a woman, other than being wealthy. Therefore, Lizzie's only aim is to destabilize the panoptic processes exercised upon her by Mr. Camperdown and the police, by every means at her disposal.[27] These practitioners apply the law, backed by the abstract power

---

[26]   Miller, *The Novel and the Police*, 27.

[27]   Michel Foucault, "Panopticism," *The Foucault Reader*, ed. Paul Rabinow (New York: Pantheon Books, 1984) 206, 209. Foucault notes that in a cultural change toward a

of someone like Mr. Dove who promotes the authority of the law through his researched opinions and pronouncements. "Let her go where she might, she would be watched," the narrator explains: "all the ingenuity, the concentrated force, and trained experience of the police of London would surely be too great and powerful for her in the long-run" (478). Lizzie agrees with the narrator's assessment as she notes, "The police were watching me every day as a cat watches a mouse" (722). Yet in the novel, Lizzie fearfully but successfully operates in the affective spaces that rational law cannot scrutinize; she confesses to Frank, "I fear nothing – nothing but being where these policemen can come to me" (513). In a text full of questionable meanings, the inept police add one more example of uncertainty as they maneuver with each other over whose theory is the correct theory, while failing to ascertain the "true facts" (485).

One of the most undecidable issues about the diamond necklace and the law consists in the very definition of truth and lies. Although a court of law would differentiate truth from perjury, it is impossible for the police to know when Lizzie tells "the truth." She engages in wishful thinking as she speaks what the text alternatively terms "blemishes" (41), "positive falsehood" (46) "incorrect versions" (660–1) "false evidence," or "a fib" (758). Because of her class status, the police treat her with belief and respect, even when she does supply them with "false evidence."

The narrator continues to undermine any surety a reader might look for in the text, opting instead for vacillating degrees of factuality. He asks this rhetorical question: "is there any difference between a lie and an untruth?" (299). The underlying point stresses that untruths—rather than lies—may be the more accurate word when the political status of the speaker comes into play: the higher the rank, the greater the ability to determine "reality," whether factual or emotional. For example, the impoverished Lucy Morris accuses Lord Fawn of telling an untruth when he says that Frank Greystock is not a gentleman; however, Lucy is made to suffer: "I have been very wrong; I know that. But I think he has been wrong too. But I must own it, and he needn't" she says bitterly (300). As Lizzie meets with Frank at Mrs. Carbuncle's and he asks her, "What is this about the diamonds?" Lizzie finds it "to be impossible to tell the true story" (451). Because Lizzie is a member of the upper class and has more money than Frank, or any other character in the text, she appears to have a right to determine what story should be told, even to the police. For most of the novel, whoever determines what is true remains a matter of who is in power, upper class members and wealth having the upper hand in establishing "truth."

However, when Lucy Morris and Lizzie converse about Frank Greystock, with Lizzie attempting to claim Frank for her husband, Lucy sincerely speaks the truth, in spite of the social difference between these two women: "If you tell him

"disciplinary society," panopticism "insidiously objectifies those on whom it is applied; to form a body of knowledge about these individuals, rather than to deploy the ostentatious signs of sovereignty."

that I do not love him better than all the world, you will lie to him. And if you say that he loves you better than he does me, that also will be a lie. I know his heart" (625). Internally, "Lizzie ... knew that she was paste, [and she] knew that Lucy was [the] real [diamond]," this, in spite of the fact that Lizzie possesses the precious diamond necklace (628).[28] Lucy speaks a truth that is beyond the rational jurisdiction of law. At this important juncture in the plot, indeterminate language no longer inserts itself halfway between the real and the imaginary, or between the powerful and the weak, but instead "truth" and "lie" become polarities, in which truth is, psychoanalytically, "full speech," and lies are, like the diamonds, an "outside garniture" with no depth of meaning (195).[29] This type of truth does not deal in rational facts, but in the emotional reservoirs of subjective experience.

When Major Mackintosh of the police force finally catches Lizzie in her lies about when the diamond necklace was stolen, she then realizes she has committed perjury and will be caught. In the ensuing court scene, the Magistrate confronts Lizzie with the facts, but her excuse is that she "was in such a state ... from fear, that [she] did not know what [she] was saying" (716). The text ironically notes that her tears make her so lovely that both the magistrate and public opinion soften their stances. Her answer to the Magistrate's questioning is simply her own tactical response in the face of the enemy, not the factual version the police, with their power to impose rational interpretations, want to hear. The narrator surmises, "People, after all did not think so very much of perjury – of perjury such as hers, committed in regard to one's own property" (689). Finally, in a second court hearing from which Lizzie is absent, a police sergeant firmly announces the facts to the public, "Lady Eustace committed perjury at Carlisle, having the diamonds in her pocket at the very moment in which she swore that they had been stolen from her" (751).

Even though Lizzie finds that factual truth, imposed by a rational system of law, is a barrier to achieving her goals, she is very stern about demanding truthful language in others when her own identity is at stake. When Lizzie and Frank are having a disagreement over Lucy Morris, Lizzie asks Frank to leave, noting, "No! ... never [will I see you] again; never, unless you will tell me that the promise you made me when we were down on the sea-shore was a true promise. Was that truth, sir, or was it a – lie?" (326) In wishing to avoid the "unwholesome" accusation of lying, Frank replies "Lizzie do not use such a word as that to me." Truth and lie, where Lizzie is concerned, become categories of tactical language usage to be called forth at her own convenience. The end result is that her language meanings have become incomprehensible, like her diamond jewelry, because their referential qualities consistently break down.

---

[28]   Like Thackeray, as discussed in Chapter 3, Trollope uses the allegorical meaning of "diamond," applying the label to what he wishes to convey is good or moral.

[29]   Jacques Lacan, "Function and Field of Speech and Language," *Ecrits* (New York: W. W. Norton & Company, 1977) 46–7.

V. Credit, Theft, Ownership

One generally overlooked plot element in the novel includes the financial dealings that Lizzie undertakes with the jeweler Mr. Benjamin, that "son of Abraham" as Lord George calls him (499). At the beginning of the narrative, Lizzie owes money to Mr. Benjamin for jewels she had purchased on credit before her father's death, yet she had actually pawned those jewels bought on credit to gain more spending money. When Mr. Benjamin asks for the jewels back, in lieu of cash, Lizzie simply says that there were "no jewels – nothing to signify" (40). Here is the one narrative section in which the reader sees Lizzie trying to maintain her status while struggling financially as a single woman.

In negotiating with Mr. Benjamin, she informs him—though she is not quite sure yet—that she will be marrying the very wealthy Sir Florian Eustace. This prospect of wealth changes everything for Mr. Benjamin, who begins to extend her money and credit, so that, even before her marriage, she can regain her pawned jewels bought on credit. After she marries, the law concerning consumer credit will actually be on Lizzie's side, for "Under the law of agency a wife could pledge her husband's credit with tradesmen for the supply of necessaries, as they were called, suitable to their station in life." In addition, the "property legally termed 'paraphernalia,' that is, the clothing and personal ornaments that a woman possessed at the time of marriage or that her husband gave her during marriage," would necessarily belong to her as a widow.[30] Beside the fashion and monetary value of the diamonds, they remained the only securely owned repository of value a wife could possess in the face of a law that favored a husband's ownership in every other instance. Even then, if the husband died in debt, a widow could be deprived of her jewels and personal effects in order to pay her deceased husband's bills; however, this caveat did not apply to Lizzie. Lizzie's desire to maintain possession of her diamond necklace throughout the narrative trajectory is, in fact, a way of looking after her self-interest: it is the only storehouse of value that she can possess outside her Scottish Castle Portray, which "they could not take away … nor could they rob her of four thousand a year" (689).

Mr. Benjamin reappears at the narrative end after he has become involved with the "second robbery" by receiving the stolen jewels and selling them in Austria. The text is unclear as to whether Lizzie has owed Mr. Benjamin money at this point. If she did still owe him money, then the irony of his being arrested and sent to prison as an accessory to the theft once again demonstrates the ways in which the text overturns reader expectations in every scene. If Lizzie does not owe Mr. Benjamin any money, then the argument the text makes here would be that all characters, including Lizzie and Mr. Benjamin, who engage in opportunistic dealings, should be stripped of the valuable diamonds or any riches the jewels represent. Of course, Lizzie and Mr. Benjamin understand the new financial *modus*

---

[30]   Lee Holcombe, *Wives and Property: Reform of the Married Women's Property Law in Nineteenth-Century England* (Toronto: University of Toronto Press, 1983) 27, 23.

operandi in which ownership of property is always subject to debt or doubt. In the end, Camperdown will not be paid for his efforts to regain the necklace for the Eustace family trust. Lord Fawn will not marry Lizzie, and Frank ends up without a seat in parliament. Lord George sums it up for Lizzie: "To be sure you have lost your diamonds for your pains. I wouldn't mind it so much if anybody were the better for it. I shouldn't have begrudged even Benjamin the pull, if he'd got it" (723).[31]

VI. Provisional Meanings

Beyond the immediate fashion statement the diamonds make in the novel, the text develops the diamonds as a source of proliferating symbolic meanings and interpretations: money, gift-giving, affection, marriage, legal possession of chattel, class, inheritance, and estates. The necklace is materially present and objectively real at the same time that any meaning it can carry is illusory, because of the shifting interpretations given it by the various characters. Any cultural artifact may thus become less meaningful through iconic overuse. In *The Eustace Diamonds*, the diamonds' meaning cannot be determined by Mr. Camperdown, the Eustace family trust lawyer, or even by Mr. Dove, the respected and impartial legal researcher. Mr. Camperdown hopes to define Lizzie's necklace as an heirloom, belonging to the Eustace family, to which he wants it returned for the patrilineal line of inheritance. After all, "the rights of [Lizzie Eustace's] baby [boy] were so serious and important that it was almost impossible not to interfere" (51). However, Mr. Dove, the authoritative and impartial legal researcher, notes that a necklace can be legally defined as an heirloom only if it belongs to the Crown (292). On the other hand, any pot or pan is an heirloom "by custom, and not by law" (262). Lizzie's possession of the necklace thus situates itself in an undecidable legal space, a site that allows a variety of conflictive interpretations. While there is no evidence to corroborate Lizzie's contestation that her husband had given her the necklace as a "love token" as part of the furnishings of her Scottish castle, neither does the novel's nebulous legal discourse contain any clear statement that could dictate the diamonds' ultimate consignment to the Eustace family trust.

---

[31]   Jonathan Freedman, *The Temple of Culture: Assimilation and Anti-Semitism in Literary Anglo-America* (New York: Oxford University Press, 2000) 10. Freedman notes that Trollope represents "parvenu Jews and excesses of capital in the seemingly stable world of Victorian London … [he represents] the Jew as a scapegoat-like speculator who embodies the author's own imaginative burdens." See also Michael Ragussis, *Figures of Conversion: "The Jewish Question" and the English National Identity* (Durham, NC: Duke University Press, 1995). Ragussis's position concerning Arnold's *Culture and Anarchy* is that Jewishness becomes absorbed by English nationalism in order to make the nation "racially pure" (Freedman, 46 quoting Ragussis, 47).

The narrative tension thus derives from all the characters' attempts to define what is, in essence, an object with fragmented meaning; as possessor of the necklace, Lizzie's tactics become apparent as she designates the diamonds' meaning according to what benefit she might gain in any given scenario. She wears it as a fashion icon. When the necklace becomes an object of legal action, Lizzie argues that the necklace was a gift, or love token; under the law, she is allowed to keep it as a personal effect. She tells Mr. Camperdown, "If a thing is a man's own he can give it away; – not a house, or a farm, or a wood, or anything like that; but a thing that he can carry about with him – of course he can give it away" (94). Not only is ownership of chattel or paraphernalia established by possession, it is easily transferable, and both definitions work in Lizzie's favor.

On the other hand, Lizzie also defines the diamond necklace as an "estate" that would determine economic and class status; she asks her companion, Miss McNulty, as she holds the necklace up to Miss McNulty's throat, "How do you feel, Julia, with an estate upon your neck? Five hundred acres at twenty pounds an acre. Let us call it 500 pounds a year. That's about it" (323). A note of irony arises in this scene: "for Trollope, the world of wealth was completely dissociated from both the world of land and the world of industry" (Betsky).[32] If Lizzie is defining an estate as a monetary value, rather than in the traditional way as landed inheritance, the conversation reveals the changes in class composition at the time: money could define a person's rank as well as inheritance of land. Here the idea that value is undergoing change is uppermost: money may buy diamonds or land, but the heritable status of diamonds is in question, whereas the heritable status of land is absolutely without question in the legal system.

In another scene, Lizzie designates the diamonds purely as money. Once the diamonds are stolen, she exclaims, "Only think that the ten thousand pounds should disappear in such a way!" (520). Frank rejoins that the theft, however, makes the diamonds "become almost valueless by the difficulty of dealing with them," a foreshadowing of Mr. Benjamin's fate. When Lizzie is trying to belittle the issue of ownership, she treats the necklace like "any indifferent feminine bauble," or as Frank describes it, "just as another man gives a trinket that costs ten shillings!" (322–3). Other synonyms for the diamond necklace deliver a barrage of meanings throughout the text: "blaze of stones" (194), "string of stones" (323), "estate of matrimony" (323), "paraphernalia" (263), "the shining thing" (436), "slate stones" (324), or "bone of contention" (650). Above all, these varied synonyms become attached to Lizzie's own fluctuating identity, as the diamond necklace and the person become interchangeable. Lizzie sleeps with the keys to the diamonds' box around her neck, and as her fetishism develops, she "thinks about the necklace every waking minute and dream[s] of it when she [sleeps]" (477). At her Scottish Castle Portray, she nurtures her class image with the diamonds, as her necklace becomes the locus of her identity and power.

---

[32]   Seymour Betsky, "Society in Thackeray and Trollope, From Dickens to Hardy," *Pelican Guide to English Literature*, Vol. 6, ed. Boris Ford, revised 1963.

Only the theft of the necklace can separate Lizzie from it. The disappearance of the necklace effaces Lizzie's identity and her autonomous power. The text thus allows her to remarry, for the theft has freed her from her tormented ties to the Eustace family, and her obsession with the "string of stones." Her image and identity finally come to rest in what Mrs. Carbuncle calls "a fixed position" (651). Although Lizzie had begun the narrative with "no jewels – nothing to signify" because she had pawned her jewelry, she ends her narrative without them, too. She marries Mr. Emilius who tells her lies, for "she like[s] lies, thinking them more beautiful than truth" (762). Lizzie enjoys the uncertainties and vacillations of meanings she perceives in the necklace, because her improvisation allows her to confront male dominance. Her tactics of flouting social convention by flaunting the necklace gain for her a certain power and recognition, while her tactics of subversion reveal the rigidity of law as an ineffective institution in a rapidly changing society. In the end, however, in order to bring the narrative to a satisfying end for the Victorian reading audience, the narrator must eventually marry Lizzie to someone: Trollope confesses, "it would be a good thing to get the widow married and placed under decent control" (645). The narrative tension dissipates with this socially acceptable ending.

As the novel builds its case for the unstable meaning of objects, things, and images in an age of transition, it also poses a conservative moral solution to the problem of determining class through the visual appeal of objects such as diamonds. Frank Greystock, the sincere and responsible young hero who is often paired with his cousin Lizzie in the narrative, eventually devalues Lizzie and her play with the fluctuating meanings of her necklace. While Lizzie herself complains that "the world is so false, so material, so worldly!" she still "desire[s] to be the possessor of the outward shows of all those things of which the inward facts are valued by the good and steadfast ones of the earth" (163). Here Trollope defines the internal meaning behind the external world of objects as a source of identity in an ideal world. Frank ultimately eschews Lizzie's arena of visible surfaces in favor of Lucy's realm of inward morality unrelated to vision. If Lizzie is "bright with outside garniture" and "rich in apparel," Lucy wears an "old grey silk dress," of which Frank Greystock eventually takes stock (195, 63). Lucy's only diamond is a "tear ... of watery brightness," and rather than trying to be a beauty, Lucy wants only to have "a purpose and a use in life" (62). Here the text acknowledges the disparity between ephemeral meanings conveyed through images and traditional, stable meaning conveyed through consistent moral practice. When the diamonds are stolen, and eclipsed from the narrative, their iconic hold on the characters' visual imagination subsides, and the moral imagination gains precedence in the end. That is how the object "steals away from us and finally becomes undecidable," and why, according to Mr. Dove, "the ultimate loss of the diamonds was upon the whole desirable, as regarded the whole community."[33]

---

[33]   Jean Baudrillard, *The Vital Illusion*, ed. Julia Witwer, Wellek Library Lectures, 753 (New York: Columbia University Press, 2000).

VII. Lizzie's Advantages

Lizzie's economic circumstances shelter her securely in the highest position imaginable. As a widow, she has legally inherited "a life's interest in her husband's land;" she owns Portray Castle in Scotland, and as Trollope notes, "there is nothing more aristocratic that you can do than go to Scotland" (329).[34] Queen Victoria's royal influence in owning a Scottish castle had translated into a new trend for the English upper classes, so that Lizzie's Castle Portray provides a fashionable place to entertain friends and acquaintances.[35] Lizzie will own the castle for the rest of her life, along with an income of £4,000 a year, enough to support her aristocratic lifestyle.[36]

In contrast to the advantage the widow Eustace enjoys in owning her own real property, married women could not own or manage real property at the time the novel was written and published: "by the act of marrying, a woman in effect made a gift of her property to her husband, while the fact that a married woman could not legally hold property prevented her husband from making over anything into her possession."[37] This law concerning a married woman's property served to keep women subordinated in all aspects of the culture, even though young women and widows, as unmarried women, could own property. Mid-Victorian writer on feminist issues, Caroline Cornwallis, argued that this division of treatment nevertheless put young girls at a decided disadvantage:

> the law with respect to the property of married women has influenced the position
> of all females; for fathers and guardians, in determining on the kind of education
> to be given a child, are guided by what is likely to be its future career in life; and
> thus, though a girl may never marry, she bears the burthen of a married woman's
> disabilities; for, marriage being the assumed end of female existence, parents
> think it needless to teach what will be useless when learned.[38]

While young women were not encouraged to learn about business, widows were equally unwelcome and out of place in the business world. Trollope, for example,

---

[34]   Lee Holcombe, *Wives and Property: Reform of the Married Women's Property Law in Nineteenth-Century England* (Toronto: University of Toronto Press, 1983) 21.

[35]   Adrienne Munich, *Queen Victoria's Secrets* (New York: Columbia University Press, 1996) 39–40. In 1868, five years before the publication of *The Eustace Diamonds*, Queen Victoria had published *Leaves from the Journal of Our Life in the Highlands from 1848 to 1861*, describing and modeling the royal family's life at Balmoral, her Scottish castle with 30,000 acres of grounds.

[36]   Roth, 13, n10.

[37]   Holcombe, 18.

[38]   Caroline Cornwallis quoted in S. G. Bell and K. M. Offen, eds, *Women, the Family, and Freedom: The Debate in Documents, Volume One, 1750–1880* (Stanford: Stanford University Press, 1983) 310.

describes the widow Eustace as "oppressed by a heavy load of ignorance which became serious from the isolation of her position" (53).

During the "property debates" in the British nineteenth century, critics argued against the constrictive law of coverture.[39] The Biblical concept of marriage on which the law was based formed a social structure that gave the husband complete authority over his wife's property.[40] In countering this traditional practice of male privilege and wealth, it was argued that all people must be free and equal in the eyes of the law: in 1869, just four years prior to publication of *The Eustace Diamonds*, J. S. Mill had reasoned that

> the legal subordination of one sex to the other—is wrong in itself, and now one of the chief hindrances to human improvement ... it ought to be replaced by a principle of perfect equality, admitting no power or privilege on the one side, nor disability on the other.[41]

What is more, nineteenth-century industrialization drew many lower class wives to work outside the home, and as they contributed financially to their household economies, these women needed to have control of their own earnings.[42] Victorian writer Barbara Bodichon argued, "There is now a large and increasing class of women who gain their own livelihood, and the abolition of the laws which give husbands this unjust power is more urgently needed."[43] Trollope's reading audience would have had some sense of the incongruities between married and single women's laws as they played out in the plot.

Trollope's novel thus considers all the ways in which contemporary property laws differed for women according to their varied social roles in relation to men: single, married, or widowed. For example, when the widow Lizzie contemplates marrying Mr. Emilius, one possible advantage she considers is that, after having had the legal status of a widow, "with Mr. Emilius, she might obtain undisputed command of her own income" (759). While discussing these cultural concerns of the time, then, the novel also anticipates, and argues for, the legal changes to come. The Married Woman's Property Act was finally adopted in 1882, nine years

---

[39]   Dolin, 3.

[40]   *The Holy Bible*, King James Version (New York: Regency Publishing House, 1976). See for example *Ephesians* 5:22 "Wives submit yourselves unto your own husbands, as unto the Lord," or *Colossians* 3:18 "Wives, submit yourselves unto your own husbands, as it is fit in the Lord."

[41]   John Stuart Mill, "From *The Subjection of Women*," *The Norton Anthology of English Literature*, 5th edn, ed. M. H. Abrams (New York: W. W. Norton & Company, 1986) 1055–66.

[42]   Holcombe, 7–8.

[43]   Bodichon, 130 (1854).

after the publication of *The Eustace Diamonds*.[44] As opposed to the previous law that dictated that a married woman could not own property, the new law held that

> a married woman shall be capable of acquiring, holding, and disposing by will or otherwise, of any real or personal property as her separate property, in the same manner as if she were a *femme sole*, without the intervention of any trustee.[45]

At the time the *Eustace Diamonds* was published, the legal circumstances of widowhood had thus given Lizzie Eustace an advantage over married women, and had significantly elevated her social prestige because of her control over real property and its sizable income of £4,000 a year. Narrating the example of an independently wealthy widow, and focusing on her advantages was Trollope's particular contribution to changing the law to benefit married women.

---

[44]   Dolin, 2; Joyce W. Warren, *Women, Money, and the Law* (Iowa City: University of Iowa Press, 2005) 190. Dolin discusses a married woman's property law of 1870, but notes that the 1882 law was the law that attained "real success." From before 1870 to 1882, then, the law was debated. Warren writes that, in the United States, the banking law of 1850 allowed a woman to have a bank account in her own name, and the Married Women's Property Act was adopted in 1860. A precedent had thus been set for the British to follow in 1882.

[45]   Holcombe, 247.

Afterword

At the outset of this work, the goal was to explore relations between human subjects and material objects by developing ideas about Victorian fiction's characters and jewels. The ultimate aim was to enlarge an understanding of subject-object relations as the basis for material culture in the West. Investigating relations between characters and jewels was considered useful because fictional people and their jewelry draw from the cultural imaginary in which the author-narrator is immersed, and these narratives would thus reveal the tenor of actual subjective experiences of objects within Victorian material culture.

In Chapter 2, objects were considered as important self-contained entities in their own right, and finding the location of meaning in the interactive space between subject and object opened up a broad historical and interdisciplinary perspective on human experience of objects in Western culture. Ensuing chapters explored the capacity of jewels to take part in building character identities across the trajectories of Victorian narratives. Looking at the apparent power of these gems to incite and absorb affect, to offer solace, to direct events, or to symbolize relations between an individual and the culture allowed insights into cultural problems.

Here one could undertake a few conclusions about human-object relations within a material culture.

In the novels discussed, it was noted that the locus of meaning production resided in between the character and the jewelry. This space for subject-object relations formed a center around which a character's consciousness would circulate, and interactions would occur whenever new circumstances arose in the storyline. The character-subject would periodically focus upon the jewel in order to internalize events, speculate about circumstances, decide how to accomplish a desired goal, or decide what to do next. The object had become an alter ego, a reflective mirror, a repository of values, and a source of meaning. By describing these interactive behaviors, narrators could use jewels to reveal the deep-set emotions experienced by the novels' characters—viable emotions for the historical time and place that were recognizable and validated by reading audiences.

Also in the narrative trajectories of the novels, jewels often allowed the characters to explore creative possibilities for themselves as they were building their identities. However, a conservative narrative outcome acceptable to readers was invariably necessary to bring the novel to a close, so that exchanges in the jewels' ownership or status would therefore take place. For instance, Samuel Titmarsh pawns his diamond, instead valuing his wife as a "diamond," while Becky's diamonds are stolen as they represent her ill-conceived project of personal social advancement through appearances. The moonstone is returned to its origins in India, because the novel considers the British post-Mutiny practice of empire as troubled. In Eliot's works, Gwendolen exchanges the Grandcourt diamonds for her turquoise necklace, while Dorothea rejects carved multiple cameos in a bracelet in favor of a single painted miniature of Will Lladislaw's aunt. Finally, Lizzie's diamond necklace is stolen, so that, having challenged the status of women in the culture and before the law, she settles on a "fixed position." These final exchanges counteract the novels' main arguments for solutions to cultural problems posed by the author-narrators, and, in the end, the problematic cultural practices authors wished to censure would have to be enacted. It is as if the ending, required to reflect the cultural status quo, was an entirely separate and opposite structure from the free play of the narrative itself.

However, other meanings await. In the novels, when jewels symbolized the moral good, they overshadowed the jewels symbolizing apparent injustice; that is why, when the gems represented established Victorian conventions that the author-narrator disparaged, the jewels were ultimately eclipsed from the narrative, undergoing a loss of meaning and a change in ownership. Jewels representing desired values were "good" jewels: the turquoise necklace belonging to Gwendolen; the miniatures belonging to Amelia in *Vanity Fair* and to Dorothea in *Middlemarch*; and the personified "diamonds": Mary Smith belonging to Samuel in *The Great Hoggarty Diamond* and Lucy Morris belonging to Frank Greystock in *The Eustace Diamonds*. These jewels—human or material—invariably survived the narrative end. By contrast, jewels representing conventions the author rejected were all diamonds: Samuel's tiepin that represented risky, immoral business investments, Becky's diamonds that signified the spectacle of an emerging upper class, Rachel's moonstone diamond that carried vexed meanings of the Indian Empire, Gwendolen's diamonds that epitomized male dominance within marriage, and Lizzie's flashy diamond necklace with its changeable and superficial meanings. None of these diamonds survived their narrative ends.

Objects inscribe their latent energies and perceived symbolic meanings into fiction's characters and reveal the characters' internal attitudes and emotions; they are therefore considered a basic source of reality in Victorian fiction because they can prompt the affective experience that forms identity. Material objects, then, mean more than calculable monetary value; rather, they exist as shared signs for established cultural values and as reservoirs of emotion brought on by individual experiences of those values. These emotions surrounding jewels could thus be quite happily positive, or then again, they could be confrontational. For example, Dorothea Brooke's sister Celia happily favors cameos while Dorothea herself rejects them, a difference arising from the sisters' opposing perspectives on women's gender roles. Because of the wide range of individual character reactions to jewels, and because of the very movement or misplacement of jewels across narrative trajectories, criticism concerning material objects in fiction is a rich source of insight into the bases of material culture, and a goal for criticism that would propel further investigation.

Many types of criticism can center on objects: fetishism; gifts; visual interpretation or spectacle; an anthropological focus on cultural artifacts; semiotic evaluations of objects as signs; the designation and use of symbols; economic discourses and monetary considerations; aesthetic judgment and interpretation; gender, class, and postcolonial studies; or ecological criticism that focuses on materials and beings in the natural world. All of these literary interpretations can arise from criticism that focuses on jewels or other objects.

Comparing character behaviors toward objects with character behaviors toward other people would underscore the importance of this type of analysis for what it can reveal about experiences of real people living in a material culture. The association of jewels with motherly affections in *Vanity Fair* would demonstrate this dynamic: little Rawdy longs for his mother Becky by gazing at her dressing table, covered with stony jewels and a metallic hand to store her rings, while Amelia Sedley lovingly cradles a painted miniature of little Georgy. The jewels' symbolic meanings show that Becky's disaffection for her son compares unfavorably with Amelia's consuming love for her son. In both cases, the jeweled objects are present *and narrated*, because the person the jewels represent is absent. Objects fill the emotional void of absences.

Therefore, one would have to question the basis for human relations with objects. Do these object relations occur because of an absence or division at the heart of Western culture, so that objects actually take the place of other people? It would seem the answer would often be "yes." Objects become excessively valued when forms of community, of communication, and of human connection are bypassed for culturally-mandated priorities that dictate absence and distance between people: planned ruptures that include empire, war, global trade, advancement in the workplace or other economic considerations, and divisions marked by class, gender, or race. These cultural priorities and practices often regulate people's lives and govern their emotions at the same time that they destroy community. When these cultural forces separate people, objects are called upon to take the place of, and symbolize, valued relationships. Understanding forces behind the very existence of objects and their roles in a culture can uncover what lies beneath "material culture": its deeper, nonmaterial meanings.

Bibliography

Abrams, M. H. *Natural Supernaturalism: Tradition and Revolution in Romantic Literature*. New York: W. W. Norton & Company, 1971.

Adorno, Theodor. "Subject and Object," *The Adorno Reader*, ed. Brian O'Connor. Oxford: Blackwell Publishers, 2000.

Altick, Richard D. *The Presence of the Present: Topics of the Day in the Victorian Novel*. Columbus: Ohio State University Press, 1991.

Anderson, Amanda. *Tainted Souls and Painted Faces: The Rhetoric of Fallenness in Victorian Culture*. Ithaca: Cornell University Press, 1993.

Appadurai, Arjun, ed. *The Social Life of Things: Commodities in Cultural Perspective*. Cambridge: Cambridge University Press, 1986.

Apter, Emily. "Introduction," *Fetishism as Cultural Discourse*. Ithaca: Cornell University Press, 1993.

Apter, Emily, and William Pietz, eds. *Fetishism as Cultural Discourse*. Ithaca: Cornell University Press, 1993.

Armstrong, Isobel. *Victorian Glassworlds: Glass Culture and the Imagination, 1830–1880*. Oxford: Oxford University Press, 2008.

Armstrong, Nancy. *Desire and Domestic Fiction: A Political History of the Novel*. New York: Oxford University Press, 1987.

Armstrong, Nancy. *Fiction in the Age of Photography: The Legacy of British Realism*. Cambridge: Cambridge University Press, 1999.

Arnold, Jean. "Cameo Appearances: Aesthetics and Gender in *Middlemarch*," *Victorian Literature and Culture* 30.1 (Spring 2002) 265–88.

Ashton, Rosemary. *The German Idea: Four English Writers and the Reception of German Thought, 1800–1860*. Cambridge: Cambridge University Press, 1980.

Austin, A. C., and Marion Mercer. *The Story of Diamonds*. Los Angeles: The Gemological Institute of America, 1939.

Aytoun, W. E. "The National Debt and the Stock Exchange," *Blackwood's Edinburgh Magazine*, 66 (December 1849) 655–78 (excerpt). In *The Financial System of the British Nineteenth Century*, ed. and intro. Mary Poovey. New York: Oxford University Press, 2003.

Babbage, Charles. "On the Identity of the Work When it is of the Same Kind, and its Accuracy When of Different Kinds," from *On the Economy of Machinery and Manufactures*. Philadelphia: Carey and Lea, 1832. In *Factory Production in Nineteenth-Century Britain*, ed. Elaine Freedgood, 138–52. New York: Oxford University Press, 2003.

Bachman, Maria K., ed. *The Woman in White/Wilkie Collins*. Peterborough, ON: Broadview, 2006.

Bachman, Maria K., and Don Richard Cox, eds. *Reality's Dark Light: The Sensational Wilkie Collins*, Tennessee Studies in Literature, 41. Knoxville: University of Tennessee Press, 2003.

Baker, William. "Wilkie Collins's Notes for *The Moonstone*," *Victorians Institute Journal* 31 (2003) 187–205.

Balfour, Ian. *Famous Diamonds*, 5th edn. Antique Collectors' Club, Ltd., 2009.

Barthes, Roland. *Mythologies*, trans. Annette Lavers. New York: Hill and Wang, 1972.

Barthes, Roland. "The Reality Effect," *French Literary Theory Today: A Reader*, ed. Tzvetan Todorov, trans. R. Carter, 11–17. Cambridge: Cambridge University Press, 1982.

Bastien, Pascal. "'Aux tresors dissipez l'on cognoist le falfaict': Hierarchie sociale et transgression des ordonnances somptuaires en France, 1543–1606," *Renaissance and Reformation/Renassance et Reforme* XXIII.4 (1999) 23–9.

Baudrillard, Jean. *Selected Writings*, ed. and intro. Mark Poster. Stanford: Stanford University Press, 1988.

Baudrillard, Jean. *The System of Objects*, trans. James Benedict. New York: Verso, 1996.

Baudrillard, Jean. *The Vital Illusion*, ed. Julia Witwer, Wellek Library Lectures. New York: Columbia University Press, 2000.

Bell, S. G., and K. M. Offen, eds. *Women, the Family, and Freedom: The Debate in Documents, Volume One, 1750–1880*. Stanford: Stanford University Press, 1983.

Benjamin, Walter. "The Work of Art in the Age of Mechanical Reproduction," *Illuminations*, intro. Hannah Arendt. New York: Harcourt Brace Jovanich, Inc., 1968.

Benveniste, Emile. "Subjectivity in Language," *Critical Theory Since 1965*, ed. Hazard Adams and Leroy Searle, 728–32. Tallahassee: Florida State University Press, 1986.

Ben-Yishai, Ayelet. "The Fact of a Rumor: Anthony Trollope's *The Eustace Diamonds*," *Nineteenth-Century Literature* 62.1 (2007) 88–120.

Betsky, Seymour. "Society in Thackeray and Trollope, From Dickens to Hardy," *Pelican Guide to English Literature*, ed. Boris Ford, 144–68. New York: Pelican, 1963.

Bhabha, Homi K. *The Location of Culture*. New York: Routledge, 1994.

Bluhm, Andreas, and Louise Lippincott. *Light! The Industrial Age, 1750–1900*. Pittsburgh: Carnegie Museum of Art, 2000.

Blumberg, Alana. "Collins's *Moonstone:* The Victorian Novel as Sacrifice, Theft, Gift, and Debt," *Studies in the Novel* 37.2 (Summer 2005) 162–86.

Bodenheimer, Rosemarie. *The Real Life of Mary Ann Evans: Her Letters and Fiction*. Ithaca: Cornell University Press, 1994.

Bodichon, Barbara Leigh Smith. "A brief summary, in plain language of the most important laws concerning women: together with a few observations thereon." 1854. Appendix One, 123–33. In *Mistress of the House: Women of Property in the Victorian Novel*, by Tim Dolin. Brookfield: Ashgate Publishing Company, 1997.

Booth, Alison. *Greatness Engendered: George Eliot and Virginia Woolf*. Ithaca: Cornell University Press, 1992.

Boundas, Constantin. "Gift, Theft, and Apology: Editorial Introduction," *Angelaki: Journal of the Theoretical Humanities* 6.2 (August 2001) 1–5.

Bourdieu, Pierre. *Distinction: A Social Critique of the Judgement of Taste*, trans. Richard Nice. Cambridge, MA: Harvard University Press, 1984.

Bowen, H. V. *The Business of Empire: The East India Company and Imperial Britain, 1756–1833*. Cambridge: Cambridge University Press, 2006.

Boyle, Sir Robert. *Experiments and Considerations Touching Colours*. London: Henry Herringman.

Brantlinger, Patrick. *Rule of Darkness: British Literature and Imperialism, 1830–1914*. Ithaca: Cornell University Press, 1988.

Braun, Marta. "The Victorian Eye: A Political History of Light and Vision in Britain, 1800–1910, by Chris Otter," *Victorian Studies* 52.2 (Winter 2010) 324–7.

Bredesen, Dagni. "What's a Women to Do? Managing Money and Manipulating Fictions in Trollope's *Can You Forgive Her?* and *The Eustace Diamonds*," *Victorian Review* 31.2 (2005) 99–122.

Briggs, John. *Francis Bacon and the Rhetoric of Nature*. Cambridge, MA: Harvard University Press, 1989.

Brooks, Cleanth. *The Well Wrought Urn*. New York: Harcourt, Brace & World, Inc., 1947.

Brown, Bill. "The Tyranny of Things," *Critical Inquiry* 28.2 (Winter 2002) 442–69.

Brown, Bill. "Thing Theory," *Things*, ed. Bill Brown, 1–16. Chicago: University of Chicago Press, 2004.

Brown, Judith C. "*Sumptuary Law in Italy: 1200–1500* by Catherine M. Kovesi Killerby," *Renaissance Quarterly* 57.1 (Spring 2004) 177–8.

Browne, Ray B. "Introduction," *Objects of Special Devotion: Fetishes and Fetishism in Popular Culture*, ed. Ray B. Browne, 1–3. Bowling Green: Bowling Green University Popular Press, 1982.

Burke, Edmund. *A Philosophical Enquiry into the Origin of our Ideas of the Sublime and Beautiful*, ed. Adam Phillips. New York: Oxford University Press, 1990.

Burnham, S. M. *Precious Stones in Nature, Art, and Literature*. Boston: Bradlee Whidden, 1886.

Bury, Shirley. *Jewellery, 1789–1910, The International Era*, Volume I, 1789–1861. Woodbridge, Suffolk: Antique Collectors' Club, Ltd., 1991.

Buzard, James. "Victorian Women and the Implication of Empire," *Victorian Studies* 36.4 (Summer 1993) 443–53.

Buzard, James, Joseph W. Childers, and Eileen Gilooly, eds. *Victorian Prism: Refractions of the Crystal Palace*. Charlottesville: University of Virginia Press, 2007.

Carlyle, Thomas. "Signs of the Times," *A Carlyle Reader: Selections from the Writings of Thomas Carlyle*, ed. G. B. Tennyson, 3–24. Cambridge: Cambridge University Press, 1984.

Caille, Alain. "The Double Inconceivability of the Pure Gift," *Angelaki: Journal of the Theoretical Humanities* 6.2 (August 2001) 23–8.

Christ, Carol T., and John O. Jordan, eds. *Victorian Literature and the Victorian Visual Imagination*. Berkeley: University of California Press, 1995.

Clark, Grahame. *Symbols of Excellence: Precious Materials as Expressions of Status*. Cambridge: Cambridge University Press, 1986.

Cohen, William A. *Sex Scandal: The Private Parts of Victorian Fiction*. Durham, NC: Duke University Press, 1996.

Cohn, Bernard. *Colonialism and Its Forms of Knowledge: The British in India*. Princeton: Princeton University Press, 1996.

Coleridge, Samuel Taylor. *Lay Sermons*, ed. R.J. White, *The Collected Works of Samuel Taylor Coleridge*, Bollingen Series LXXV. Princeton: Princeton University Press, 1972.

Collins, Wilkie. *The Moonstone*, ed. J. I. M. Stewart. New York: Penguin Classics, 1986.

Cottom, Daniel. *Social Figures: George Eliot, Social History, and Literary Representation*, foreword Terry Eagleton, Theory and History of Literature Series, 44. Minneapolis: University of Minnesota Press, 1987.

Crary, Jonathan. *Techniques of the Observer: On Vision and Modernity in the Nineteenth Century*. Cambridge, MA: MIT Press, 1990.

Culler, Jonathan. *Ferdinand de Saussure*. Ithaca: Cornell University Press, 1986.

Cvetkovich, Ann. *Mixed Feelings: Feminism, Mass Culture and Victorian Sensationalism*. New Brunswick: Rutgers University Press, 1992.

Darwin, Charles. *Voyage of the Beagle: Charles Darwin's Journal of Researches*, ed. and intro Janet Browne and Michael Neve. New York: Penguin Books, 1989, originally published by Henry Colburn, 1839.

Darwin, Charles. *The Origin of Species By Means of Natural Selection, or, The Preservation of Favoured Races in the Struggle for Life*, ed. and intro. J. W. Burrow. New York: Penguin Books, 1985.

Daston, Lorraine, ed. "Introduction," *Biographies of Scientific Objects*. Chicago: University of Chicago Press, 2000.

David-Menard, Monique. "How the Mystery of Conversion is Constructed: Hysteria from Freud to Lacan," *Body and Language in Psychoanalysis*, trans. Catherine Porter. Ithaca: Cornell University Press, 1989.

Dawes, Ginny Redington, and Corinne Davidov. *Victorian Jewelry: Unexplored Treasures*, Photographs Tom Dawes. New York: Abbeville Press Publishers, 1991.

Debord, Guy. *The Society of the Spectacle*, trans. Donald Nicholson-Smith. New York: Zone Books, 1995.

De Certeau, Michel. *The Practice of Everyday Life*, trans. Steven Rendall. Berkeley: University of California Press, 1984.

De Certeau, Michel. *Heterologies: Discourse on the Other*, trans. Brian Massumi, foreword Wlad Godzich, Theory and History of Literature, Volume 17. Minneapolis: University of Minnesota Press, 1986.

de Man, Paul. "The Rhetoric of Temporality," *Blindness and Insight: Essays in the Rhetoric of Contemporary Criticism*, 2nd edn, revised with introduction by Wlad Godzich, Theory and History of Literature, Volume 7. Minneapolis: University of Minnesota Press, 1983.

de Man, Paul. *The Rhetoric of Romanticism*. New York: Columbia University Press, 1984.

Dickens, Charles. *Little Dorrit*, ed., intro., and notes John Holloway. New York: Penguin Books, 1967.

Dolin, Tim. *Mistress of the House: Women of Property in the Victorian Novel*. Brookfield: Ashgate Publishing Company, 1997.

Douglas, Mary. "Foreword," *The Gift: The Form and Reason for Exchange in Archaic Societies*, trans. W. D. Halls. New York: W. W. Norton, 1990.

Duncan, Ian. "*The Moonstone*, the Victorian Novel, and Imperialistic Panic," *Modern Language Quarterly* 55.3 (September 1994) 297–319.

Eagleton, Terry. "Foreword," *Social Figures: George Eliot, Social History, and Literary Representation*, Theory and History of Literature, 44. Minneapolis: University of Minnesota Press, 1987.

Eagleton, Terry. *The Ideology of the Aesthetic*. London: Blackwell's, 1990.

Edlin, Douglas E. *Common Law Theory*. Cambridge: Cambridge University Press, 2007.

Eliot, George. *Letters*, I, ed. Gordon Haight. New Haven: Yale University Press, 1954.

Eliot, George. *Middlemarch: A Study of Provincial Life*, ed. and intro. Gordon S. Haight, Riverside Editions. Boston: Houghton Mifflin Company, 1956.

Eliot, George. *Daniel Deronda*, ed. and intro. Barbara Hardy. New York: Penguin Books, 1967.

Eliot, George. *Adam Bede*, ed. and intro. Stephen Gill. New York: Penguin Books, 1980.

Eliot, George. "John Ruskin's *Modern Painters*, Vol. III," *George Eliot: Selected Critical Writings*, ed. Rosemary Ashton, 247–59. New York: Oxford University Press, 1992.

Elise, Diane. "Beauty and the Aesthetic Impact of the Bejeweled Mother: Discussion of Papers by Debra Roth and Elaine Freedgood," *Studies in Gender and Sexuality* 7.2 (2006) 207–15.

Ellegard, Alvar. *Darwin and the General Reader: The Reception of Darwin's Theory of Evolution in the British Periodical Press, 1859–1872*, with a new foreword by David L. Hull, 194–5. Chicago: University of Chicago Press, 1990.

Emanuel, Harry, F.R.G.S. *Diamonds and Precious Stones: Their History, Value, and Distinguishing Characteristics*, 2nd edn. London: John Camden Hotten, 1867.

Ender, Evelyn. *Sexing the Mind: Nineteenth-Century Fictions of Hysteria*. Ithaca: Cornell University Press, 1995.

Federer, Laura Sue. *The Female Bildungsroman in English: An Annotated Bibliography of Criticism*. New York: The Modern Language Association of America, 1990.

Ferguson, Niall. *Empire: The Rise and Demise of the British World Order and the Lessons for Global Power*. New York: Basic Books, 2002.

Ferris, Ina. "Thackeray and the Ideology of the Gentleman," *The Columbia History of the British Novel*, ed. John Richetti, 407–28. New York: Columbia University Press, 1994.

Flint, Kate. *The Victorians and the Visual Imagination*. Cambridge: Cambridge University Press, 2000.

Flower, Margaret. *Victorian Jewellery*, foreword Margaret J. Biggs. Chapter on collecting by Doris Langley Moore. New York: A. S. Barnes and Company, 1973.

Flugel, J.C. *The Psychology of Clothes*. New York: International University Press, 1930.

Forrest, Denys. *Tiger of Mysore: The Life and Death of Tipu Sultan*. London: Chatto and Windus, 1970.

Foucault, Michel. *The Order of Things: An Archaeology of Human Sciences*. New York: Vintage Books, 1973.

Foucault, Michel. "Panopticism," from *Discipline and Punish*, in *The Foucault Reader*, ed. Paul Rabinow, 206–13. New York: Pantheon Books, 1984.

Foucault, Michel. "The Repressive Hypothesis," from *The History of Sexuality*, Volume in *The Foucault Reader*, ed. Paul Rabinow, 301–29. New York: Pantheon Books, 1984.

Free, Melissa. "'Dirty Linen': Legacies of Empire in Wilkie Collins's *The Moonstone*," *Texas Studies in Literature and Language* 48.4 (Winter 2006) 340–71.

Freedgood, Elaine. "Banishing Panic: Harriet Martineau and the Popularization of Political Economy," *The New Economic Criticism: Studies at the Intersections of Literature and Economics*, ed. Martha Woodmansee and Mark Osteen, 210–28. New York: Routledge, 1999.

Freedgood, Elaine, ed. *Factory Production in Nineteenth-Century Britain*. New York: Oxford University Press, 2003.

Freedgood, Elaine. *Ideas in Things: Fugitive Meaning in the Victorian Novel*. Chicago: University of Chicago Press, 2006.

Freedgood, Elaine. "Commodity Criticism and Victorian Thing Culture," *Contemporary Dickens*, ed. and intro. Eileen Gillooly and Deirdre David. Columbus: Ohio State University Press, 2008.

Freedman, Jonathan. *The Temple of Culture: Assimilation and Anti-Semitism in Literary Anglo-America*. New York: Oxford University Press, 2000.

Freud, Sigmund. *On Sexuality*, intro. Steven Marcus, trans. and ed. James Strachey. New York: Basic Books, Inc., 1962.

Geertz, Clifford. *The Interpretation of Cultures: Selected Essays*. New York: Basic Books, 1973.

Gilbert, Katharine Everett, and Helmut Kuhn. *A History of Esthetics*. New York: Macmillan, 1939.

Gilbert, Sandra M., and Susan Gubar. *The Madwoman in the Attic: The Woman Writer and the Nineteenth-Century Imagination*. New Haven: Yale University Press, 1979.

Gillooly, Eileen, and Deirdre David, eds. *Contemporary Dickens*. Columbus: Ohio State University Press, 2008.

Godelier, Maurice. *The Enigma of the Gift*, trans. Nora Scott. Chicago: University of Chicago Press, 1999. Originally published as *L'eginma du don*. Paris: Librairie Artheme Fayard, 1996.

Goffman, Erving. "Symbols of Class Status," *The British Journal of Sociology* 2.4 (December 1951) 294–304.

Graff, Gerald. *Professing Literature: An Institutional History*. Chicago: University of Chicago Press, 1987.

Guth, Deborah. "George Eliot and Schiller: Narrative Ambivalence in *Middlemarch* and *Felix Holt*," *Modern Language Review* 94.4 (October 1999) 913–25.

Hahn, Emily. *Diamond: The Spectacular Story of Earth's Rarest Treasure and Man's Greatest Greed*. Garden City: Doubleday & Company, Inc., 1956.

Haight, Gordon. *George Eliot: A Biography*. New York: Penguin Boooks, 1968.

Hall, Dorothy. "Aesthetics and the New Ethics: Theorizing the Novel in the Twenty-first Century," *PMLA* 124.3 (May 2009) 896–905.

Harden, Edgar F. *Thackeray's English Humourists and Four Georges*. Newark: University of Delaware Press, 1985.

Harper's New Atlantic Monthly Magazine, "More of the Great Show at Paris," 35.210 (November 1867) 787.

Harper's New Atlantic Monthly Magazine, "Holland and the Hollanders," Second Paper, 44.261 (February 1872) 349–64.

Hayward, Maria. "Fashion, Finance, Foreign Politics and the Wardrobe of Henry VIII," *Clothing Culture, 1350–1650*, 165–87. Burlington: Ashgate Publishing Company, 2004.

Hegeman, Susan. "Franz Boas and Professional Anthropology: On Mapping Borders of the Modern," *Victorian Studies* 41.3 (Spring 1998) 455–83.

Heller, Tamar. *Dead Secrets: Wilkie Collins and the Female Gothic*. New Haven: Yale University Press, 1992.

Henry, Nancy. "'Rushing into Eternity': Suicide and Finance in Victorian Fiction," *Victorian Investments: New Perspectives on Finance and Culture*, ed. Nancy Henry and Cannon Schmitt. Bloomington: *Victorian Studies* and Indiana University Press, 2009.

Herbert, Christopher. *Culture and Anomie: Ethnographic Imagination in the Nineteenth Century*. Chicago: University of Chicago Press, 1991.

Herbert, Christopher. *War of No Pity: The Indian Mutiny and Victorian Trauma*. Princeton: Princeton University Press, 2008.

Hibbert, Christopher. "The Tower of London: A History of England from the Norman Conquest," *Newsweek*, 1981, 112–15.

Hilton, Boyd. *The Age of Atonement: The Influence of Evangelicalism on Social and Economic Thought, 1785–1865*. Oxford: Oxford University Press, 1986.

Hinks, Peter. *Nineteenth Century Jewellery*. London: Faber & Faber, 1975.

Hobsbawm, Eric. *The Age of Capitalism*. New York: The World Publishing Company, 1962.

Hobsbawm, Eric. *Nations and Nationalism Since 1780: Programme, Myth, Reality*. Cambridge: Cambridge University Press, 1990.

Holcombe, Lee. *Wives and Property: Reform of the Married Women's Property Law in Nineteenth-Century England*. Toronto: University of Toronto Press, 1983.

Holman, C. Hugh, and William Harmon. *A Handbook to Literature*, 5th edn. New York: Macmillan Publishing Company, 1986.

Howe, Irving. "The Self in Literature," *Constructions of the Self*, ed. George Levine, 249–67. New Brunswick: Rutgers University Press, 1992.

Hunt, Alan. "The Governance of Consumption; Sumptuary Laws and Shifting Forms of Regulation," *The Consumption Reader*, ed. David B. Clarke, Marcus A. Doel, and M.L. Housiaux, 62–8. London: Routledge, 2003.

Hyde, Lewis. *The Gift: Imagination and the Erotic Life of Property*. New York: Vintage Books, 1979.

Irwin, Jane, ed. *George Eliot's Daniel Deronda Notebooks*. New York: Cambridge University Press, 1996.

Itzkowitz, David C. "Fair Enterprise or Extravagant Speculation," *Victorian Investments: New Perspectives on Finance and Culture*, ed. Nancy Henry and Cannon Schmidt. Bloomington: Indiana University Press, 2009.

Jacobus, Mary. "The Difference of View." *Women Writing and Writing about Women*. Ed. Mary Jacobus, 10–21. Totowa, NJ: Barnes & Noble Books, 1979.

Jaffe, Audrey. *The Affective Life of the Average Man: The Victorian Novel and the Stock-market Graph*, Victorian Critical Interventions, Donald Hall, Series ed. Columbus: Ohio State University, 2010.

Jameson, Fredric. *The Political Unconscious: Narrative as a Socially Symbolic Act*. Ithaca: Cornell University Press, 1981.

Jameson, Fredric. *The Cultural Turn: Selected Writings on the Postmodern, 1983–1998*. London: Verso, 1998.

Jameson, Fredric. "Postmodernism and the Consumer Society," *The Cultural Turn: Selected Writings on the Postmodern, 1983–1998*, 1–20. New York: Verso, 1998.

Janson, Dora Jane. *From Slave to Siren: The Victorian Woman and Her Jewelry from Neoclassic to Art Nouveau*. Durham, NC: The Duke University Museum of Art, 1971.

Jaritz, Gerhard. "*Ira Dei*, Material Culture and Behavior in the Late Middle Ages: Evidence from German-speaking Regions," *Essays in Medieval Studies* 18 (2001) 53–66.

Kant, Immanuel. *The Critique of Judgement*, trans. James Creed Meredith. Oxford: Clarendon Press, 1952.

Kasser, Tim. *The High Price of Materialism*. Cambridge, MA: MIT Press, 2002.

Kaul, Suvir. *Thomas Gray and Literary Authority: A Study in Ideology and Poetics*. Stanford: Stanford University Press, 1992.

King, C. W. *Antique Gems: Their Origin, Uses, and Value as Interpreters of Ancient History; and as illustrative of Ancient Art: with Hints to Gem Collectors*. John Murray, Albemarle Street, 1860.

King, C. W. *The Natural History, of Ancient and Modern Precious Stones and Gems, and of The Precious Metals*. London: Bell and Daldy, 1865.

Kopytoff, Igor. "The Cultural Biography of Things: Commoditization as Process," *The Social Life of Things: Commodities in Cultural Perspective*, ed. Arjun Appadurai, 64–91. New York: Cambridge University Press, 1986.

Krips, Henry. *Fetish: An Erotics of Culture*. Ithaca: Cornell University Press, 1999.

Labovitz, Esther Kleinbord. *The Myth of the Heroine: The Female Bildungsroman in the Twentieth Century: Dorothy Richardson, Simone de Beauvoir, Doris Lessing, Chrisa Wolf*. New York: Lang, 1987.

Lacan, Jacques. *Ecrits*. New York: W. W. Norton, 1977.

Lacan, Jacques. "Function and Field of Speech and Language," *Ecrits*, 30–113. New York: W. W. Norton, 1977.

Levine, George. "Introduction: Reclaiming the Aesthetic," *Aesthetics and Ideology*, ed. George Levine. New Brunswick: Rutgers University Press, 1994.

Lindner, Christoph. *Fictions of Commodity Culture: From the Victorian to the Postmodern*. Burlington: Ashgate, 2003.

Lipovetsky, Gilles. *The Empire of Fashion: Dressing Modern Democracy*, trans. Catherine Porter, foreword Richard Sennett, New French Thought. Princeton: Princeton University Press, 1994.

Logan, Peter Melville. *Victorian Fetishism: Intellectuals and Primitives*. Albany: SUNY Press, 2009.

Lootens, Tricia. "Hemans and Home: Victorianism, Feminine 'Internal Enemies' and the Domestication of National Identity," *PMLA* 109.2 (March 1994) 238–53.

Loxley, Diana. *Problematic Shores: The Literature of Islands*. New York: St. Martin's Press, 1991.

Lutz, Catherine, and Geoffrey M. White. "The Anthropology of Emotion," *Annual Review of Anthropology* 15 (1986) 405–36.

Mao, Douglas. *Solid Objects: Modernism and the Test of Production.* Princeton: Princeton University Press, 1998.

Marx, Karl. "The Value-Form," Appendix to the First German edition of *Capital,* Volume 1, 1867, trans. Mike Roth and Wal Suchting, 1978, *Capital and Class* 4 (Spring 1978) 130–50. www.marxists.org/archive/marx/works/1867-c1/appendix.htm#n1, 7/20/2009.

Marx, Karl. *Capital: A Critique of the Political Economy,* ed. Frederick Engels, revised Ernest Untermann, trans. Samuel Moore and Edward Aveling. New York: Modern Library, 1906.

Mastai, Marie-Louise d'Otrange. *Jewelry,* ed. Brenda Gilchrist. Cooper-Hewitt Museum: The Smithsonian Institution's National Museum of Design, 1981.

Mauss, Marcel. *The Gift: The Form and Reason for Exchange in Archaic Societies,* trans. W. D. Halls, foreword Mary Douglas. New York: W. W. Norton, 1990; first published as *Essai sur le Don,* Paris: Presse Universitaire de France, 1950.

McCallum, E. L. *Object Lessons: How to Do Things with Fetishism.* Albany: SUNY Press, 1999.

M'Carthy, Justin. Untitled Essay, *Westminster Review* (July 1864). In *Norton Anthology of English Literature,* ed. M. H. Abrams, 5th edn, 2, 1635–6. New York: W. W. Norton & Company, 1986.

McMaster, Roland. *Trollope and the Law.* New York: St. Martin's Press, 1986.

Mehta, Jaya. "English Romance: Indian Violence," *The Centennial Review* 39.3 (1995) 611–57.

Mill, John Stuart. "The Spirit of the Age," *Essays on Politics and Culture,* ed. Gertrude Himmelfarb. Garden City: Doubleday, 1962.

Mill, John Stuart. "From *The Subjection of Women,*" *Norton Anthology of English Literature,* 5th edn, 2, 1055–66. New York: W. W. Norton & Company, 1962.

Miller, Andrew H. *Novels Behind Glass: Commodity Culture and Victorian Narrative,* Literature, Culture, Theory 17. Cambridge: Cambridge University Press, 1995.

Miller, D. A. *The Novel and the Police.* Berkeley: University of California Press, 1988.

Milligan, Barry. *Pleasures and Pains: Opium and the Orient in Nineteenth-Century British Culture.* Charlottesville: University Press of Virginia, 1995.

Miskimin, Harry A. *The Economy of Early Renaissance Europe, 1300–1460.* Englewood Cliffs: Prentice-Hall, Inc., 1969.

Mitchell, W. J. T. "Representation," *Critical Terms for Literary Study,* ed. Frank Lentricchia and Thomas McLaughlin. Chicago: University of Chicago Press, 1990.

Moretti, Franco. "The Comforts of Civilization," *Representations* 12 (Fall 1985) 115–38.

Munich, Adrienne. *Andromeda's Chains: Gender and Interpretation in Victorian Literature and Art*. New York: Columbia University Press, 1989.

Munich, Adrienne. *Queen Victoria's Secrets*. New York: Columbia University Press, 1996.

Nayder, Lillian. *Wilkie Collins*. Twayne's English Authors Series, ed. Herbert Sussman. New York: Twayne Publishers, 1997.

Nichols, Nina DaVinci. *Ariadne's Lives*. Madison: Fairleigh Dickinson University Press, 1995.

Nunokawa, Jeff. *The Afterlife of Property*. Princeton: Princeton University Press, 1994.

Nussbaum, Martha C. *Love's Knowledge: Essays on Philosophy and Literature*. New York: Oxford University Press, 1990.

O'Connor, Brian, ed. *The Adorno Reader*. "Introduction" to "Subject and Object" by Theodor Adorno, 137. Malden: Blackwell Publishers, 2000.

Ofek, Galia. *Representations of Hair in Victorian Literature and Culture*. Burlington: Ashgate Publishing Company, 2009.

Osgood, Mrs. "The Language of Gems," *The Magnolia, or, Southern Apalachian [sic]: A Literary Magazine and Monthly Review*, new series, 1.3 (July 1842–June 1843).

Osteen, Mark. "Gift or Commodity," *The Question of the Gift; Studies Across Disciplines*, ed. Mark Osteen, Routledge Studies in Anthropology, 229–47. New York: Routledge, 2002.

Osteen, Mark, ed. *The Question of the Gift: Essays Across Disciplines*, Routledge Studies in Anthropology. New York: Routledge, 2002.

O'Sullivan, Simon. "The Aesthetics of Affect: Thinking Art Beyond Representation," *Angelaki: Journal of the Theoretical Humanities* 6.3 (December 2001) 125–35.

Otter, Chris. *The Victorian Eye: A Political History of Light and Vision in Britain, 1800–1910*. Chicago and London: University of Chicago Press, 2008.

Page, Norman, ed. *Wilkie Collins: The Critical Heritage*. Boston: Routledge & Kegan Paul, 1974.

Peters, Catherine. *Thackeray's Universe*. Boston: Faber & Faber, 1987.

Phillips, Kim M. "Masculinities and the Medieval English Sumptuary Laws," *Gender & History* 19.1 (April 2007) 22–42.

Pietz, William. "The Problem of the Fetish," pt. 1, *Res* 9 (Spring 1985).

Pietz, William. "Fetishism and Materialism," *Fetishism as Cultural Discourse*, ed. Emily Apter and William Pietz. Ithaca: Cornell University Press, 1993.

Plotz, John. *Portable Property: Victorian Culture on the Move*. Princeton: Princeton University Press, 2008.

Plotz, John. "'*Victorian Fetishism: Intellectuals and Primitives*,' by Peter Melville Logan," *Victorian Studies* 52.2 (Winter 2010) 282–4.

Poovey, Mary. *Uneven Developments: The Ideological Work of Gender in Mid-Victorian England*. Chicago: University of Chicago Press, 1988.

Poovey, Mary. "Aesthetics and Political Economy in the Eighteenth Century: The Place of Gender in the Social Construction of Knowledge," *Aesthetics and Ideology*, ed. George Levine, 79–105. New Brunswick: Rutgers University Press, 1994.

Poovey, Mary. *The Financial System of the British Nineteenth Century*, ed. and intro. Mary Poovey. New York: Oxford University Press, 2003.

Price, David. *Memoirs of the Early Life and Service of a Field Officer*. London: Wm. H. Allen & Co., 1839.

Prior, Kathleen, and John Adamson. *Maharajas' Jewels*. New York: The Vendome Press, 2000.

Psomiades, Kathy Alexis. "Heterosexual Exchange and Other Victorian Fictions: *The Eustace Diamonds* and Victorian Anthropology," *Novel: A Forum on Fiction* 33.1 (Fall 1999) 93–118.

Pykett, Lyn, ed. *Wilkie Collins: Contemporary Critical Essays*. New York: St. Martin's Press, 1998.

Ragussis, Michael. *Figures of Conversion: "The Jewish Question" and the English National Identity*. Durham, NC: Duke University Press, 1995.

Ray, Gordon N. *Thackeray: The Uses of Adversity, 1811–1846*. New York: McGraw-Hill Book Company, Inc., 1955.

Redfield, Marc. *Phantom Formations: Aesthetic Ideology and the Bildungsroman*. Ithaca: Cornell University Press, 1996.

Reed, John R. "English Imperialism and the Unacknowledged Crime of *The Moonstone*," *Clio* 2 (1973) 281–90.

Renfrew, Colin. "Varna and the Emergence of Wealth in Prehistoric Europe," *The Social Life of Things: Commodities in Cultural Perspective*, ed. Arjun Appadurai, 141–68. New York: Cambridge University Press, 1986.

Richards, Thomas. *The Commodity Culture of Victorian England: Advertising and Spectacle, 1851–1914*. Stanford: Stanford University Press, 1990.

Richardson, Catherine, ed. *Clothing Culture, 1350–1650*. Burlington: Ashgate Publishing Company, 2004.

Riffaterre, Michael. "How Do Images Signify," *Diacritics: A Review of Contemporary Criticism* 24 (Spring 1994) 3–15.

Rischin, Abigail S. "Beside the Reclining Statue: Ekphrasis, Narrative, and Desire in *Middlemarch*," *PMLA* 111 (1996) 1121–32.

Roberts, Jane, ed. *Royal Treasures: A Golden Jubilee Celebration*. London: The Royal Collection Enterprises, Ltd., St James's Palace, 2002.

Rogers, Frances, and Alice Beard. *5,000 Years of Gems and Jewelry*. New York: J. B. Lippincott Company, 1947.

Rose, Jacqueline. *Sexuality in the Field of Vision*. New York: Verso, 1986.

Rosenberg, John D., ed. *The Genius of John Ruskin: Selections from His Writings*. Charlottesville: University of Virginia Press, 1998.

Roth, Alan. "He Thought He was Right (But Wasn't): Property Law in Anthony Trollope's *The Eustace Diamonds*," *Stanford Law Review* 44.879 (April 1992).

Roy, Ashish. "The Fabulous Imperialist Semiotic of Wilkie Collins's *The Moonstone*," *New Literary History* 24.3 (Summer 1993) 657.

Rushby, Kevin. *Chasing the Mountain of Light: Across India on the Trail of the Kohinoor Diamond*. New York: St. Martin's Press, 2000.

Ruskin, John. *Praeterita: The Autobiography of John Ruskin*, intro. Kenneth Clark. Oxford: Oxford University Press, 1949.

Ruskin, John. *The Genius of John Ruskin: Selections from His Writings*, foreword Herbert Tucker. Charlottesville: The University of Virginia Press, 1998.

Said, Edward. *Culture and Imperialism*. New York: Vintage Books, 1993.

Schiller, Friedrich. *On the Aesthetic Education of Man: In a Series of Letters*. Oxford: Clarendon Press, 1967.

Schrift, Alan D. *The Logic of the Gift: Toward an Ethic of Generosity*. New York: Routledge, 1997.

Sedgwick, Eve Kosofsky. *The Coherence of the Gothic Convention*. New York: Methuen, 1986.

Sewell, William H., Jr. "Geertz, Cultural Systems, and History: From Synchrony to Transformation," in *The Fate of "Culture": Geertz and Beyond*, ed. Sherry Ortner, 35–55. Berkeley: University of California Press, 1999.

Sharpe, Jenny. *Allegories of Empire: The Figure of Woman in the Colonial Text*. Minneapolis: University of Minnesota Press, 1993.

Showalter, Elaine. "Feminist Criticism in the Wilderness," *The New Feminist Criticism: Essays on Women, Literature, Theory*, ed. Elaine Showalter. New York: Pantheon Books, 1985.

Shrimpton, Nicholas. "'Even these metallic problems have their melodramatic side': Money in Victorian Literature," *Victorian Literature and Finance*, ed. Francis O'Gorman. New York: Oxford University Press, 2007.

Simmel, Georg. *The Sociology of Georg Simmel*, trans., ed., and intro. Kurt H. Wolff. New York: The Free Press, 1950.

Simmel, Georg. "Fashion," *The Journal of Sociology* 62.6 (May 1957) 541–58; originally published in *International Quarterly* X (October 1904) 130–55; also published in *On Individuality and Social Forms: Selected Writings*, ed. Donald N. Levine, 294–323. Chicago: University of Chicago Press, 1970.

Simmel, Georg. *The Philosophy of Money*, ed. David Frisby, trans. Tom Bottomore and David Frisby. New York: Routledge, 1978.

Smith, Adam. *An Inquiry into the Nature and Causes of the Wealth of Nations*. Gen. ed. R. H. Campbell and A. S. Skinner. Text edited by W. B. Todd. New York: Oxford University Press, 1976.

Spyer, Patricia, ed. *Border Fetishisms: Material Objects in Unstable Spaces*. New York: Routledge, 1998.

Stein, Richard L. "Street Figures: Victorian Urban Iconography," *Victorian Literature and the Victorian Visual Imagination*, ed. Carol T. Christ and John O. Jordan, 233–63. Berkeley: University of California Press, 1995.

Stone, Donald. *The Romantic Impulse in Victorian Fiction*. Cambridge, MA: Harvard University Press, 1980.

Sussman, George. *Selling Mother's Milk: The Wet Nursing Business in France, 1715–1914*. Champaign: University of Illinois Press, 1982.

Tarshis, Dena K. "The Koh-I-noor Diamond and its Glass Replica at the Crystal Palace Exhibition," *Journal of Glass Studies* 42 (2000) 133–43.

Tavernier, J.-B. "Of Diamonds and the Mines and Rivers where they are found; and in the first place of the Author's Journey to the Mine of Raolconda," *A General Collection of the Best and Most Interesting Voyages and Travels in All Parts of the World*, 8, ed. John Pinkerton, 235–57. Philadelphia: Kimber and Conrad, 1810–12.

Thackeray, William Makepeace. *The History of Samuel Titmarsh and the Great Hoggarty Diamond*. *The Works of William Makepeace Thackeray*, VIII. Adamant Media Corporation: Elibron Classics series, 2007. Unabridged Facsimile of edition published by Smith, Elder & Co., London, 1872.

Thackeray, William Makepeace. *The History of Samuel Titmarsh and the Great Hoggarty Diamond*, in *The Christmas Books of Mr. M.A. Titmarsh, Thackeray's Complete Works*, The Household Edition. Boston: Estes and Lauriat, 1884.

Thackeray, William Makepeace. *Vanity Fair: A Novel Without a Hero*, ed., intro., and notes Geoffrey and Kathleen Tillotson, Riverside Editions. Boston: Houghton Mifflin Company, 1963.

Thomas, Nicholas. *Entangled Objects: Exchange, Material Culture, and Colonialism in the Pacific*. Cambridge, MA: Harvard University Press, 1991.

Thoreau, Henry David. *The Portable Thoreau*, ed. and intro. Carl Bode. New York: Penguin Books, 1975.

Trollope, Anthony. *Thackeray*, ed. John Morley, English Men of Letters. London: MacMillan and Co., 1892.

Trollope, Anthony. *The Eustace Diamonds*, ed. Stephen Gill and John Sutherland. New York: Penguin Books, 1969.

Vaughan, Richard. "Chasing a Sphinx," *History Today* 37 (May 1987) 28.

Veblen, Thorsten. *The Theory of the Leisure Class*. Toronto: Dover Publications, 1994.

Ver Eecke, Wilfried. "Hegel as a Source for Necessity in Psychoanalytic Theory," *Interpreting Lacan*, ed. Joseph H. Smith and William Kerrigan. New Haven: Yale University Press, 1987.

Voillot, Patrick. *Diamonds and Precious Stones*, trans. Jack Hawkes. New York: Harry N. Abrams, 1998.

Warren, Joyce W. *Women Money and the Law: Nineteenth Century Fiction, Gender, and the Courts*. Iowa City: University of Iowa Press, 2005.

Waters, Catherine. *Commodity Culture in Dickens's Household Words: The Social Life of Goods*. Burlington: Ashgate Publishing Company, 2008.

Watt, Ian. *The Rise of the Novel: Studies in Defoe, Richardson, and Fielding*. Berkeley: University of California Press, 1957.

Weiner, Annette B. *Inalienable Possessions: The Paradox of Keeping-While-Giving*. Berkeley: University of California Press, 1992.

Weiskel, Thomas. *The Romantic Sublime: Studies in the Structure and Psychology of Transcendence*. Baltimore: The Johns Hopkins University Press, 1976.

Weiss, Barbara. *The Hell of the English: Bankruptcy and the Victorian Novel*. Lewisburg: Bucknell University Press, 1986.

Weltman, Sharon Aronofsky. "'Be No More Housewives, but Queens': Queen Victoria and Ruskin's Domestic Mythology," *Remaking Queen Victoria*, ed. Margaret Homans and Adrienne Munich, 105–22. New York: Cambridge University Press, 1997.

White, Hayden. *The Content of the Form: Narrative Discourse and Historical Representation*. Baltimore: The Johns Hopkins University Press, 1987.

Whorf, Benjamin Lee. "Subjectivity in Language," *Critical Theory Since 1965*, ed. Hazard Adams and Leroy Searle, 710–23. Tallahassee: Florida State University Press, 1986.

Wolf, Kurt H. "Introduction," *The Sociology of Georg Simmel*, trans. and ed. Kurt H. Wolf. New York: The Free Press, 1950.

Woodmansee, Martha, and Mark Osteen, eds. *The New Economic Criticism: Studies at the Intersection of Literature and Economics*. New York: Routledge, 1999.

Yan, Yuxiang. "Unbalanced Reciprocity: Asymmetrical Giving and Social Hierarchy in Rural China," *The Question of the Gift: Essays Across Disciplines*, ed. Mark Osteen, 67–84. New York: Routledge, 2002.

Yolton, John W. *Perception and Reality: A History from Descartes to Kant*. Ithaca: Cornell University Press, 1996.

Zimmerman, Bonnie. "George Eliot and Feminism: The Case of *Daniel Deronda*," *Nineteenth-Century Women Writers of the English-Speaking World*, ed. Rhoda B. Nathan, 231–77. New York: Greenwood Press, 1986.

Index

172

Victorian Jewelry, Identity, and the Novel

Tarshis, Dena K., 19
Tavernier, 41, 77
Thackeray, W.M., 11-12, 15-18, 30-31, 48,
    49-50, 49fn, 50fn, 51, 57-59, 58fn,
    59fn, 62-66, 65fn, 66fn, 68-70,
    70fn, 72, 127, 138fn
theft(s), 2fn, 27fn, 77-78, 84, 84fn, 87-90,
    98-99, 139, 141-42
Tipu, 77-78, 88, 88fn
translucence, 18, 41, 54, 60
Trollope, Anthony, 31, 127-29, 13, 140fn,
    141-45
truth, 17, 43, 68, 91, 97, 99, 102-103, 109,
    125, 128fn, 137-38, 142
turquoise, 2fn, 21-27, 21fn, 78fn, 127, 148

van Berghem, Louis, 52
Vanity Fair, 10-13, 16-17, 23-27, 148-49
Vasco da Gama, 51
Vatican, 107, 114, 116-17
Veblen, Thorsten, 2, 2fn, 4fn, 39

Ver Eecke, 104fn
vision, visual, visible 2, 5-6, 9-11, 10fn,
    11fn, 16, 18, 18fn, 21, 24-25, 27,
    28, 37-40, 39fn, 44, 53, 71, 87,
    105-106, 113-114, 122, 142, 148
Voillot, Patrick, 77fn

Warren, Joyce W., 145fn
Waters, Catherine, 3
wealth, 2, 4fn, 5, 7, 9, 11-12, 24, 58, 60,
    66, 78-79, 90, 110, 130-32, 136-41,
    144
Weiner, Annette B., 91, 92fn
Weiskel, Thomas, 60, 60fn
The Westminster Review, 108
White, Hayden, 28fn, 108
Whorf, Benjamin, 35
widow, 128, 130-32, 136, 139, 142-45
Williams, William Carlos, 47
Wolff, Kurt H., 20fn, 133fn
The Woman Question, 108